A Journey into the Arms
of the Father's Love

Grace
Orphans No More

Dr. JAMES G. JOHNSON

Dedication

To the Fathers in my life:
Charles E. Johnson, who adopted me as his own son.
Dean Hatfield, who led me to the One
Who adopted me as His SON.
Jack Ailes and Ron Fish, who filled my life
with stories and wisdom.
Fred Barshaw, who filled my heart with His Stories.
To You, ABBA Father, Who are Father of All.

Acknowledgments

To Cheryl, my best friend and companion in life — you have my heart. Thanks for providing the support, encouragement and kindness the Lord has used to help me see the truth about myself, and for encouraging me to stay the course.

To my children, Brent, Jeremiah, Cory, and Kristin. In you I see how much a father can love a son or daughter, and through our mistakes become a family and grow together.

No work is that of a single creative genius; it is the compilation of a lot of significant contributors who stood behind the writing:

To Pauly Heller, without your input, corrections, style and editing, this would have remained another intellectual study. Thank you.

To Lisa Hainline, not only are you an award-winning graphic artist, but you have also been our friend and companion on this journey. Thanks for listening to the vision.

To Jack Frost, Bob Munger, Ed Piorek, Gordon Dalbey and many others, I never met you personally, yet your lives changed mine.

To Ramon and Angela Lago, Joe Gee, Dan Lind, Jeff Chariker, Erik Thein and the elders and class at Faith Bible Church for praying with us and giving us a place to teach these things and grow them.

To Phil Volgraf, George and Sue DeCelle, John and Rhonda Riva and Trent Hamlin for your prayers and advice.

To Evi and Steve Fulford, Diane Fillmore, Mark and Jennifer Byum and all the reviewers who corrected my theology, grammar and sentence structure — Mount Everest would have been easier.

To pastors Tom Bell, Fred McCormick and Leith Anderson, and the team who took so much time to believe in me, and to Craig and Linda Coffman, I was obedient to the process.

To Mike Smith, Sue McCornack, Gary Lee and all the others in our class at Wooddale — you were my first try.

And I am thankful for those I saw as my "enemies." Though you may have meant evil, God meant it for good. Through His sovereign GRACE, He used you to help me see that more times than not, I was the one wrong.

Endorsements

"Out of his own pain and healing Jim brings hope and healing to others."
—Dr. Leith Anderson
President of the National Association of Evangelicals and
former Senior Pastor, Wooddale Church, Eden Prairie, Minnesota

"Jim gets to the heart of Grace. With powerful and honest stories from his own life, and testimonies from people who've attended his events, this book is nearly impossible to put down! When you finally stop crying from the trials Jim and his wife experienced, you realize that God really does love you and His grace is what ultimately saves!"
—Dr. Michael Smalley
The Smalley Institute, Houston, Texas

"In *Grace: Orphans No More*, Dr. James Johnson takes us on a personal journey sharing remarkable insights that lead us back to a Heavenly Father's Heart of Grace. Can Grace actually be experienced and lived out?

"Can it be? On this journey with Pastor James you will come to understand that Grace can not only be felt and lived out, but it will also change your soul and release a freedom bathed in God's Love that will refresh you spiritual walk. I encourage you to join others in this journey in Grace as you read *Grace: Orphans No More*."
—Dr. Darryl DelHousaye
President of Phoenix Seminary

"Reading *Grace: Orphans No More* is like taking a bath in the Father's love. Dr. Johnson identifies the dirt that infects our orphan thinking and presents practical solutions to return to (or begin) our Abba Father intimacy. I highly recommend this book for anyone at any stage of their journey with God, whether someone who needs a fresh reminder of the Father's love, a 'prodigal' who needs to return home, or an 'older brother' who needs to be awakened to the Father's love in his mist. This book is a page-turner, and you will be tempted to do just that. Don't!

Read it slowly and devotionally, and it will be like receiving a welcomed
dose of the Father's love every morning."

—Dr. Charles Rasmussen
Pastor, retired, Glendale, Arizona

"Dr. Jim Johnson takes on the greatest challenge we face living in our
broken world in *Grace, Orphans No More.* He helps us embrace the truth
that we are deeply loved by the Living God. Through practical learnings
from his own faith journey and ministry and from the Scriptures, he
gives insights that enable us to thrive in a relationship with God, so we
can become the salt and light our world so desperately needs."

—Dr. Wendell Nelson
Pastor of Spiritual Formation, Christ Community Church, Omaha,
Board of Trustees, Crown College, Saint Bonifacius, Minnesota

"Jim Johnson's love for God, knowledge of the Bible, and concern for
hurting people resound throughout this impressive book. Having experienced the healing Grace of God that transforms emotional and spiritual
orphans into beloved children, Jim provides guidance and resources to
help his readers along that life-changing journey."

—Sandra D. Wilson, Ph.D.
Retired family therapist and seminary professor
and author of *Released From Shame* and *Into Abba's Arm*

"You are holding in your hand a manual for life. Jim's delightful style
and practical insights will lead you into a deeper understanding of God's
eternal, unconditional, relentless Love and Grace. It will show you how
your relationship with Him, as the Apostle Peter writes, will give you
everything you need for life and godliness. This book is loaded with
essential life skills. You will have to read it slowly, absorb it thoughtfully,
and live it out joyfully!"

—Dr. Gary Kinnaman
Pastor and author of *Experiencing the Power of the Cross* and
My Companion Through Grief

"Jim Johnson's take on Grace, the Father's Love, and how we as believers live as either orphans or sons is a message we need to read and heed.

His book is full of honest transparency regarding his personal struggles and insights, as well as practical solutions we can put into practice in our lives. Take the time to absorb this book. Your relationship with God as your Father will never be the same."

—Gary Barkalow
Founder, The Noble Heart ministry and author of *It's Your Call*

"For far too long, Father God has been misrepresented and misunderstood. Dr. James Johnson brings a much needed course correction, sharing the love and beauty of the Father's heart. He begins with examining the source and life impact of our misunderstandings and leads us to a discovery of Abba Father."

—Faith Cummings
Pastor Adult Education, Living Streams Church, Phoenix, AZ

"Grace: Orphans No More is a journey from lost to found, striving to rest, absent to present. James Johnson has joined the ranks of those who have encountered God as a loving Father, and he knows the personal and relational transformation that results. Using his training as a counselor, James communicates God's grace in a way that anyone can receive, and in so doing he brings God closer to every life. The truths in this book are not new; they have been taught by a variety of teachers over the years and they can be traced back to Jesus and even to the principles in the early chapters of Genesis. What is new is the careful compilation and personalization of eternal truths for transformation and liberty. This makes the book useful for seeker and helper alike. When we come into the arms of our Father, and experience grace, we are truly orphans no more.

—Mark Burlinson
Executive Pastor, Christ Community Church, Myrtle Beach, SC

"Jim Johnson's book is all about being 'amazed by Grace' from discovering that until we open our hearts to Him, we wallow as orphans, our souls unable to find the nourishment that comes only from a proper understanding of and embracing our Abba Father. Along with his vulnerable sharing, Jim gives practical tools to move from where the reader is today to that soul-healing, nurturing place close to God. *Grace: Orphans*

No More guides a reader through the dysfunctions, wounds and hurts we all have so we can make the connection between the desire God has for none to be lost, and finding our way home."

—Don Farr
Marriage Pastor, Scottsdale Bible Church, Scottsdale, Arizona

"I have been privileged to partner with James Johnson in ministry as he asks us all to answer the question, 'Dare we bask in the Father's love?' For pilgrims and pastors alike, Jim shows us that if we not only understood but also believed our position in Christ, our lives would be radically different. The candor and credibility of Jim's writings will stir the soul to wonder and worship. Read it. Think about it. Be changed by it ... we are orphans no more."

—Dr. Dan Lind
Senior Pastor, Faith Bible Church, Phoenix, Arizona

"Every reader will greatly appreciate the openness and honesty applied to James's writing, and realize the great amount of prayer, thought, and study, as well as the life experience shared throughout this book.

"The ability to utilize this book in teaching, training and coaching, and its importance/relevance to men in the church are extensive. Very few are teaching the importance of the Father heart of God today, how to apply it to our lives, and to take action with regard to our God-given purpose and call."

—Lindon Gareis
Co-author with Sherry Gareis of *Declutter Now!*, Peoria, Arizona

"For those of us whose self-worth is largely determined by what others say about us, by what we own, by what we have achieved, or because of who likes us, this book is a must read. Dr. Johnson's story is riveting; his teaching is transformational; the applications at the conclusion of each chapter are practical. Once you've read it, I believe you'll want to share it with your friends and family."

—John M. Palmer
President, EMERGE Counseling Services, Akron, OH

"I write this with tears flowing down my cheeks for the thousands upon thousands of God's children who have felt like orphans. Dr. James Johnson, thank you from the bottom of my heart for your life-changing book. This is more than another book to read. It is a manual to freedom and hope. Just a few years ago, I was one of those orphans, when grace fetched and found me. There is a desperate cry from those poisoned by hopelessness in our world and *Grace: Orphans No More* is the antidote. This book will be healing for those who have been running from God's love. When you are done reading this book, you will be running into the arms of the Father's love. Ready yourself for this life-changing journey and enjoy the ride to a healed, stronger, better more fulfilled you!

—Sam Hinn

Pastor and Motivational Speaker, Toronto, Ontario, CANADA

FOREWORD

I have never pictured myself as an orphan. I hadn't the remotest need to. I was raised in a Jewish home with loving, supportive parents who were married more than 50 years before my dad passed away. And what a dad he was! Reliable, loving, funny. Lenny Burger was well known in our southwestern Pennsylvania community as a jokester, yet a natural leader — successful Charter Life Underwriter, several times local president of the B'nai B'rith (Jewish men's association), actively involved on committees at our local Jewish Community Center (as was my mother also). Daddy loved firing the starting gun at our summer swim meets almost as much as he enjoyed cheering us on once the races were underway. "Uncle" Lenny to most of my peers, my dad loved them one and all.

So when Dr. Jim Johnson asked me to edit his doctoral thesis on *Grace: Orphans No More*, I thought I'd have a hard time relating to his theme. In fact, few people will share his life experience of learning in his early thirties that he was adopted by the man he thought was his biological father. The shock of this discovery during a difficult season in a challenging pastorate escalated what was already an emotional and spiritual tailspin.

Yet Jim didn't "crash and burn" — though he came mighty close on several occasions. This book describes how this broken man found God's Grace in the midst of meltdown. But it's far more than the success story of a pastor who found redemption, renewal, self-respect and personal healing. Jim's purpose in writing his story is not to draw you to him and his successful healing, but to point you to the greatness and Grace of Abba, Father God, who drew him, like Moses, out of the waters of his slavery to self, and freed him to lead others on the way to that Grace.

In editing this book, I have come to realize how many "orphan" behaviors I share with Jim and many other believers who struggle with performance, perfectionism, fear of rejection, and the gamut of self-directed, self-serving, self-rewarding behaviors we Christians employ to try make ourselves acceptable in the sight of God and those around us.

I encourage you to take your time with this book. Don't rush through it. Let Jim's voice become your friend. With humility and gentleness, he will guide you on the path to the One Who is not hidden from us, yet we fail to recognize even though He is with us. We fear Him as Judge, yet He loves us as Abba Father. We cover our eyes in shame, yet He lifts our faces and gazes at us and welcomes us into His arms.

Like our Abba-Father-Poppa-Daddy God, Jim Johnson is gentle and compassionate. Trust him to guide you along the way to Grace. You, too, will discover that you are no longer an orphan.

Pauly Heller
Editor, *Grace: Orphans No More*

CONTENTS

INTRODUCTION

"I have been a Christian for more than thirty years and have sat through hundreds of hours of classes and seminars that were all about learning and knowledge, but nothing has changed my life like this ministry and teaching."
— Rick, seminar participant

SIMPLY put, this book is about GRACE. Its chapters radiate from the passion and excitement of my own walk with God and 35 years of experience as a pastor, counselor and master coach. And it flows from my own frustration with how much Christian teaching fails to address the true meaning of God's GRACE.

This book is about *starting* with GRACE, the GRACE that appeared in Jesus who died to re-introduce us to a Father who loves us. A Father Who doesn't judge us, as "angry God" theology would have us believe. A Father Who isn't impressed with our rituals, religion, requirements, rules, rites, and regulations. A Father Who longs to do what He created us for — to walk with us, fellowship with us, enjoy us (and we Him). God the *Father* longs to share His heart with us; and *Jesus, the Son of God* longs for a bride to cherish and nourish; His *Holy Spirit* abides in us to prepare us as the SONS and DAUGHTERS He wants.

This book is about *seeing* Grace — what GRACE means to God, how it became the life-changing force of the early church, how the core essence of GRACE was lost, and how you can discover the powerful impact of GRACE in your life. I want you to not only know God's Love but also to experience Him on a daily basis, "knowing and believing" what God means when He says, "You are the one I love in whom My heart is well pleased."

This book is about *applying* GRACE as it was meant to be applied through reforming a foundation of BASIC TRUST in your life. I don't mean repackaging worn-out "Christianese" clichés about God's Love, but learning how His Love welcomes us to His Presence every day of our lives.

GRACE allows you to live in ABBA Father's house, "HOME," a place where He embraces you, a place where you belong, where you are important, where you have value, comfort, provision, protection, affirmation, acceptance, inheritance, and identity, a place of light and warmth and intimate love. GRACE is about *allowing God to change your life by focusing not on your behavior but on the driving emotions beneath the behaviors at their very root.*

GRACE rightly understood changes us from the inside out. My mentor Dean Hatfield would say, "It's not a problem of fruit as much as it is root." In other words, people's outward behaviors and daily actions express or reflect the inner motivations of their heart. Like a fruit tree, a person's life has roots below the surface that determine the type or quality of the external "fruit" they bear. Crabapple roots produce crabapple trees, which produce crabapples.

I want to bear good fruit in my life — apples, not crabapples. When crabapple behaviors show up — sour, bitter, angry, hurtful behaviors — *the primary problem is not the crabapple behavior that looks and tastes like a crabapple. It's that the roots of my heart are still crabapple roots. This book is all about changing those roots.*

The writer of Proverbs addressed this issue saying, "Watch over your heart with all diligence, for from it flow the springs of life."[1]

The point is, *if the water is bad, don't clean the pond; check the source.* My friend John, for example, found himself constantly irritated at work, so he attended an "I will not be irritated anymore" seminar to control his behavior. But John's primary emotion was not irritability; it was the fear that if he couldn't produce more, faster, harder, and better, he would be terminated.

Explosive pressure dominated this primary emotional area. Driven by the root of fear, John was emotionally exhausted and angry, but couldn't say anything. His behavior — the secondary "crabapple" of anger — originated from his primary root of fear. Life change is not about conforming to a new law — "Thou shalt not be angry at thy neighbor" — but about transforming the inside, because the outside is most often an expression of the inside heart. Establishing and following a whole new set of behavior-conforming laws will only *displace* the basic heart problem, *not resolve* it. If transformation is to take place, the heart problem has to be identified, exposed and surrendered to the Spirit's/ Father's scrutiny. Additionally the believer must accept a new identity, one founded on the reality of who he/she is under the blood of the cross. In our coaching sessions, John saw his root fear. He realized he was not believing God for His provision, and the anger at others' behavior amazingly disappeared. With an understanding of Father's Love (GRACE), treating the root led to natural changes in the fruit.

Jesus said:

> *For there is no good tree which produces bad fruit, nor, on the other hand, a bad tree which produces good fruit. For each tree is known by its own fruit. For men do not gather figs from thorns, nor do they pick grapes from a briar bush. The good man out of the good treasure of his heart brings forth what is good; and the evil man out of the evil treasure brings forth what is evil; for his mouth speaks from that which fills his heart.* [2]

On another occasion Jesus explained the heart issue to his disciples while simultaneously confronting religious leaders.

Jesus said,

> *Are you still lacking in understanding also? Do you not understand that everything that goes into the mouth passes into the stomach, and is eliminated? But the things that proceed out of the mouth come from the heart, and those defile the man. For out of the heart come evil thoughts, murders, adulteries, fornications, thefts, false witness, slanders. These are the things which defile the man; but to eat with unwashed hands does not defile the man.* [3]

Lastly this book is about *beholding* GRACE. I want you to see a full picture of a relationship with God, and set yourself in it, personally. I want you to see what the disciples saw in Jesus, when they "beheld Him full of GRACE and truth." Then as the Spirit touches you, to let Him do what He came and died to do: introduce you to His Father.

Its three sections describe (1) the problem we Christians have of being God's SONS and DAUGHTERS yet living like spiritual ORPHANS, (2) the prodigious GRACE poured out on us by the Father, and (3) the practical steps we need to take to displace our old distorted ways of thinking with the positive Truth that sets us free.

Don't rush through this book. I want you to mull it over, interact with it, apply it to your life. Each chapter concludes with a personal application section to help you *"Learn to Hear the Shepherd's Heart"* based on the guidelines of Habakkuk 2:1-2:

> *I will stand on my guard post and station myself on the rampart; and I will keep watch to see what He will speak to me, and how I may reply when I am reproved. Then the LORD answered me and said, "Record the vision and inscribe it on tablets that the one who reads it may run. For the vision is yet for the appointed time; it hastens toward the goal and it will not fail. Though it tarries, wait for it; for it will certainly come, it will not delay. Behold, as for the proud one, His soul is not right within him; but the righteous will live by his faith."*

I want this book to be a resource for you, so its appendices are loaded with additional resource material, excerpts from the research of a slew of experts, links to websites, and so on. I hope that those who help others — encouragers, pastors, counselors and coaches who have a passion to see hurting souls healed — will use this material. People have told me, time and again, "I've been in counseling for years, with multiple counselors, and you have taught me more in 45 minutes than I received in five years of counseling." God's GRACE is truly life changing. Rightly communicated, it will do just that.

Living the Grace Embrace,
Dr. James Johnson, Ph.D.
Executive Director, Keys4-Life:
Faith-based Counseling and Coaching
May 1, 2015

SECTION ONE: THE PROBLEM WITH ORPHANS

CHAPTER 1: JEREMIAH'S STORY

"You will live your life as if you have a home or you will live your life as if you don't."

—Henri Nouwen[4]

"WHAT? What did you do? But you didn't tell us anything was wrong! What have you done with our son?" From the next room, I hear panic distorting my wife's voice as she talks on the phone with "Peggy," (not her real name) our babysitter. It's late. We have just returned home, exhausted, from three days of medical testing at the Allergy Institute in Oakland, California. If my migraines weren't so frequent and debilitating, we never would have left our 13-month-old son in a sitter's care for so long.

My wife drops the phone into its cradle, tears flooding her blinking eyes. Usually so competent and nurturing with Jeremiah, Peggy had been unable to stop him from crying after we left him with her. Rattled by his nonstop wails, Peggy told "Bob," her deputy-sheriff husband that something was wrong. When the sheriff stopped by to pick up Bob for work, the sheriff intoned, "That child looks abused." Without consulting us, they whisked Jeremiah off to a Bakersfield hospital — a 45-minute drive away — where a first-year resident diagnosed him with "failure to thrive" and said he belonged with Child Protective Services (CPS). That's all it took for my wife and me to be charged as child abusers.

Incredibly, unbelievably, Peggy never indicated to us in any of our frequent phone calls to check on Jeremiah that anything was seriously wrong with him. She mentioned that he cried a lot, but not that he was frantic, inconsolable, or wouldn't eat. We had thought two to three days of separation might even be healthy for his social development.

We could not have been more wrong. Jeremiah experienced what we later learned was "anaclytic depression," which can afflict babies and young toddlers when separated from their parents. At this stage of life, children normally become clingy and cry when their parents lay them down or leave the room. Anaclytically depressed babies, however, can die from this reaction to separation, but neither the medical community nor we knew about this condition in those days.

For the next thirty days, we endured gut-wrenching legal battles to get our child back from the grip of authorities seemingly set on proving us to be unfit parents. "No you cannot see your son until we tell you." But why? When we were finally allowed to see Jeremiah, it had been eight days since we had left him at Peggy's, and now the foster parents assigned to him could not get him to "thrive."

On day 10 we appeared in an initial hearing, then a full hearing some days later. Sixty-seven witnesses from our church drove 45 miles to wait in the hot sun to be called as character references on our behalf. The appointed referee got through the first five. LAPD Vice Detective Arnie Rios, Kern County school teacher Stan Chapman, and Kern County Sheriff Jim Armstrong all stated they knew us and our family, that we would never do anything to harm our child. Unnerved, the referee dismissed the court. Whether to save embarrassment in front of the press or for some other selfish reason, he offered us a way out — a lie.

"Here's the deal," our attorney said. We were sitting in a stark prisoner holding room. "If you lie to say you neglected your son, we release him; he goes home with you and you get him back right now. Don't sign and you may never see him again."

For years, the Lord had been convicting me of my tendency to tell half-truths to others and myself — those "little" deceptions that spring from my self-protective heart. I thought of Abraham and his willingness to sacrifice his son Isaac to the Lord. I knew God was saying to me, "Do you love Me more than your son? Will you sell out your devotion to Me and save your son by a *lie?*" I was a pastor. I could not make that compromise.

I watched in helpless agony as our 13-month-old son was trundled away in the foster parent's car. Because of my allergies and headaches, we kept daily written records of everything Jeremiah ate. What did the foster parents know or care about my baby's food and dairy sensitivities?

Time and again I cried, "What is my crime?" We were a cozy family of three. "Why are they taking my son away from me? I'm a GOOD FATHER!" I would never desert Jeremiah as my own birth father had deserted my mother and me. But how could I prove that to my baby boy when I was only allowed to see him in supervised visits for one hour a day every other day?

Panic-stricken and out of control, I tumbled through a pounding surf of emotional pain that kept tossing me onto the rocks of my past.

Not until November a year and a half later would I learn why the term "father" held such conflicting emotions for me. At Thanksgiving dinner I joked that I didn't look like anyone else in the family. Sudden silence. Embarrassed looks. Cleared throats.

"Well, Jim ..." I was 35 years old that day when I learned that my dad was not my biological father, who had long since disappeared. I was adopted. Adopted! The man I called Dad had loved my mother and had compassion on me and made us his family. True, they were both flawed — she, daughter of the town drunk, and he, son of a man who abandoned his family for another woman. But what did I know or care of compassion in that moment? My life turned inside out. My heart froze. How could I trust that anything I associated with the word "father" was true? It would be years before I would understand the limitless value and deep emotion of what adoption meant.

Now I was a father myself, and I agonized over how to show the son I adored that I was there for him. As much as I wanted to assure Jeremiah that Daddy would get him home, I was thwarted at every turn. How could my toddler know Daddy's good intentions when we were allowed to see him, at best, only two hours a day in a stranger's house?

The foster parents still could not get Jeremiah to "thrive." He would eat and throw up everything. His weight kept dropping, ultimately from around 20 to 9.7 pounds! Finally their pediatrician had them check him into L.A. County Children's Hospital. We met them there. All the medical staff stared at us as if we were child abusers.

But we were a family again, if only in Jeremiah's hospital room. When he woke up, we were there. Each day his health improved. We smiled and laughed again. And we stayed until end of day and he went to sleep. Then we drove 60 miles home, only to return the next day before he woke up. On day three or four, he became violently ill. I happened to see on his chart that at 2 a.m., he had been force-fed milk.

I was enraged — I had struggled with anger management for years — but exerted self-control at the nurses' station. "Who fed my son milk last night?" No one moved. In anger I slammed my hand on the counter. "Who ... fed ... my ... son ... milk ... last ... night!" Hearing the commotion, a kind, grandfatherly man stepped out from among the filing cabinets. "Would you mind going down to the end of the hall to the waiting room for me?"

We sat in the avocado-green vinyl chairs and built our case, spreading our charts and records of Jeremiah's previous doctor visits across the coffee table. The man patiently allowed us a few moments. We looked up through bloodshot eyes. Then he said, "We have put your son through every test known to medicine. There is nothing wrong with him. Nothing at all. He needs to be in your family again. So I want you to take your son home."

"What? Sir, whoever you are, you don't understand. We have been accused of neglect. They say we are child abusers." It came out in shameful sobs.

"We think you should just take your son home."

"You don't understand, we can't. The courts won't allow it."

Then came the words I'll never forget: "I am the head of Los Angeles County Children's Hospital. If I say you take your son home, you take your son home!" With that, we packed up our papers, our son's clothing and our hearts. I tucked Jeremiah into my arms and whispered, "We're going home, son." And WE WENT HOME!

In the midst of that trial, God was working in my heart. One conversation with God would change my life forever.

One day, praying by a stream, I told Him, "No matter what, Lord, I'm going to follow Abraham's example with Isaac. Jeremiah belongs to You, and I refuse to try to control things anymore. I give up my son to You, because I choose to love You more than anything or anyone else."

I will never forget, in the midst of all my anguish, alone in the gravel, the words I felt God say, still and small in my inner spirit: "If you can love Me so much ..." And here I interrupted Him to say, "And I do, I love you so much!"

There was a long pause and I realized I had interrupted God. He patiently began again, "If you can love me so much, why do you find it so hard to understand that *I love you so much more?*"

It was May 1983 and the beginning of my walk toward LIFE and GRACE. There would be many failures to come, but this was the start of my journey into Father's arms, my walk to Father's HOME. God began to grind through the emotional cement of my inability to see His Love. The foundations of my past dysfunction and misunderstanding began to crumble.

Father God knew what I needed (and each of us needs) to hear:

1. God will test the heart of His "Abrahams" as He chooses to do so. He has the right to test the integrity of His servants. The question is: How far can He test you? Trials test and reveal the limits of your integrity. This was not as much about Jeremiah as it was about my integrity and the need to be unyielding in the face of a lie.

2. When you think God can't, He can. Like that kind hospital administrator, God says, "My Name is Jesus. I am Almighty God. If I say you can count on this promise, then you simply count on that promise."

3. Always know that God is in the midst of the storm and will be trying to speak to your heart. *Wait* and *watch* for Him.

4. The depth of the trial will be equal to the depth of the emotional lies you are believing about God.

5. In the context of my life's worst horror, when every-thing had been stripped — my son, my job, my health, even a place to stay — and I had nothing, there Father God spoke.

My prayer for you, reader, is that you will learn to look through the storm to find His face. He is there. He wants to show you Himself and His Love for you. As you relinquish your own strength, and become as weak and trusting as a child, you will feel Father tucking you close to His chest and whispering in your ear, "I've got you. I know the way. I'll get you HOME."

ORPHANS *and* SONS *Defined*

Scripture describes two types Christians — those who live *by striving to perform according to religious law* and those who live *by faith in promise*. The distinctions between the resulting lifestyles form the foundational principles of this book. I refer to them as ORPHANS and SONS.

The believers in the early church at Galatia struggled with understanding how to live out their freedom in Christ. In Galatians 4:21-28, Paul writes to them, "Tell me, you who want to be under law, do you not listen to the law? For it is written that Abraham had two sons, one by the bondwoman and one by the free woman. But the son by the bondwoman was born according to the flesh and the son by the free woman through the promise."

Abraham had received the promise of a son, but he jumped the gun in making his dream come true through his union with Hagar, his wife Sarah's slave. Their resulting offspring, Ishmael, is associated throughout Scripture with the impulses of the flesh, lack of faith, trust in one's self rather than in God. Eventually, to keep peace in the family, Abraham sent Hagar and Ishmael away into the wilderness. Sarah's son, Isaac, however, was a true miracle baby, the "child of promise," born long after menopause, when Sarah was 90 years old and Abraham 100. Paul makes a clear, specific declaration to his audience when he writes, "and you brethren, like Isaac, are children of promise."

ORPHANS: What is an ORPHAN spirit? An ORPHAN is one without a home. Christians with an ORPHAN spirit believe they are like Ishmael, rejected, turned out. They depend solely on themselves, instead of on their Father God. ORPHANS believe the following:
1. I am who I am *because of what I do.*
2. I am who I am *because of what people say I am.*
3. I am who I am *because of what I own.*

4. I am who I am *because of the good times I have.*
5. I am who I am *because of what and whom I control.*
6. I am who I am *because everyone likes me.*
7. I am who I am *because of what I achieve.*
8. I am who I am *because somebody needs me.*

ORPHANS live in fear; they cannot trust, so they must fight for what they can get. They struggle to know peace or joy or rest or loving someone else. ORPHANS cannot hear, "It's not about you." Though they are Christians, ORPHANS live, like Ishmael, as "children of the bondwoman," rejected and forever striving to earn the Father's Love and forgiveness through their self-effort and love of law. They have forgotten the value of God's Love for them, and that God is their only source of Life and power. They have "fallen from grace" in the sense that they continue to try to earn what God freely gives them. Although they are legitimate children of God the Father, they live as if they are Fatherless. These believers face the challenges of losing their freedom by yielding to the appeal of the world's values and returning to the illusion of security found in legalistic behavior.

ORPHANS have the inner spirit of a child living life without a parent, and an adult living life apart from fully depending on God as Father. Spiritually, it is the human spirit severed from the Father's heart.

SONS: SONS know:

1. I am who I am *because of who my Father says I am.*
2. I am who I am *because I am loved by my Father.*
3. I am who I am *because He has given me a significant work.*
4. I am who I am *because He values me greatly.*
5. I am who I am *because He approves of me.*
6. I am who I am *because He protects and provides for me.*

SONS, like Isaac, live in awareness of their standing as children of promise. They are free of the world and its values, free of pressure to perform under some religious laws, rules, regulations, rituals, requirements or restrictions. SONS learn to live by the Law of Love; they bask in God's Presence, receiving His Love first. Then in loving response to hearing His commands, they obey, asking for His insight through the practice of prayer.

> ORPHANS *live by faith in self-dependence — self-solutions, self-strength, self-wisdom, self-sufficiency, self-centeredness, self-protection, self-vindication, self-promotion, self-exaltation. They try harder to do it right or, failing to do so, give in and become embittered toward God.*

> SONS *learn that life is about intimacy and trusting God, practicing His Presence every day in their daily lives. Pleasing Him comes as an overflow of trust.*

CHAPTER 2: LOCKED OUT

"All my Christian life I have felt I was standing at the door of a house, hearing the laughter and warmth inside but couldn't figure out how to open the door to get in. Your ministry gave me the keys to open the door of Father's Presence; I will never be the same."

—Steve, seminar participant

"IF A PASTOR struggles at the Christian walk and finds some amazing answers, it sure helps regular folks like me." Steve barely meets my gaze as he speaks. I met him after teaching at his church a week ago, and now he is sharing his heart with me.

"When I first became a Christian," Steve explains, "everything seemed so filled with joy. But as I tried to walk with God, I had a feeling of not being good enough, not measuring up. I knew there was this Presence, something more that was just beyond my reach but I don't understand how to get through. It feels like I am always at the doorway to God's Presence and power. It's like standing outside a wonderful home where, on the inside, are all these sounds of laughter, acceptance, and peace. I can hear it, but with my best efforts, I can only peek through a crack in the door. I can't get in. It's always just out of reach.

"And the worst thing is that I know this is my HOME — where I belong — but I can't find the keys to get in. I try, but I can't seem to do it right, or do enough, or be good enough, or stay in control or whatever. And then I go to a conference, or hear a message or someone tells me to read the latest book, and I try new things, learn new things that help for a while. But they don't last. They wear off."

Steve leans forward, "I believe you have found the keys I am missing, the keys to help me open that door and live inside my Father's house, where I belong."

I smile at Steve. I know exactly what he is talking about. I have been where he is.

A Great Start — But the Glasses Stayed On

I started out on my own Christian journey with great intentions of pleasing God. I tried hard to obey, to surrender and work at those things I thought would make me look good in God's eyes. From my past, I knew that I had to work really hard to gain approval. At least that was how it was in the family I grew up in. Very little I did met with any approval from my parents. My grades weren't good enough, my behavior wasn't acceptable and my life goals were too shortsighted. My interests were not theirs. Clearly to me, I did nothing right in their eyes.

Wordlessly my parents could communicate their disapproval to me with just one look or facial expression that spoke volumes of disdain and disappointment. That early training — with its emphasis on what I did and how I looked in every arena of my life — became the value system I used to filter everything. Like Dorothy and her companions entering the Emerald City in *The Wizard of Oz*, I wore spectacles that colored everything I experienced in my world. Only my world wasn't emerald-colored; it was cloudy gray. Was I good enough? Did I do enough? Was I successful? Did I look right? Own the right stuff? That's who I was before Christ came into my life.

Initially, after accepting Christ as my Savior, I experienced overwhelming love and affirmation. I couldn't get over the joy, contentment and peace I felt. But I didn't understand at the time that I came to Christ with a performance-based value system in place. I still wore the self-centered spectacles through which I saw my life and filtered all my perceptions of my basic value to Him.

I started out feeling God's Presence, peace and contented joy. But the feelings wore off. Then came that "look" again, this time from God. I felt His displeasure. The Christian groups I attended seemed to point to a clear direction. I believed that to feel that initial joy again I had to work hard, strive more, be more disciplined, do things right, look good, make the performance grade, have the right degrees, impress the right people and excel in all my assignments. Then, somehow, maybe, I would avoid the "look" and be accepted again by God.

I went to college then seminary. I was a youth pastor, Bible study leader, held a couple of pastorates then finally became a senior pastor with a fairly good-size church and staff. But I still hadn't arrived at the place of feeling accepted. There were more standards to live up to, to be judged by: the size of my church, my level of education, my salary, how many books and pamphlets I'd written, how many radio interviews I'd conducted. I thought that if I just did it right or better than anyone else, I would have God's Presence, and would know His smile. *Am I doing it right, God? Am I becoming super godly man? I'm still empty inside! I must need to pray more, share more, work harder, get another God-fix from a conference or reading a book or talking to a big-name speaker. Now am I doing it right, God? Are you pleased with me? Am I something special now? Am I better than the others? Can you love me? Will you bless me?*

A Great Fall — When Glasses Distort Rather Than Correct

In college, I took a mandatory class, Psychology 101, in which we watched (and laughed at) an experiment done on a willing volunteer who was given a set of glasses that altered his normal vision. Everything he saw appeared upside down. The floor seemed to be the ceiling, and the ceiling was the floor. From his perspective he walked across the ceiling, came to a doorway and saw the upper doorjamb as something he had to step over. He waved his hands in the air because, for him, the couch was on the ceiling. When he tried to pour water into a glass, he put the glass above the pitcher and poured the water on the floor. Everything was upside down.[5]

Walking outside was an even bigger challenge (and, of course, more hilarious for us) because the sky became the ground and the ground the sky. He would fall down hills, try to step over tree limbs or hit his face because he didn't duck. (You can see what this experiment was like by lying on the floor and imagining you're walking on the ceiling, stepping over doorways. You'll get the idea).

But slowly, the volunteer's mind began to adapt to the glasses. Soon he was able to function normally. Abnormal became normal, and normal became abnormal (a principle of dysfunctional thinking, by the way). The process was given a name: perceptual adaptation. The volunteer's brain adapted to upside-down perception so he could survive. Here is an important point: When the upside-down glasses were taken off, the man's perceptions did not automatically return to what they had been like before. He had to go through a retraining process in order to see, or even to walk, normally. The filter remained in his brain.

So it was with me. And so it may be with you. Reared in their families of origin, people are trained to think about themselves with certain values and beliefs about themselves and the world they inhabit. We are custom-fitted with value-system glasses from very early on.

Becoming a believer does not automatically remove the distorted lenses that filter one's thinking. God's normal way of thinking is foreign to people, even born-again ones. The concept "normal is abnormal and abnormal is normal" applies here. Most believers live in an opposite reality to what God sees.

A Great Announcement — He Knows What to Do

Now, the great news is when Christians come to know Christ as Savior, they hear the promise, "You shall know the truth and the truth shall set you free."[6]

Jesus told His followers that Father God would send the Spirit of Truth. "But when He, the Spirit of truth, comes, He will guide you into all the truth; for He will not speak on His own initiative, but whatever He hears, He will speak; and He will disclose to you what is to come."[7]

So the potential to find the truth and change what you believe is available to you. In essence, the good news is, *the glasses can come off.*

But a problem occurs when the Spirit gives the truth, and the receiver doesn't change right away. People cling to their filter systems that make abnormal seem normal and normal seem abnormal. Having been taught about what group they need to belong to, what things they must do to make themselves important, how they must prove their value and measure up to gain approval and appreciation, to be provided for and protected, they will go to great lengths to do or get those things to feel good about themselves. Like orphans starved of what they need, they rummage through the dumpsters of a world value-system in search of counterfeit affection. They will do anything they can to perform and people-please and pretend and try to control in an effort to feel good about themselves and their world.

I brought all of my performance and people pleasing and pretending and control issues right into my Christian life. When things weren't going my way, I tried harder to look better and please more people and network more extensively. When my efforts in the flesh ran out of gas, I fell away from Christ, not wanting anything to do with Him or things about Him.

Did my Christian life fail because I wasn't trying? No, I tried with all I had. The breaking point came because I was struggling with controlling my tongue. In those early days, my words spewed bitterness and anger punctuated with curse words. As I read the Word of God, I realized my cursing was wrong. I wanted desperately to change. I would get on my knees by my bed and pray that God would change me.

One day, I was kneeling at the end of my bed, hoping that God would see me and know I was doing right for Him. I got up from prayer and turned, my eyes still a little foggy, and smacked myself on a door my roommate had left open. I proceeded to tell the door where it could spend eternity under the judgment of Almighty God. Then a realization hit me even harder than the door had. I couldn't change my behavior for even five minutes, despite the time I had spent praying on my knees. That was when I quit. Christianity was a joke.

For a while, I made it my mission to see that no one would be fooled by this Jesus stuff like I had been. Like the Apostle Paul, I "persecuted the Way." I argued with Christians, slashing their simple faith with my sharp, angry logic. "Winning" arguments and proving them wrong or duped was all that mattered to me.

I later understood that I quit because my filter system said that I could make God happy with me by my own self-righteous behavior. Unwittingly, I was trying to fill my internal God-shaped hole — that "I feel good about me" feeling — by committing self-righteous acts designed to impress God and make Him proud of me so I could receive more of His blessing and get that "I feel good about me" feeling back.

Still in college, I continued my assault on Christianity until, one evening, I met Dean Hatfield, a campus missionary. He used a word I hadn't heard before and it gave me insight into something I had not known. The word was GRACE. As I got to know Dean, I saw him live out this word in front of me. This godly man simply brought me into his home and poured loving encouragement into a very empty hole.

Unfortunately, I still did not grasp the meaning of GRACE. I heard the definition spoken over and over — God's Riches at Christ's Expense — and I knew He had made me righteous in Christ, but my understanding of the concept remained superficial. I heard the words but they didn't have the emotional substance to challenge my filter or remove my world-value-system glasses. I was still "walking on the ceiling." I had clutched GRACE, but I couldn't hang on. I knew I was *saved*; I didn't know I was *loved — that was the problem*. I wanted desperately to be valued, to be important, to know my future was secure. Again the glasses stayed on.

This time I tried harder, worked at it more, and discovered that through my prideful knowledge of the Bible, I could outperform others, I could excel, I could teach. I would go to seminary so I could be licensed to teach others. But the glasses and the filter remained stubbornly in place. My normal and God's normal still didn't coincide. I wasn't ready yet.

In his book *Victory over the Darkness*, Dr. Neil Anderson recounts the story of Jesus healing a blind man from Mark 8:22-25. "And they brought a blind man to Jesus and implored Him to touch him. Taking the blind man by the hand, He brought him out of the village; and after spitting on his eyes and laying His hands on him, He asked him, 'Do you see anything?' And he looked up and said, 'I see men, for I see them like trees, walking around.'"

Wow! Imagine that! This blind man could see, for the first time in his life. A miracle had occurred. But something wasn't quite right. The gospel account continues: "Then again He laid His hands on his eyes; and he looked intently and was restored, and began to see everything clearly." Notice something here — Jesus healed him the first time but the man says, "I can see but I see men walking about as trees." So had Jesus just not "tweaked" him enough?

Press this a bit. Did the Lord of the Universe, who created the man in the first place and who created his eyes, not know him well enough to get it right the first time? Had Jesus made a mistake? I think not. As Anderson points out, this eyewitness account reveals Jesus emphasizing an important principle: *One touch isn't always enough.* In His wisdom, Jesus teaches that people often must come back for another touch of His healing GRACE and mercy. Otherwise, they simply see men vaguely, like trees, blurred and without understanding. That was me. I needed a second touch.

I pastored churches and dealt with people, all the while a hungry ORPHAN-leader trying to teach ORPHAN-followers what it felt like to be full and loved. I was trying to lead others to a place I'd never been myself. I studied the Word with the best of teachers. I learned to practice a Christian walk in the Spirit through the teaching ministry of Campus Crusade for Christ (now Cru). But though I could get it right some of the time, most of it was all about me. Driven to be successful, I needed to keep things under control; I had to do everything right, to impress others to feel good about myself. Like a juggler spinning plates atop sticks, I had to keep them all spinning, running from plate to plate and adding more plates.

Following the loss of a ministry due to a theological stance I had to take, I strove with diligence and sheer will to plant a church and keep it going. I worked way more hours than I should have, pushing with everything in me to be "the best" in the game. I believed I could be a successful pastor (in the world's view) by working harder and harder. I met every new frustration and obstacle with greater effort, beating myself into submission. This was how my ORPHAN spirit worked within me.

Fueled by competitive comparison and my co-dependency on my work — which was my little god — my "life" cord plugged in (welded in) I sucked like an addict every ounce of hope I could find in how I was performing. When work was up, I was up, and when it was down I was depressed. So it went for years, each new wound cutting deeper into a very defective foundation until my building simply crumbled.

Finally, after 21 years and the exit of another group of people from my life and ministry, I gave up. Literally … on everything. Too tired to try anymore, I simply stopped caring. The plates fell and I let a lot of people down. Deep inside I believed God could bless others, but not me, because I was not good enough (a lie Satan spits at Father's children). The picture of failure, I fled.

Incredibly, God never gave up on me. I left ministry, brokenhearted, hopeless, immersed in a dark night of the soul. I took a job managing a fast-food restaurant. What else could a divorced, used-up failure do? Sometimes my hands shook so badly I couldn't make a simple sandwich. On my second day of training, sitting in the back-room utility area, watching instructional videos, the other manager trainee turned to me and said, "You're a pastor." I smiled weakly, panicked and wanted to run. But I stayed and said yes, I was. She then said, "Last night, at my church, during a circle of prayer, someone stopped, looked up at me and said, 'You are working with a pastor, and you must tell him he has to go back, for he will help many people.'"

I couldn't believe it. There was no human explanation for her knowledge; I had told no one I was a pastor. *Good grief,* I thought, *give me a break. Seriously, God, are You kidding me? My life is a mess, my hands can't even hold a hamburger, my heart barely takes one more beat and You give me this?* I politely asked the woman never to mention this again … to anyone.

God didn't give up on me, even as He'll never give up on you. *He takes our mess and makes it His Message.* I finally brought all my emotional stuff to Him and said, "You fix it, because I'm so done and I haven't even a clue what to do." One December dawn in 1995, driving to work on a snow-packed road in Iowa, with the rising sun blinding my eyes through the windshield, I felt Him say in my inner spirit, "I won't give up on you, I love you. I want you to go back, and re-learn from Me, because you don't understand Me or our relationship at all. Start from the beginning; just be My SON."

So I did. This book is a chronicle of my walk with God that began at that point and changed everything about my thinking and my life and how I came to be so amazed by GRACE. It started when I realized I knew virtually nothing about God's Love.

All my formal education, reading, seminars, sermons, and accomplishments did nothing to teach me that God really loved me and delighted in me and rejoiced over me and gathered me in His everlasting arms and wanted me back to Himself. I had interpreted GRACE through my world value-system. God began to show me so much more.

A Great Relief — You Are Not Alone

I went back and engaged in a process with a kind and caring group of mature believers who loved me, trusted me and picked me up. Pastors Tom Bell, Fred McCormick and Leith Anderson, with elders from Wooddale Church, helped me see myself and the pain I had caused. They put me in charge of a divorce recovery group. *Oh great*, I thought, *this is just what I need — a discouraged, depressed failure leading a group of depressed people whose marriages have failed.*

However, we must never forget these two mighty words: "But God." The Creator/Carpenter started helping me rebuild my thinking. I began reading and studying from a different perspective — not to impress God or others with my knowledge but to learn about my relationship with Him. From that foundation came the passion to build healthy relationships with the people God loves. I knew there had to be answers somewhere. As I studied I began to teach what I was learning, and people kept coming back.

After several years of being single I met Cheryl on a blind date. (I like to jokingly say she was blind and I was the date.) We were married in May 1999. One day, listening to the radio together, we couldn't believe our ears. Cheryl exclaimed, "That man sounds just like you!"

David Seamands, author of *Healing for Damaged Emotions*, speaking from his years of counseling and preaching, was sharing exactly what I was experiencing. I stared at the radio, listening to this man who could have been reading my diary. Then I went out and bought *Healing for Damaged Emotions*.

Seamands describes two groups of people whom he was unable to help through regular preaching, teaching, prayer, committing to Christ, filling of the Spirit, communion, and other church involvement. One group "tried every Christian discipline, but with no results," and eventually fell into despair and disillusionment. The second group became phony, "repressing their inner feelings and denying anything that was seriously wrong, because, Christians can't have such problems. ... The denied problems went underground, only to later reappear in all manner of illnesses, eccentricities, terribly unhappy marriages, and sometimes even in the emotional destruction of their children."[8]

What was I reading? These people sound just like me! Well, some of it anyway. Seamands continues:

> *During this time of discovery, God showed me that the ordinary ways of ministry would never help some problems. And He began to enable me to open up my heart to personal self-discovery, and to new depths of healing love through my marriage, my children, and intimate friends. In the 20 years that I have been preaching, teaching, counseling, and distributing tapes on this subject, I have heard from thousands of formerly defeated Christians who have found release from emotional hang-ups and who have experienced the healing of crippling memories of the past.*

My experience was not unique! Over the years, I have counseled many people and found very similar experiences. I've learned that other pastors saw the same things. In fact, 82 percent of evangelical Christians in churches today come from a very dysfunctional background.[9]

My research gradually revealed the same percentage for Christian pastors, leaders and teachers as for their congregations. Something is wrong, not merely with people's behavior, but at the core, with their hearts. Damaged emotions emanate from the emptiness of people's God-shaped hole. They need to be healed.

Churches are filled with well-meaning and hardworking performance-oriented Christians trying to live out the Christian life in their own strength. Something is wrong on the inside. They are wearing their own upside-down glasses.

I realized that my flesh, my orphaned spirit, was still in control, as it was before Christ was in my life. It had just taken on a different expression.

Nor was I alone. Others experienced it, too. Some of the most notable testimonies of something being wrong on the inside came from men I deeply respect. Pastor of First Baptist Church of Atlanta since 1971, Charles Stanley wrote the following during a time when, as an internationally successful preacher, he was in the midst of an emotional identity crisis:

> *One of these fellows said, "Charles, put your head on the table and close your eyes." So I did. Then he said to me very kindly, "Charles, your father just picked you up in his arms and held you. What do you feel?" I burst out crying. And I cried and I cried, and I could not stop crying. Finally when I*

stopped, he asked me again, and I said that I felt warm and loved and secure and good, and I started weeping again. For the first time in my life I felt God emotionally loving me. All these years I preached about trusting God and believing Him and obeying him. And I had. But I came back and I looked through my sermon file, and in all of those years I had only preached one sermon on the love of God and it was not worth listening to. The reason was because I didn't know what it meant to feel the love of God because my dad had walked out on me in death at seven months of age."[10]

Here was a man, still one of my heroes of the faith, who had a worldwide ministry on thousands of radio stations, yet a vacuum remained down deep inside him. Coming from a terribly dysfunctional background by his own admission, even Stanley, at a crisis point in his life, did not have a finger on the pulse of God's emotional Love for him.

So, my reader, I invite you to walk with me. I'd like to show you some of the depth of God's Love, break through some of your preconceived notions, and dig down until you not only know He loves you but you also *believe* it at your very core. At the outset I can tell you this will hurt a little. No, in fact, if you seriously apply yourself to the Scriptures and principles in this book, it will hurt a lot.

No one likes it when the glasses come off. No one likes to feel exposed and uncertain. People grow to like living in their prisons. Prison is consistent and predictable — there are four walls, well-defined boundaries, rules to follow, scheduled meals, and everything is in order. But there is also no freedom, no truth, nor opportunity for change or growth. A.W. Tozer wrote, "It is doubtful whether God can bless a man greatly until He has hurt him deeply."[11]

APPLICATION: LEARNING TO HEAR THE SHEPHERD'S HEART — HABAKKUK 2:1-4

I have learned in my counseling and coaching practice that there is only one starting point that matters. It is simply *Building a Vertical Relationship with God.* Jesus, knowing His followers intimately, provided for the generations of believers to come the greatest Counselor of all. "And I will ask the Father, and he will give you another Counselor to be with you forever," He told His disciples in John 14:16. He also said that relying on Him would "lead [us] into all truth." Furthermore, He said, "My sheep hear My voice, and I know them, and they follow Me."[12]

He had already promised His disciples in John 7:38 that from their "innermost being will flow rivers of living water."

If I can do nothing else for you, I want to teach you to start spending time with the Wonderful Counselor and learn to hear His voice, His inner leading, in your heart every single day. Doing so was never intended to be complicated — it is Father's gift to His children. For the most part, the church has made it too hard. Habakkuk 2:1-2 presents some guidelines I will use to enhance your understanding throughout this book:

> *I will stand on my guard post and station myself on the rampart; and I will keep watch to see what He will speak to me, and how I may reply when I am reproved. Then the LORD answered me and said, "Record the vision and inscribe it on tablets that the one who reads it may run. For the vision is yet for the appointed time; it hastens toward the goal and it will not fail. Though it tarries, wait for it; for it will certainly come, it will not delay. Behold, as for the proud one, his soul is not right within him; but the righteous will live by his faith.*

I want you to learn the following four principles from this passage:

1. GET SERIOUS: "Stand and station yourself to wait on God alone."

The first necessity for time with God and hearing His voice is shutting off every other voice in your head. People's minds are filled with thoughts, worries about the day, goal setting for tomorrow, rehearsing the frustrations of yesterday. Forcibly shut them off. Quiet your heart to stand like a soldier fixed on hearing what God has to say to you. I love to remind myself, "*Stop listening to the thoughts your mind is thinking and start telling your mind what thoughts to think.*"

2. BE FOCUSED: "And I will keep watch to see what He will speak to me."

A person keeping watch over something constantly turns his or her eyes, scanning every detail, usually to protect the object. In your times with God, as you hear Father's voice, you need to be protecting your heart from all distractions. Father God has given you the Holy Spirit as your internal guidance system. Professor Howard Hendricks of Dallas Theological Seminary would say that God is far more interested in giving you His will than you are in finding it.

Practice spiritual breathing, inhaling God's Word by reading His Bible and letting it wash through you. Try reading one book in the New

Testament every day for thirty days. Soak it in, "letting the Word of Christ dwell within you richly." [13]

Soon you will start to hear and sense the Holy Spirit guiding you internally. You will start hearing His voice as you learn to watch for Him, listening for His still, small nudges within you. Picture Him speaking to you, as you sit by your Father's chair or in His lap. Learn to see with your spiritual eyes. Journal with your Father or with Jesus as you see in the eyes of your spirit. Listen to His Spirit as His voice leads you.

3. PRACTICE AUTHENTIC HUMILITY: *"And how I may reply when I am reproved."*

The core of your walk with God is hearing how loved you are, which leads to a repentant, or humble, heart. The essence of sin is self-dependence, and the goal of the believer's life is to respond to God's Love in humility. Often, before Father God begins a discussion with you, the Holy Spirit will identify the self-prioritizing, self-centering, or some particular sin you are doing, which keeps Him from flowing through you. "For God is opposed to the proud but gives grace to the humble. [14]

Breathing in His Word and exhaling selfishness opens up the rivers of GRACE flowing through your heart. As that happens, God's power flows through you. You will see this important concept expressed in every chapter of this book. Father won't spend long on "reproof" in your life; He seldom mentions more than a couple of areas that need cleansing. John 1:9 says that when "we confess our sins, He is faithful and just to forgive us our sins and to cleanse us from all unrighteousness." The Greek word for "confess" comes from HOMOLOGEO, meaning "to say the same thing." So confessing is simply feeling the same thing God feels about your sin.

4. WRITE IT, CHECK IT, RUN IT: *"Record the vision and inscribe it."*

Learn to journal your conversations with God. Sit with your Bible and a notebook. Write down what you say to Him then what your heart (not your ears) hears Him saying to you. Listen quietly and let Him speak or lead however He chooses. (He is God, remember.) Learn to check your heart by sharing what you've written with at least three trusted advisors. When they agree with what you have heard, then you have a checking system that keeps you from going in some drastically wrong direction.

At this point, you run in the strength of the vision God is giving you for your life. I am indebted to Dr. Mark Virkler, whose excellent materials on this subject give guidance for recording your conversations with God.[15]

He writes that there are five conditions that should be met to safely hear God's voice:

1. You are a born-again Christian, having accepted Jesus Christ into your heart as your Lord and Savior, and having had your sins washed away by His cleansing blood.
2. You accept the Bible as the inerrant Word of God.
3. You demonstrate your love and respect for God by your commitment to knowing His Word. You follow a plan for reading through the entire Bible regularly (such as once each year), as well as enjoying more in-depth meditation on books, characters, or topics.
4. You have an attitude of submission to what God has shown you from the Bible.
5. You have two or three spiritual advisors/counselors to whom you go for input on a regular basis.

I also strongly recommend Dr. Virkler's book *Hearing the Voice of God* for an excellent treatment of this subject.[16]

CHAPTER 3: IN THE BEGINNING: ORPHANS AND SEVERED HEARTS

"As doctors, when they examine the state of a patient and recognize that death is at hand, pronounce, 'He is dying, he will not recover' so we must say from the moment a man is born: 'he will not recover.'"

—St. Augustine

In the Beginning

"IN THE BEGINNING God created. ..." He chose that action. He did not have to do it; He wanted to. Creating human beings was not a passing craze that sprang from a cosmic ego, not random chance oozing from wandering goo. God chose to create man deliberately. People are not accidents. No matter what you look like, or what talents you do or do not possess, God gave you value in the simple act of creation.

With the potential contained in the first man and woman, God created you, and He delighted in doing so. With every other created thing, God simply spoke and it came into being. God spoke and vegetation grew. God spoke and light shined. God spoke and land was formed. God spoke and animals propagated the earth.

But notice: God did not speak to create man. Instead, Genesis 2:7 says, "Then the Lord God formed man of dust from the ground, and breathed into his nostrils the breath of life; and man became a living being." *He did not create man by speaking, but rather, created man by forming him with His own hands, like precious pottery, forming him from the ground in His Image.* Then, even stranger, God breathed His own LIFE into man's body.

As I awakened to the revelation contained in this familiar passage, I was overwhelmed by an observation I had not previously recognized: Whose was the first face man saw when his eyes opened? It was the face of his Heavenly Father. And God intended it that way. Man's first memory was a Father's smile.

My mom, who struggled with her own pain in so many ways, had a saying that helped her throughout her life. Pinned to her refrigerator, it read, "God made me the way I am, and He don't make junk."

God Said, "Let Us Create Man in OUR Likeness."

God decided to create man in His own image. God is a triune being — One God with three distinct parts, or persons, or expressions — Father, Son and Holy Spirit. When God designed people in His likeness, He gave them a soul — a spiritual nature with the capacity to appreciate and respond to their Creator. Like their Maker, these souls also have with three parts: a *mind* with which to think, *emotions* with which to feel, and a *will* with which to make decisions.

God Created Man "for His Glory," for His DELIGHT!

Creation was for God's own good pleasure. "Thou hast created all things, and for Thy pleasure they are and were created," says Revelation 4:11. Proverbs declares how Wisdom, the pre-incarnate Son of God, took delight with the Creator in the people He made:

> *When He established the heavens, I was there / When He inscribed a circle on the face of the deep / When He made firm the skies above / When the springs of the deep became fixed / When He set for the sea its boundary / So that the water would not transgress His command / When He marked out the foundations of the earth / Then I was beside Him, as a master workman / And I was daily His delight / Rejoicing always before Him / Rejoicing in the world, His earth / And having my delight in the sons of men."[17]*

God delighted in creating men! This is not "angry God" theology at all. God rejoiced over man as a new father rejoices over the birth of his children. In their book *We Would See Jesus*, Roy and Revel Hession write:

> *The story of man began when God, who is complete in Himself and therefore could have no needs, deliberately chose, it would seem, to be incomplete without creatures of His own creating. ... It was for this purpose and no other — that of existing for the pleasure of God — that man was brought into being. He was intended to be the delight of God and the object of His affection. ... Man knew that he had only been created to delight God, and his only concern was to respond to the Divine affection, to live for Him, and*

to do His will. ... To insist, then, that to see God and be in living relationship with Him is the supreme goal of life is not to insist on anything strange or unnatural. It is the very purpose for which we were recreated, the sole raison d'etre for our being on the earth at all.[18]

Are you seeing something new? You were not created for yourself; you were created for the joy and pleasure of Almighty God. You were created to be dependent upon Almighty God for everything in your life, created *in* joy *for* joy.

From ORPHAN to SON

For the person without God, the spiritual ORPHAN, life's meaning does not include God — or if it does, God sits on a shelf; life is all about what one can achieve or do by oneself, and ultimately for the glory of one's self. There is no sense of God's pleasure or delight, but rather an angry God to either please or avoid.

But for the SON, life is not about self at all — it is about respecting then adoring the Creator; for He was Father before He was the Creator who delighted in making man.

Eden's Failure: The Severed Heart

In Genesis, a major "fail" occurred. Here is the context:

The Lord God took the man and put him into the Garden of Eden to cultivate it and keep it. And the Lord God commanded the man, saying, "From any tree of the garden you may eat freely; but from the tree of the knowledge of good and evil you shall not eat, for the day that you eat from it you shall surely die."[19]

God promised if man disobeyed God's one command, man would die. When you choose "Not God," you get "Not LIFE." God is the only source of LIFE. Man sinned, by his own choice. Man chose "Not God." Obviously, man did not die physically immediately, because Adam and Eve were alive when God confronted them and escorted them from the garden. God placed an angel who stood guard to keep them from re-entering and gaining access to the Tree of Life. Adam and Eve were physically alive, but spiritually dead.

In his letter to the Ephesian church, the Apostle Paul comments on the hopeless spiritual-death state Adam and Eve left as their legacy for all mankind:

And you were dead in your trespasses and sins, in which you formerly walked according to the course of this world, … but God, being rich in mercy, because of His great love with which He loved us, even when we were dead in our transgressions, made us alive together with Christ (by grace you have been saved) and raised us up with Him, and seated us with Him.[20]

The Bible says all people are born dead. Dead means *dead*, not partially alive, not swooned but recovering, not injured but healing. When a person becomes a Christian, when he is "born again" to a "new creation," his or her spirit is made alive and receives LIFE.

According to John's Gospel, God is the only source of LIFE. "ZOE," the Greek word for life used in John 14:8 and 17:3, denotes not physical life but the spiritual LIFE that God gives us. The other word for "life" in the New Testament is BIOS and refers more to the physical or biological aspects of being alive. In a 1979 message, Dr. Darryl Delhousaye defined "life" as "functioning as intended or designed," whereas "death" means "to cease to function as intended or designed." So man was alive in spirit before sin, functioning as intended or designed. But when man sinned and "died," he ceased to function in the capacity for which he was intended or designed.

Vine's Expository Dictionary of Old and New Testament Words says, "Death came through sin, Romans 5:12, which is rebellion against God. Sin thus involved the forfeiting of the 'life.'"[21]

So when sin entered the human race, everyone died, not physically — though that would come eventually — but the part of man that is in the spirit was severed from God, its LIFE-source. As a consequence of choosing "Not God," mankind received a *"severed heart."* All people thereafter *ceased to function as designed or intended.* But by GRACE, the person who accepts Christ as Savior is born again and made alive in Him. Barring that acceptance, all remain dead — severed, orphaned from their Father, cast away from their HOME.

Five Needs of "Life"

This loss of LIFE means that certain basic needs are no longer fulfilled. Philosophers, theologians, psychologists and researchers over the years have tried to categorize these needs. Though given different terms and slight variations of groupings by various experts, these basic needs are recognized as residing within the heart of every human being. American psychologist Abraham Maslow arranged a hierarchy of needs into a pyramid shape, expressed in his 1954 book *Motivation and Personality*.[22]

In Maslow's pyramid, the most basic fundamental needs are at the bottom, the broad base of the pyramid. From that point upward, the categories narrow in size and relative importance. Interestingly, Maslow would write, "if these 'deficiency needs' are not met, the body gives no physical indication *but the individual feels anxious and tense*" (emphasis mine)."[23]

Below is a brief overview of Maslow's pyramid of needs:

1. **Physiological Needs** For the most part, physiological needs are obvious — they are the literal requirements for human survival. If these requirements are not met, the human body simply cannot continue to function. Clothing and shelter, for instance, provide necessary protection from the elements.

2. **Safety Needs** With one's physical needs relatively satisfied, the individual's safety needs take precedence and dominate behavior. Personal security, financial security, health and wellbeing, protection from accidents and illness and their adverse impacts all fall under this category.

3. **Love and Belonging** After physiological and safety needs are fulfilled, the third layer of human needs is social and involves feelings of belonging. Humans need to feel a sense of belonging and acceptance. This may come from large social groups, such as clubs, office culture, religious groups, professional organizations, sports teams, gangs and so on, or from small social connections like family members, intimate partners, mentors, close colleagues or confidants. People need to love and be loved by others. In the absence of these elements, many people become susceptible to loneliness, social anxiety, and clinical depression.

4. **Esteem** All humans have a need to be accepted, valued and respected by others, and to have self-esteem and self-respect. People need to engage in activities (such as their profession or hobbies) to gain recognition and give them a sense of contribution, to feel self-valued.

5. **Self-actualization** "What a man can be, he must be."24 This quotation forms the basis of the perceived need for self-actualization. This level of need refers to what a person's full potential is and the realization of that potential. Maslow describes this level as the desire to accomplish everything that one can, to become the most that one can be.

From my personal research and experience, I have observed similar basic human LIFE needs, which I have distilled as follows: 1) Belonging, 2) Significance, 3) Worth, 4) Approval and 5) Protection/Provision. Unlike Maslow, I do not order them in a hierarchy, as all are necessary for people's survival.

When these five needs are lacking sufficiency, people live in a world of anxiety and tension, striving, control, depression and anger. Human hearts were designed to be dependent on God to fulfill these needs. People need to know they are loved. Prior to the renewal of salvation, people without LIFE in Christ are unable to function according to God's original design. Sin has caused a separation from God's Presence, and His LIFE is no longer automatically dwelling within. I believe that these five needs reflect the deadness of the spirit part of all mankind. People's spirits are dead, and they no longer function as God intended. They are independent of Him and His LIFE.

I believe that a huge pool of anxiety, hopelessness, striving and aggressiveness —all related to fear — is the byproduct of a dead spirit separated from LIFE. Note in Maslow's observation above, a person may feel "anxious and tense" without showing any physical signs. Could it be that the reason people feel anxiety, stress, tension, lack of hope, discouragement and depression is largely due to these five needs no longer being met in a relationship with God? In desperation, like poverty-stricken orphans, mankind "digs in dumpsters" to satisfy those needs in their own strength.

In *The Search for Significance*, Robert McGee writes of Christians who have "deadened themselves to their own feelings to the point that they have many relational problems they cannot even recognize." He contends that people are driven "from life's outset" to "satisfy some inner, unexplained yearning" for love and acceptance. But though people search throughout life for the right others to fulfill this unquenchable thirst for acceptance and love, even Christians have difficulty recognizing that "its true source is the love and acceptance of God. He created us. He alone knows how to fulfill all our needs."[25]

Of the utmost importance to me in my personal struggle to please God as a pastor is McGee's observation: "But if we base our work on our abilities or the fickle approval of others, the behavior will reflect the insecurity, fear, and anger that comes from such instability."

When Adam and Eve were exiled from the Garden of Eden, they were separated not only from the Tree of the Knowledge of Good and Evil but also from another tree — the Tree of LIFE. Severed from LIFE, people experience two things: 1) *fear* and 2) *hopelessness.* You may call them what you will — being burdened, weighed down, stressed, concerned, worried, irritated, frustrated. McGee used the words insecurity, fear, anger and instability. But basically the products of living death are fear and hopelessness. That is the essence of life without God. Why wouldn't it be? Only the Creator can give LIFE, only the Creator can sustain LIFE, and only the Creator can protect LIFE.

My Upside-Down Glasses

God had to tear down my world-based value-system trappings and to address these issues of my need for His Love. LIFE comes only from a vertical relationship with God. Growing up, I was subjected to many negative influences. I was rejected by my biological father and reared by a mother who, as the daughter of the town drunk, already had issues. The last thing she wanted was a kid, but she got pregnant and she was stuck with me. (If abortion had been an option in 1952, I'd have never made it.) My mom got married and my adoptive dad graciously took me in. But he had been hurt deeply by his own dad, who had abandoned him and his mom in his teenage years.

I became a Christian in November 1970 at age 18, but try as I might, I just could not live the Christian life. Some inner compulsion drove everything I did. I could never be at rest. I was never good enough. I found peace only for brief moments, but not often; and joy was always elusive, a formula I couldn't figure out.

I felt irritated by other people's lack of commitment, while I was in bondage to many things. I would cycle through some success from a conference or new teaching, some Bible discovery, and gain hope that I would change soon if I just stayed faithful. The "spiritual high" would last a couple weeks then dissipate. A sort of autopilot fueled my actions, but I couldn't see it. I was like the man in the upside-down glasses, only I was driven by fear, anxiety and hopelessness.

I brought this world-performance filter into my Christian walk with God. I quickly learned basic Christian growth principles, such as how to walk in the filling of the Holy Spirit. But that "how to" became another formula. Even as a pastor, I tried to perform to get God's acceptance. Despite my daily devotional times and Bible study, change was marginal. I was definitely not living the "wonderful life." Instead, in my ORPHAN's mismanagement of relationships, I left a trail of injury and hurt behind. I competed for status and respect, believing I had to work more hours, try harder, pray more. I took every ministry failure personally.

Then came a round of disappointments in our church-planting ministry. The worship pastor, my dear friend was leaving; one elder was quitting; another elder moving; another close confidant moving as well. Our church had nearly finished a local evangelism campaign when a pastor from a bigger, more affluent church seemingly elbowed into our allotted neighborhoods because they were more upscale. I cried out to God, "Why can You bless other pastors, but You can't bless me?"

I immediately envisioned a beautiful white church building and people being blessed. Then I saw an old, unpainted wooden shed behind it with broken shingles and grease-covered windows. What went through my heart was a direct lie from Satan. The white church represented other pastors in the area, blessed and growing and helping others. But my ministry was the shed, and it was all I deserved. These words went through my heart like a spear: "You are not blessed because God can't bless you. You aren't good enough, you don't measure up, you don't deserve His love. You aren't blessed because you aren't worth it."

I sank into emotional discouragement that resulted in my leaving the ministry and then, in 1995, divorce. All because I was sucking my "life" from a world value-system that says: 1) the blessing of God is measured in size and numbers, 2) if you work hard and do it better, then you are guaranteed success, and 3) if you are in a bad situation, you cannot make necessary changes, you are stuck.

I was striving and pushing and doing everything I could to fulfill those five human LIFE needs. I was picking through the garbage dump of the world, trying to measure up to the world's demands so I could impress God enough to get what I wanted out of life.

> *In the* ORPHAN'*s heart exists an inner compulsion, a driving anxiety on one end and a gnawing hopelessness on the other. At the core,* ORPHANS *are severed from the springs of* LIFE, *so they search for it in the horizontals of the world, seeking security, peace or hope, diving in dumpsters for counterfeit affection, fighting over scraps and always starving.*

> SONS *learn to recognize fear and hopelessness as the results of a severed heart. They know the only solution is to refuse being driven into the world. They let their fear and hopelessness drive them to live vertically, to be completely dependent on God, saying, "Whom have I in Heaven but Thee? And besides Thee I desire nothing on the earth."*

APPLICATION: LEARNING TO HEAR THE SHEPHERD'S HEART — HABAKKUK 2:1-4

1. GET SERIOUS: Stand and station yourself to wait on God alone.

Make sure you are spending some time every day with God. He is your Father and He wants to fellowship with you. Shut off the voices, pull to the side, stand and station yourself. Don't merely read this book — start living it. Remember that God is Spirit and those who worship Him must worship in spirit and in truthfulness (John 4:10-24).

"He who is joined to the Lord is *one Spirit* with Him" (1 Corinthians 6:17).

Learn to meditate with God, to fill your mind with His written Word, and let Him guide your spirit and thoughts. Remember He will communicate with you, Spirit to spirit. Hearing His voice and practicing His Presence involves learning to walk with Him "filled with the Spirit."

2. BE FOCUSED: "And I will keep watch to see what He will speak to me."

Read His Word with intentionality. Then reflect through the principles discussed here about how God created you and His Love for you. Reflect on His creation and the joy He felt in making you. Let him kiss your forehead and call your name. He longs to do that. Learn to let Him lead your heart with an inner dialogue, inner leadings. Let Him speak to you. He will when you give Him permission.

3. PRACTICE AUTHENTIC HUMILITY: "*And how I may reply when I am reproved.*"

When God speaks, your self-centeredness will float to the top. Don't make a big deal out of it; just confess it to Him and let Him be in control. Inhale His Word, exhale your heart; inhale His encouragement, exhale your concerns; inhale His promises, exhale the lies Satan would have you believe.

Look for the **PEACE STEPS**. Ask yourself, "Is there …"

+ a **P**romise to keep?

+ an **E**xample to follow?

+ an **A**ttitude to change?

+ a **C**ommand to obey?

+ an **E**rror to avoid?

+ any **S**in to confess?

+ any **T**ruth to apply?

+ an **E**xhortation to heed?

+ any **P**rayer or **P**raise to pray?

+ **S**omething to thank God for?

4. WRITE IT, CHECK IT, RUN IT: "*Record the vision and inscribe it.*"

Journal … journal … journal. If you and your Heavenly Father are sharing and He is leading you, then journal that. Listen with intentionality; deal with your selfish attitudes, then be prepared for His Presence and blessings. Let Him guide your heart then check it with your trusted godly advisors. Do this daily for 60 days, and see what He shows you. Don't wait until you hear God speaking to you, then try to find a paper to record your impressions. Get the journal now, in faith believing He will speak to you.

Chapter 4: Dumpster Diving

From the very beginning, God planned to provide mankind — through a relationship with Him — with the five basic needs of Life: belonging, significance, value, approval, provision/protection. God intended and designed human beings for a close personal relationship with Him, their Creator, so people's need to know they are loved would be met.

Because mankind was orphaned, Father sent His Son as His Life-giving remedy for the human race's severed hearts. The Apostle John described Jesus' Life-giving purpose in several Scriptures, including the following:

"In Him was life, and the life was the Light of men. The Light shines in the darkness, and the darkness did not comprehend it" (John 1:4-5).

"The thief comes only to steal and kill and destroy; I came that they may have life, and have it abundantly" (John 10:10).

"I am the way, the truth and the life" (John 14:6).

You are intended to get your Life from Jesus.

Getting Life from God Alone

In John 15, Jesus uses a specific teaching illustration to show man's dependence on God: a familiar sight in Israel — a grapevine. "Look," He says, "just as a cluster of grapes gets its life by remaining attached to the vine where it constantly receives its life-giving flow of nutrients, so are you to be attached to and get your Life from Me. When the grapes are separated from the life-giving flow of nutrients in the vine, they begin to die. Their life comes from being attached to the vine. In the same way, being attached to Christ gives you the Life you desperately need. You are to abide, to remain, to adhere, and to be attached to Him for your Life.

Jesus uses these words: "I am the true vine and My Father the vine-dresser." Follow my logic and you will see what I did not see for so many years: If there is a *true* vine as Jesus says, then there must be a *false* vine. If I hand you a one-hundred-dollar bill and say this is a *true* one-hundred-dollar bill, then I am assuring you it is *not false or counterfeit*. In Jesus' day, because of Biblical messianic prophecy, several military and political leaders were claiming to be the Messiah. In this passage from John, Jesus is saying, "I am the *real* Messiah, I am the real deal, I am the *true vine*."

What you may miss (as I missed for years) is the implication that there are other false, fake impostors that you think you can plug into for LIFE, but they are not true. These false vines appear real, but cannot provide that long-term flow of nourishment necessary to sustain LIFE. They cannot supply the nutrients it takes to survive. If you plug into that vine expecting to find LIFE, you will starve to death.

The same *feel-good feeling* that comes from LIFE in Jesus can come in another form — from a false vine, a counterfeit source. What happens is this: Instead of living vertically, getting all your needs met in God, you turn to the world and its value-system to try to get your needs met. When you operate within the world, you may feel that *feel-good feeling* by measuring up to the world's standards or acquiring the things of the world. You may feel good if you perform correctly on a test in school, and feel a sense of "life." You may get "life" from performing to some standard of others' judgments. You may know the right people, receive people's praise, be connected to and loved by some right person. If you are a self-satisfied, self-developed individual others look up to, or if you have power and can control others, then you may get that *feel-good feeling* about yourself. You may get that feeling of "life."

But when you don't have that feeling, then what do you have? Anxiety and hopelessness.

I have identified eight world value-systems to help you see the false vine that works its way through every area of life. Feeding on the scrap heap of the world's garbage dump, this vine entangles ORPHANS' feet with its counterfeit affections and empty promises of fulfillment. If you draw your sense of value from this false vine and define yourself by its nutrients, then when you can't get it, you fight other ORPHANS for it, compete for it, strive for it, and on it goes. In fact, when you start to see the ramifications of the human condition in these terms, you begin to see that the whole world system is based on these false vines. You will see the false vine in education, politics, careers, sports, everyday life, family structures, the entertainment industry and, with the help of popular figures/famous personalities, it flows almost unchallenged into the church.

The Eight World Value-systems Identified

1. Performance: Getting "life" from What You Do — Believing the Lie "I am who I am because of what I do."

Bearing in mind that each of these eight value-systems has multiple expressions, know that the world's value-system works primarily by measuring a person's importance or worth by what he or she *does* and how well he or she *performs*. In performing well, a person gets that *feel-good feeling* of "life," that sense of importance, of belonging to, of being approved. In turn, they rate others with a sense of how they measure up as well.

This sizing-up is easily seen in men and career-based women meeting other people for the first time. Typically, after "Hello, my name is so-and-so," comes the next question, "What do you do?" People measure themselves by what they do and how they do it. One need not look far to find illustrations of value by performance. In education, value is assigned by grades — straight-A students have more value than non-straight-A students.

In politics, voter approval determines value. In the marketplace or one's career, value is tied to performance and titles. Athletes are valued by scoring touchdowns or goals, racking up trophies, getting their name in the press, contract bonuses and commercial endorsements. Society is geared toward performance systems that promise "life" but are simply well-camouflaged counterfeits.

Obviously, some degree of performance evaluation is necessary for quality control. Unfortunately, Christians often drag this same performance system right into their walk with God. People's perception of their value to God is warped by this world value-system. They become convinced that they are valued by God for what they do, how well they are able to perform. *They are deluded that somehow, something they do can im-*

Hated that? Hated people looking confused at me

press God! In reality, what they have is a works-based religion. Even if their theological knowledge is correct, they are duped into thinking that they need to pray more or serve more or be happier in order to regain that *feel-good feeling* with God.

Jesus refused to be pulled into this mindset. No one was more performance-oriented than the religious rulers of Jesus' day. Time and again they challenged Jesus with their religious rules, requirements, rituals, rights and regulations. Jesus repeatedly made it penetratingly obvious that He was interested only in the Audience of One, living vertically before God, and not sucking "life" from the world's horizontal value-system.

On one occasion, they asked Him why His disciples did not practice the ritualistic washing before a meal. Against this background, He made two statements about the religious system: First, "This people honors Me with their lips," then "...but their heart is far away from Me" (Matthew 15:8). In other words, they try to honor me with their actions, but it's their motives, what comes from their hearts that matters to God. Simply put, the important thing to God is not what you do but why you do it.

Jesus could not be more emphatic. Man's performance in keeping strict dietary rules as the religious leaders did had no value without the engaged, intimate heart. In explaining a parable to Peter in Matthew 15:15-20, He put it another way: "Do you not understand that everything that goes into the mouth passes into the stomach, and is eliminated? But the things that proceed out of the mouth come from the heart, and those defile the man. For out of the heart come evil thoughts, murders, adulteries, fornications, thefts, false witness, and slanders. These are the things which defile the man; but to eat with unwashed hands does not defile the man."

Translation: It's the heart that I'm interested in. *What* you do is not nearly as important as *why* you do it. It's not the abundant performance of rules and rituals, which you claim to do in My name, that pleases Me. It's what is in your heart — it's why you do it.

The rules and requirements are not wrong. The world cannot operate without performance standards because the world is under law. Law is the basic foundation of behavior. However, what is of *greater importance* is the *why* of what you do. Jesus was not interested in religion. He was, and still is, interested in relationship. He wants our hearts.

> ORPHAN *thinking measures self-worth on a performance standard of comparison, basing treatment of others on a value system that allows one to say, "I'm better than him / her."*

> SONS *learn that every person they meet has a value placed on him or her by a Father who loves them dearly, and they learn to love each person for who he or she is.*

There is a very serious hidden agenda in this system. It creates an undertow that will pull you in. Having performance as the basis of relationship involves a spirit of comparison and competition. "Am I good enough?" usually carries with it a "compared to what?" clause. How do you know if you are good enough? By comparing yourself to others and coming up with the unspoken statement, "I'm OK, because I'm as good as or better than they are." This spirit of performance and comparison is the rocket fuel of shame.

> ORPHANS *measure everything by rules, rituals, requirements, regulations and restrictions, and find themselves justified by how they perform* — *never looking at what splashes from the heart.*

> SONS *live by a principle that guides their thinking and actions; spiritual practices and right living are not as important as why they do what they do.*

2. Projection or Pretending: Getting "life" from How You Look — Believing the Lie "I am who I am **because of how I look.***"*

The second way our world value-system works is by measuring people's importance or worth by how they look, the image they project, and the person they want people to see when they look at them. As in each of these world value-systems, there are multiple expressions. People think they are valued, important, belong, or approved of because of how they appear to others. This outward projection includes the way one behaves, speaks or dresses, hoping to turn heads when one enters a room. Some people name drop: "I know so-and-so; I'm friends with such-and-such a person." Others dress to impress: "I'm carrying this designer purse or wearing that designer shoe."

Here the perfectionist is born and thrives. What becomes important is having the admiration, respect and approval of others. However, the true-vine value system says "It's not how good you look, but the reflection of Christ in you, that defines you." Jesus said that if you want to know how to measure greatness, look at John the Baptist, the forerunner of Christ. "I say to you, among those born of women there is no one greater than John; yet he who is least in the kingdom of God is greater than he" (Luke 7:28). Meaning, John was the best of the best from the kingdom of man. But the truth is in Christ, you are a blood-bought citizen of the kingdom of heaven, and the *least* in that kingdom is *greater* than the greatest in the world value-system. Get it?

But people pretend. People can't stand the thought of being seen as they really are, so they wear masks. Wearing masks allows one to keep people from seeing who one really is. The word "hypocrite" comes from the Greek word for actor. In ancient Greece, all actors were males, even for female parts. They would simply hold masks in front of their faces to play whatever role was needed. So actors were "hypocrites," people behind masks pretending to be what they were not.

A mid-thirtyish friend of mine, who was beginning to see this, one day came to me and said, "Jim, I think the light bulb has come on." Over the weekend her father and mother had come to visit. Although she always felt nervous and edgy around her parents, she could not figure out why. Yet she enjoyed her relationship with them very much.

On this occasion, her father looked around her home and noticed she had left her shoes downstairs. "This is out of character for you," he remarked. "And it's certainly not how you were raised."

My friend said she snatched up her shoes and took them upstairs. When she came back downstairs, her father said, "I noticed the windowsills have a lot of dust on them."

Obediently, she went to the kitchen for a rag and Windex to improve the windowsill situation. Then her dad called out, "Oh, by the way, as long as you're in the kitchen, I noticed your refrigerator light has burned out."

At that moment, rag in hand, reaching for the car keys to run to the store and buy a replacement bulb, she had a revelation. "The light came on," she told me. "I was so determined to get my value from how I looked to my father, my sense of belonging to his family, my sense of value and importance, of approval and appreciation, and my sense of provision. I realized that my entire identity as a person was derived from the approval I received from my dad in doing the things that made me look good to him."

In our society, at every turn you can see that image rules. In sales, it's more the sizzle that sells the steak than the quality of meat. Even Christian sales people must push image rather than substance, and function with the detrimental mindset that perception is everything.

Hollywood celebrities provide very public examples of how Americans judge value, importance and approval on the basis of looks, rather than intrinsic quality. Many of the most popular stars are total failures at life. But judging only by its horizontal standards, society reveres them.

I'm amazed how willing we are to listen to these people as if their opinions were based in truth. *People* is one of the best-selling magazines on the newsstands. Featuring drug-addicted, sexually inappropriate, debt-ridden, alcoholic, immature, coddled narcissists, it reveals how easily duped the American public can be. Addicted to the world value-system, fans flock to hear a celebrity speak, and listen to every word as if it were gospel. Many of Hollywood's elite possess very little formal education. Some, to be sure, are wonderful exceptions, but most filmgoers/ TV viewers take little time to evaluate the stars' academic degrees. Instead those shining lights are valued by their glittering images.

I am not putting down acting as a profession. But I want to focus on the truth. Believers must stop valuing people based on their presentation and performance. Image may be everything in the world value-system, but not in God's eyes.

Jesus was not interested in appearances as much as He was in what was in people's hearts. He frequently fellowshipped with His society's outcasts. For example, He should have shunned the Samaritan woman because of her religion. Instead, engaging her not only in conversation but also in one of the greatest theological discussions in the Bible, Jesus revealed to her the true meaning of worship. Instead of being sent away in humiliation, she left refreshed, with an inexhaustible source of Living Water.

His critics thought the sinless Son of God should have rejected the woman caught in adultery, but instead He rescued her from her accusers and sent her on her way with an admonition to sin no more. When lepers came to Him crying out, He should have shunned and rebuked them, but instead He gave them what they craved most — He reached out as He healed them and did something He didn't have to do, something that the dictates of Law said He must never do — He touched the unclean and untouchable.

Touch

A church elder once told my wife and me, "You'll never be successful until you have a book, a hook, and a look to your ministry." Struggling over my lack in this area, I looked at the face of Jesus and it occurred to me that He never wrote a book, never had a hook and never pushed an image. He was convinced that what He needed was the power of prayer. Why did He do so few miracles in relation to all those who could have been healed with one word? He had no interest in image development. His "branding" was prayer.

Don't get me wrong — branding and marketing are important marketing tools in our consumer-driven economy. But as a Christian, you must not get your value from them.

> ORPHANS believe that the one who looks better and measures up better possesses greater value and is accorded much greater respect.

> SONS know that how one looks on the outside and what image one projects diminish in importance. They come to understand it really is what is in the heart that counts.

3. Possessions: Getting "life" from What You Have — Believing the Lie "I am who I am *because of what I own.*"

The third way our world value system works is by measuring one's importance or worth by one's possessions. Who has not been jealous of the person who drives the brand-new car? Almost by second nature, most people assign high value to a person driving an expensive car. Possessions matter greatly when it comes to assigning relative value or importance to people. The one with the larger or newer home seems more distinguished than someone residing in a manufactured home or rented apartment.

"Conspicuous consumption" is an economic term that refers to people's worth as displayed by the things they can do and purchase, valuing people according to their possessions. This value-system has a pecking order determined by brand names, neighborhoods, vacation destinations, club memberships, and the like.

Inherent in this value system is a strong feeling of satisfaction from purchasing new things. There's nothing wrong with feeling good about getting new things. But you may move into wrong thinking if your horizontal possessions become the system on which you base your value, define your self-worth. Once your goal becomes getting all the things you need and want plus more, you will never have enough.

The true vine is Jesus. According to His vertical value system, "A person's life is not made up of his possessions." [26]

The make, model and year of your car, the location of your home or office do not matter in God's view of your value or worth.

"New car fever" is the industry name for the obsessive, "I just have to have it" mind-set that most of us, at times, fall prey to. In the moment you may feel desperate, as though you cannot live without this thing; you are obsessed with getting it. A few years after the purchase, it is rotting away or gathering dust in the garage. Possessions cannot satisfy. They rust and rot away. Jesus said, "Do not store up for yourselves treasures on earth, where moth and rust destroy, and where thieves break in and steal. But store up for yourselves treasures in heaven, where neither moth nor rust destroys, and where thieves do not break in or steal; for where your treasure is, there your heart will be also" (Matthew 6:19-21).

In other words, Jesus said, if it can be attacked by a moth, rusted out or stolen, then don't treasure it, don't get "life" from it, don't assign it worth. Why? "Because where your treasure is, there is your heart also." *Live life vertically!* If you don't, your valuables will be moth-eaten, rusted out, waiting-to-be-stolen junk. Who needs that?

God says a lot about people's lives being summed up in their possessions. The most powerful statement by God regarding this world's value-system is written in stone, in the list of Ten Commandments. Where is that, you say? It is Number Ten. Chiseled out, right after "Don't murder," "Don't have sex outside of marriage," "Don't steal," and "Don't lie," comes, "You shall not covet your neighbor's house; you shall not covet your neighbor's wife or his male servant or his female servant or his ox or his donkey or anything that belongs to your neighbor." *Envy or coveting is simply an attitude that expresses that one's values are horizontal.* That is why it is one of the Ten Commandments. It is that important. *Don't try to get* LIFE *from stuff.*

Much of Jesus' teaching dealt with the lack of value He placed on possessions. Remember His reply to the rich young ruler? "Go and sell all that you have ... ."[27]

Jesus could read this young man's heart and knew that his possessions held too high a priority in his life — ahead of following God. Material things did not matter much to our Lord. At one point He simply said, "The Son of Man has nowhere to lay His head."[28]

This was not a rejection of possessions, just a reminder to keep them in their rightful place.

In another setting, Jesus taught that material possessions tend to assume a controlling force, seeking mastery over a person. While material things are tools to sustain life and can be used to serve God, the pressure for mastery always exists. The horizontal value-system strives to usurp the vertical priority of God first. Jesus said, "No servant can serve two masters; for either he will hate the one and love the other, or else he will be devoted to one and despise the other. You cannot serve God and wealth."[29]

Does that mean money is bad? Is having abundance wrong? No. To exemplify this point, the "rich young ruler" story of Luke 18 is followed by the story of Zacchaeus, just 16 verses later. And it says, "And he was very rich." Yet Jesus took the time to go and fellowship with him. His visit had such an impact that Zacchaeus gave away half of his wealth to the poor and repaid fourfold anyone he had cheated. His actions demonstrate that although Zacchaeus was very wealthy, his possessions did not control him or have priority over God's place in his life and heart.

God is interested in your heart attitude toward money and possessions, not the possessions themselves.

> ORPHANS *place a huge emphasis on what they own, and give great homage to the one who has much. The rich, the famous, and the popular are their gods.*
>
> SONS *know that what a person owns is not a measure of what he is inside. They understand that the greater the stature of a person, the less that person values "stuff."*

4. *Pleasures and Escapism: Getting "life" from the Good Times You Experience — Believing the Lie "I am who I am* **because of the good times I enjoy.***"*

This fourth component of a horizontal world value-system is found in getting "life" from the amount of fun, pleasure or enjoyment one experiences through certain activities. The types of pleasure seekers in this group range from the constant partygoer, through the dance-till-she-drops barfly, to the hopelessly chemically addicted junkie. But escapism also takes other, more socially acceptable forms as well: the beach-bum surfer, the waterskiing enthusiast, the daredevil skydiver/bungee jumper/mountain biker, the hobby addict. Who does not enjoy having fun, whiling away the days without thought for the future or the effect of one's actions on one's family? But these people go a step further and find "life" in the caliber of pleasures in which they indulge.

It's not that God doesn't want us to have fun, but "good times" cannot be the source of our "life." Such escapes from life's ho-hum drudgery must not form the core of what makes me feel good about me. These carefree, happy-go-lucky hedonists need to get a dose of reality.

Unfortunately, this world value-system has huge negatives. Picture the man who can't retire because he's afraid of losing the sense of being needed. Or the woman who can't let go of chairing a time-consuming bridge club (she might as well be bar hopping) because the fun gives her value. Some husbands go out with "the guys" because they can't get along with their wife. A classic auto hobbyist drags his spouse to car shows (and she despises car shows). His wife has closets overflowing with knitting yarn, and she can't stop buying more. And golfers abandon their families for five hours at a time, sometimes more than once a week, to go hit a little ball around a grassy course.

The activities in themselves are not wrong. But drawing "life" from these things rather than from the Lord is dissipation. As Pastor Chuck Swindoll has said, these people "worship their work and work at their play and play at their worship."

In agreement with Romans 14:12, the true-vine value-system says, "There is coming a day when every man shall give an account of his life." Whether or not you are prepared, you will be called upon to give an account of your life and to be held responsible to God. You must have a focused mind and a focused heart in order to give an account to Him.

1 Peter 1:13-19 admonishes believers:

> Therefore, *prepare* your minds for action, *keep* sober in spirit, *fix* your hope completely on the GRACE to be brought to you at the revelation of Jesus Christ. As obedient children, do not be conformed to the former lusts which were yours in your ignorance, but like the Holy One who called you, *be holy* yourselves also in all your behavior; because it is written, "YOU SHALL BE HOLY, FOR I AM HOLY." If you address as Father the One who impartially judges according to each one's work, conduct yourselves in fear during the time of your stay on earth; knowing that you were not redeemed with perishable things like silver or gold from your futile way of life inherited from your forefathers, but with precious blood, as of a lamb unblemished and spotless, the blood of Christ.

In observing people who live life as though it's one big party, I find that this behavior is often an anesthetic to deaden the pain of not living productive lives, seeking "life" from their popularity or drug-induced euphoria.

> For ORPHANS who live for the next party or the next good time, "life" is about escape — anesthetizing the pain of feeling as though they have no place in their Father's heart.

> SONS know that LIFE cannot come from a party or good time, and one cannot inject/draw LIFE through a drug. A SON recognizes the hole in his heart and doesn't try to cover up the pain with drugs; he/she learns to be filled in Father's Love.

*5. Power and Control: Getting "life" from What and Whom I Control — Believing the Lie "I am who I am **because of what and whom I control.**"*

A fifth way the horizontal world value-system works is by measuring one's importance or worth by one's ability to control one's circumstances and have control over others. Remaining safe or keeping things under control gives people that false sense of "life." People functioning within this world value-system have an inordinately overpowering need to control circumstances, which have the potential to hurt or cause a sense of insecurity. Such people manipulate and control to their advantage.

A person who has been significantly hurt in life often becomes very defensive and tends to control circumstances and/or people as protection from ever being hurt again. While this reaction may be understandable, it demonstrates the world value-system of power and control.

Instead of trusting God, this person derives his or her sense of importance — and especially of protection — by controlling everyone and everything around them. This can easily be observed in the hyper-meticulous, vigilante office manager who monitors coworkers' actions and attitudes, so that nothing is misplaced, miscommunicated or misstated, and nothing is accomplished without their control.

This kind of control provides not only a sense of protection, but also a sense of significance and importance, a sense of worth and value, because this person thinks, *"After all, this office (this family, this group, etc.) would fall apart were it not for me."*

On a certain occasion, I saw this attitude in an elder of a church I pastored. Following the service, I was greeting people as they exited. This man seemed unsettled, different from his normal self, and paused as if he wanted to talk.

"I'm feeling depressed," he said as we stepped aside. When I asked why, he said, "There's recently been a change in my job. I used to be in charge of 120 people, but they've cut my responsibilities. Now I only oversee about 70." The company had provided him with a significant salary increase. And due to the decreased responsibility, he was required to work fewer hours.

I could not believe my ears! He had less responsibility, fewer work hours and greater pay! All I could think was, *What in the world is wrong with that?*

"Why is this such a disappointment?" I asked.

In tears now, he looked me straight in the eye and said, "I am not as important because I don't manage as many people." He was shaking as he said this.

I have seen families, businesses and churches run by those who need to exercise control. Anytime anyone steps out of line, whether in a moment of spontaneity or of genius, or out of pure, unbridled joy, they do everything possible to make sure that it never happens again.

 The problem with needing to be in control is, you never really are. Pontius Pilate thought he was in control of the destiny of Christ. He told Jesus that he held authority over him. Jesus said to Pilate, "You would have no authority over Me, unless it had been given you from above." [30]

There are so many ways to control that it would be impossible to name them all. Dominating conversations, using an intimidating tone of voice or body language, talking loudly, interrupting, manipulating events to go one's way, judging people, talking about people behind their backs, isolating others, displaying facial expressions of disappointment, outbursts of anger or dissolving in tears are just a few.

This false vine produces an inner feeling of power. I have witnessed personality changes in controlling people who have attained leadership positions. Whereas such people may have previously appeared humble and willing to work hard — showing up early, leaving late — once they come into power, they may become more tyrannical and power hungry.

> ORPHANS *seize on the counterfeit "life" through control and power over others. It is imperative for the* ORPHANED *heart to remain in or hold control.* ORPHANS *live in fear and feel that the only way they can be safe is if they are in control.*

> SONS *have learned that people matter to God. People are to be loved and not controlled. All control is ultimately in God's hands and* SONS *know they need to use what influence they have wisely.*

6. Popularity (or the Praise of Men): Getting "life" from People-pleasing — Believing the Lie "I am who I am *because everyone likes me.*"

The sixth way the world value-system works is by measuring people's importance or worth — their value — by how others think of them. Like each of these world value-systems, this one also has multiple expressions. It is often seen in the desire to please, to be well thought of in order to receive the praise of men and gain popularity.

This desire flows from God's design for man. *Pleasing God was the original intent of His design.* However, as misguided, fallen beings, (controlled by the ORPHAN spirit) we misdirect our intended purpose, and seek to satisfy our need to please God by pleasing others instead. We long to find a sense of "well done" in the eyes of other people.

In the award-winning movie, *Babe*, there's a point where the gate latches, the sun breaks through a hole in the clouds, the music crescendos and farmer Hoggett looks down and says, "That'll do pig; that'll do." The popularity of movies like *Seabiscuit* and *Secretariat* shows how much ordinary people relate to underdog-racehorse-wins-derby stories. People long to hear cheers as they cross the finish line and naturally want others to speak well of them.

Yet when people live for that applause, when they make decisions based on someone else's approval without giving thought to God's heart in the matter, they place themselves in the world's value-system of seeking the praise of others.

Christians should find it interesting, maybe even unsettling or terrifying, that God says those who make the flesh their strength are cursed:

> *Thus says the LORD, cursed is the man who trusts in mankind and makes flesh his strength, and whose heart turns away from the LORD. For he will be like a bush in the desert and will not see when prosperity comes, but will live in stony wastes in the wilderness, a land of salt without inhabitant. Blessed is the man who trusts in the LORD And whose trust is the LORD. For he will be like a tree planted by the water, that extends its roots by a stream and will not fear when the heat comes; but its leaves will be green, and it will not be anxious in a year of drought nor cease to yield fruit.[31]*

Seeing yourself as a people pleaser is a hard step to take. Recognize that you do it when you drop names in a crowd: "I know so-and-so," or "I'm endorsed by such-and-such an expert." It gives us a sense of importance, of worth, and approval by others. In an article from Psybersquare.com, licensed clinical social worker Mark Sichel identifies eight characteristics of people pleasers:

1. People pleasers rarely consider their own needs, wants, and desires.

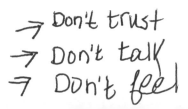

2. People pleasers take any criticism as fact, and immediately suffer a deflation in their own self-esteem.
3. People pleasers feel an extraordinary fear of abandonment.
4. People pleasers blame themselves for everything that ever goes wrong.
5. People pleasers are more concerned with others' feelings than their own.
6. People pleasers have an overdeveloped sense of responsibility, expecting of themselves magical abilities to fix the significant others in their lives.
7. People pleasers learned early in their lives to bury their own feelings, needs, and wants, and keep them buried until they get help for their problems.
8. People pleasers chronically confuse pity with love and self-sacrifice with caring for others.[32]

Craig Groeschel of Lifechurch.tv lists four additional characteristics:

1. People pleasers take most criticism personally.
2. People pleasers feel an extraordinary fear of rejection.
3. People pleasers find it hard to express their true feelings because they don't want to hurt others.
4. People pleasers have a hard time saying "no."[33]

I saw much of this in my own life. Even now, when someone says something good about me, I think, *That felt really good.* Because I received so little affirmation growing up, I was like an empty cup, needing desperately to know that I pleased someone. Or if they didn't say something good about me, I'd probe to see if they were OK with me. I'm hypersensitive to what others may think about me and easily lean toward building myself up by mentioning some well-known connection's name.

People pleasers struggle as leaders, and yet, quite frequently can be found in leadership positions. These individuals either avoid what needs to be said or done in order to make others happy, or they will forge ahead with their plan/idea/proposal, and then be eaten alive when others don't see the value or point of their decisions.

Often as a pastor, I would sacrifice my self-image on the altar of another person's ego, simply because I was afraid of losing their vote of approval. I didn't want to make waves. I didn't want someone to be mad at me.

People pleasers take all forms of rejection personally. When they sense a negative response from one they are trying to please, they will do whatever they can to make it right, putting up with all kinds of injustices and abuse from that person. They can't look someone who has rejected them in the eye; they may not even be capable of being in the same room, as they dread a possible confrontation.

In reality, when you remain in a vertical relationship with God, drawing LIFE from Him, instead of getting "life" from horizontals, it doesn't matter what others think of you. It matters what the Father thinks — of you and the people in your life. Paul dealt with this subject when he wrote to the Corinthians, "But to me it is a very small thing that I may be examined by you, or by any human court; in fact, I do not even examine myself. For I am conscious of nothing against myself, yet I am not by this acquitted; but the one who examines me is the Lord."[3]

Paul lived the best he could to maintain a clear conscience and let the Lord deal with the rest. Although this mindset is not easily accomplished, it is mandatory. Otherwise, if you are a people pleaser, the controlling people will look down on you and you will feel small, unimportant, devalued, as though you don't belong, you are disapproved and unprotected. Get the picture? Turning your natural inclinations against you, controller-types use the world value-system and your inborn need to please to control you.

Jesus stalwartly resisted pleasing men. In Luke 4:14-30, Jesus was in His hometown synagogue and was handed the scroll of Isaiah as part of a normal Sabbath service. He read a passage from Isaiah then rolled up the scroll midway through. "Today," He said, "this scripture [about the Messiah and His kingdom] is fulfilled in your hearing." Instantly, the same people who had spoken so well of Him moments before, now wanted to kill Him.

Obviously, Jesus was not a people pleaser.

An ORPHAN lives to receive the praise of man, the acceptance of another, the approval that comes from doing what another person wants.

A SON learns to live for the approval of God and God alone. If others are pleased, it feels good, but pleasing others is not the source of a SON's LIFE.

7. Pursuits of Me: Getting "life" from My Agenda — Believing the Lie "I am who I am *because of what I achieve."*

The seventh component of a horizontal world value-system is personal, self-centeredness. These people measure their importance, worth or value by their pursuits and personal achievements. Even beyond performance orientation, this is about a larger-than-life global view. This person works 60, 70, 80 hours a week, driven to be top salesman, no matter the cost. His controlling personality micromanages everyone around him. He magnetically attracts others with his passion, his cause, his vision, even though his personal life may be in ruins.

This value-system expresses itself in a multiplicity of forms. As an artist, this person starves his family in pursuit of his dream. As a rejected lover, she's the woman who can't forgive. He's the husband who can't lay down his resentments; the wife who has to control every detail; the son who refuses to honor his parents; the thrill seeker who takes too many uncalculated risks. She's the showgirl past her prime still awaiting discovery as a young ingénue, absorbed in the fantasy of Hollywood fame.

This value-system involves a sense of a personal, self-centered pursuit to build something, to make an improvement in oneself or in someone else's life. It may be expressed by working for causes such as world peace, the environment, supporting orphans, feeding homeless children, or even saving the whales. One's source of "life" becomes engagement with a certain cause or group; and being separated from the group causes distress, anxiety and hopelessness. Instead of involvement for some sort of reward, or driven by fear of punishment, as in performance orientation, this person has an inner drive to achieve.

Some businessmen have to do it right, make it bigger, be an icon and leave a legacy. As a pastor, I had an inner passion to be the best there ever was. It became a passion about just improving me — I wasn't all that bad, but I believed I could be better. I realize I wanted to appear godly, while striving to glorify myself instead.

This type of person is driven by urgency to be better than anyone else, to be the hero when one is called for. They must stand above the crowd because of what they have accomplished. The drive can describe the lawyer who won't leave the office until every lead has been pursued; the theologian who devotes himself to research at the expense of relationships. It thrums through mechanics and medical students and musicians.

The pursuit of excellence to create a legacy is a good thing. But when it becomes a monster that pushes aside and makes people neglect their families and destroy their relationships, it ceases to be God-honoring. In my case, I was so in love with the Great Commission[35] that I sacrificed everything, including my emotional health and time spent with my family. Too late, I realized that the Great Commission was not to be prioritized ahead of the great commandment to love God above all, and my neighbor as myself — my family had to come first.

The story is told of early-20th Century historian and social critic Brooks Adams. When he was eight years old, Brooks wrote in his diary, "I went fishing with my father; the most glorious day of my life." Throughout his life, his diary reflects the influence of that day on his life.

There is another side of the story, however. Brooks' father, Charles Francis Adams, grandson of President John Adams and son of President John Quincy Adams, served as a Massachusetts state senator, as a U.S. congressman and as ambassador to Great Britain under Abraham Lincoln. He wrote about that same day in his diary: "Went fishing with my son; a day wasted."

A legacy of greatness is difficult to maintain. Charles, the father whose time 8-year-old Brooks wasted, often complained to his diary that he thought he was wasting time. Charles confided in his voluminous journal that he felt "crushed by the weight of two generations of distinction ... let me take it for granted that my life must be ... a verdict of failure against myself." And Brooks later wrote regarding his grandfather John Quincy and his great-grandfather John, "They were pretty formidable men. The rest of us leave nothing."[36]

Passions are good things as long as they are based on God's princi-ples and are not at the expense of loving others. But some of the pas-sions that drive people can never be satisfied. Nothing is enough, never enough.

ORPHANS, valued according to horizontals, are driven by all-important earthly pursuits and making a name for themselves. Having titles such as "ambassador" or "senator" is more important than being called "father."

SONS experience a change within their thinking; relationships and people have greater value than names, titles, pursuits and passions. While passions in life are important, they are balanced by a higher respect for others.

8. Personal Codependency: Getting "life" from a Significant Other — Be-lieving the Lie "I am who I am because somebody needs me."

The eighth way the horizontal world value-system works is by measur-ing one's belonging, importance, worth, approval and provision by spe-cific people or significant others in one's life.

The personal codependent plugs his or her "life" cord into other peo-ple to feel affirmed by having them in his or her life. The codependent's life has meaning through being needed or wanted by the other person. Needing another person for a sense of self-significance or self-worth is the essence of codependency. The codependent person gets a sense of "life" from a certain person or group. He or she thinks, *I can't live without them.* Even if the object of his or her devotion is highly dysfunctional and/or abusive, the codependent person doesn't give up on the relation-ship because that person or group gives a sense of needed approval and of belonging.

In this system, the codependent's emotions are entangled with those of the significant other, going up and down with theirs. When the new girlfriend or boyfriend says, "Yes, I want you, I need you," the code-pendent is walking on clouds. And when "Susie" or "Billy" says, "It's over," the codependent is devastated; life is over; he or she can't go on.

Codependent thinking can affect business people regarding their ca-reer. The job is everything; advancement is the only goal that matters. Everything is sacrificed on the altar of serving one's career goals. Over-night business trips ransack family time; late nights working at the office supersede social engagements; the next big deal trumps budding friendships. Sunday church attendance serves merely as a source of business connections in pursuit of the golden pat on the back.

For pastors and spiritual leaders engaged in serving others, codependency takes even more insidious forms. In my case, the ministry became a god. God was no longer the Lord of the ministry; but I began serving and catering to the ministry itself. It became a living nightmare, like the man-eating plant in *Little Shop of Horrors*. My church, my ever-growing "empire," demanded, "Feed me," more and more. When the organization did well, I felt good about me, at least until the next Sunday. And when Sunday was a bad day, I would repeat Scriptures out of Job: "I sought the Lord to take my life."

Following is a group of questions I use to help others see codependency issues in their thinking. (We will return to these issues in a self-assessment in Chapter 9, "Five Provisions of Grace."):

1. Do you keep quiet to avoid arguments?
2. Are you always worried about others' opinions of you?
3. Have you ever continued to live with someone with an alcohol or drug problem?
4. Have you ever continued to live with someone who hits or belittles you?
5. Are the opinions of others more important than your own?
6. Do you have difficulty adjusting to changes at work or home?
7. Do you feel rejected when significant others spend time with friends?
8. Do you doubt your ability to be who you want to be?
9. Are you uncomfortable expressing your true feelings to others?
10. Have you ever felt inadequate?
11. Do you feel like a "bad person" when you make a mistake?
12. Do you have difficulty receiving compliments or gifts?
13. Do you feel humiliation when your child or spouse makes a mistake?
14. Do you think people in your life would go downhill without your constant efforts?

15. Do you frequently wish someone could help you get things done?

16. Do you have difficulty talking to people in authority, such as the police or your boss?

17. Are you confused about who you are or where you are going with your life?

18. Do you have trouble saying "no" when asked for help?

19. Do you have trouble asking for help?

20. Do you have so many things going at once that you can't do justice to any of them?

Jesus refused to be pulled into this type of relationship. In Matthew 12:46-50, the following scene occurred during a public meeting:

While He was still speaking to the crowds, behold, His mother and brothers were standing outside, seeking to speak to Him. Someone said to Him, "Behold, Your mother and Your brothers are standing outside seeking to speak to You." But Jesus answered the one who was telling Him and said, "Who is My mother and who are My brothers?" And stretching out His hand toward His disciples, He said, "Behold My mother and My brothers! For whoever does the will of My Father who is in heaven, he is My brother and sister and mother."

Think about it — Jesus' mom was outside wanting Him to interrupt everything and come out to her. But Jesus was not codependent on anyone but His Heavenly Father. He simply said no.

In another passage, Peter, in all his brashness, pulled Jesus aside and admonished Him for saying He was going to Jerusalem to give His life in serving His Father.

From that time Jesus began to show His disciples that He must go to Jerusalem, and suffer many things from the elders and chief priests and scribes, and be killed, and be raised up on the third day. Peter took Him aside and began to rebuke Him, saying, "God forbid it, Lord! This shall never happen to You." But He turned and said to Peter, "Get behind Me, Satan! You are a stumbling block to Me; for you are not setting your mind on God's interests, but man's."

Jesus refused to let Peter drag him into a codependent relationship based on worry about what others thought rather than what God thought. There is another important lesson here: You need to pull away from dependency on others so that you can be *more* dependent on God. God intended for you to be codependent ... on Him. Christians need to depend on Him for everything in life.

> ORPHANS *are pulled into thinking that someone else has the ability to give them "life," so they plug in their "life" cord and suck the vitality from their relationships, making themselves dependent on their significant others.*

> SONS *learn to live vertically, drawing* LIFE *from a vertical relationship with God. God intended for His people to be codependent on Him and Him alone.*

APPLICATION: LEARNING TO HEAR THE SHEPHERD'S HEART — HABAKKUK 2:1-4

Needing LIFE, people strive to plug into any vine that promises "life" in the world value-systems. When those systems fail — and they will always fail — people are hit with the realization that they have defined themselves by a faulty value-system.

The issue for you is what defines you — your education, your possessions, your heritage, your achievements, or worse, your shortcomings and your failures? Are you like Debbie, a participant in a divorce-recovery group I once led? With tears of desperation, she said, "After years of trying, I want to stop being defined by my divorce." In the true-vine value-system, it is not the "what" that defines us but rather, the Who.

1. GET SERIOUS: "I will stand and station myself ..." to wait on God.

Take time in the Lord's Presence to take a personal inventory. Consider your life priorities. Ask Him to shine His spotlight into the corners of your life as you ask yourself:

What is it in your life that is defining you?

+ Your job?
+ Your church?
+ Your career?
+ Your education?
+ Your friends?
+ Your possessions?
+ Your children?

- ✦ Your spouse?
- ✦ Your accomplishments?
- ✦ Your projected image to others?
- ✦ Your popularity?
- ✦ Your passions?
- ✦ Your politics?
- ✦ Your _____? (What gives you "life" apart from God?)

What false vine are you plugged into for "life?"

Which one of the eight world value-systems are you plugged into?

Which one would your wife/husband or children say?

2. BE FOCUSED: "and I will keep watch to see what He will speak to me."

Sit quietly in the Lord's Presence with your journal and write the Lord's responses to this inventory. Don't try to edit what comes to your mind. Listen and take note of:

- ✦ Mental pictures of past events that you remember in this moment.
- ✦ Snippets of conversations that run through your mind.
- ✦ Scripture verses or phrases or song lyrics that you recall at this time.
- ✦ Emotions — they may be seemingly in conflict with one another (happy/yet sad; amused/yet angry; confused/humiliated/defeated; anxious about something/yet peaceful about something else).

3. PRACTICE AUTHENTIC HUMILITY: "how I may reply when I am reproved."

If you are not already part of a small group of believers, find one through your church, or ask people to join you in one specifically for the purpose of studying this material.

+ Ask one another to share what you are gleaning from your reading and processing and from these *Application* questions.

+ Accept one another's responses without judgment.

+ Keep yourselves accountable by following up with one another
  between sessions, asking, "How's it going with such-and-such
  that you shared in the group?"

+ Pray for one another.

+ And above all, maintain one another's strict confidence by sharing nothing with individuals outside the group.

4. WRITE IT, CHECK IT, RUN IT: "Record the vision and inscribe it."

Sit with God daily and dialogue with Him about these items. Write in
your journal what He leads you to hear and sense spiritually. Share your
insights with your trusted advisors and small-group members. Then
apply what you are learning, that is, *run with it as one who has vision and
passion.*

CHAPTER 5: MY DUMPSTER

EACH of us comes with a "life" cord we want desperately to plug into one or more of the world value-systems. Facing the first hurdle of denial, most of my clients won't admit they are "jacked in." But eventually, several false "outlets" surface in their lives.

How can a person identify what he or she has plugged into for "life"? Typically, a person's dependency on a false vine is revealed in those hard moments when God removes the vine. A person is devastated by the loss of a significant other. Or someone loses a job, and sits staring into space, paralyzed with fear, feeling like life has ended. Another person is angry and depressed over a stolen possession. Someone else falls apart because of a coworker or friend's criticism. "Plugging into" the wrong outlet occurs at many levels.

See the Splash from Your Cup

Here's a simple principle to use in your daily life — *The Principle of Splash: Evaluate your heart by seeing what "splashes from your cup."* If you want to see real life transformation, you need to develop a daily discipline that asks yourself, "What is splashing from my cup?"

The everyday "bumps" in your life reveal the state of your heart and what outlet you're plugged into. If you're carrying a cup of coffee and someone bumps your elbow, you don't splash out a Popsicle do you? No, you splash out exactly what is in your cup. That principle also applies spiritually and emotionally. Whatever is filling your heart is going to come out when you get bumped. And bumps can come from any horizontal circumstance of life, whether accidental or intentional.

Maybe you're doing all you can to hold on to your job, or maintain a certain relationship, or pass a class at school. You feel frustrated because something or someone is threatening your false-vine source of "life." Then unexpectedly someone bumps into you (physically or emotionally), and you blow up at that person. He might not have deserved it, but he got it.

This is how road rage works. Day after day someone's life cord is plugged into getting somewhere on time, but instead of leaving earlier or sitting back and enjoying the rush, he allows himself to become angry in the crush of traffic. Then some other driver cuts him off or criticizes his driving, complete with hand gestures. *Why you so-and-so!* he thinks. *I oughtta show you a thing or two! I've had it with guys like you!* Something snaps and he blows up, retaliates.

Now maybe you don't chase down other drivers, force them off the road and beat them up, but you may be just as guilty — because you are considering such actions. The anger is there in your heart.

Christian motivational speaker Zig Ziglar used the following illustration of "Kicking the Cat" in his seminars:

Running late on his way to work, a boss gets pulled over for speeding, which makes him even later. He storms into his office, calls in the sales manager and chews her out for not meeting their goals (even though she's great at her job). Now she, too, is agitated and takes out her anger on another employee. This guy stews over their encounter during his commute and arrives home furious with the world. He sees a bike in the driveway and takes it out on his wife. She goes inside and yells at little Johnny, who storms out of the house, slamming the door. On the porch lies the family cat, napping. Johnny kicks that cat into the air and over the fence. Zig concludes, Wouldn't it just have been better for the boss to drive over to the employee's house, pick up that cat, and dropkick it himself?

Repeat the principle out loud: *What is in your heart will "splash out" of your life cup — in your words or in your actions — when you "get bumped."*

When a person "gets bumped," three types of reactions demonstrate his or her misplaced "life" plug. That person may:

1) Get Big
2) Get Little
3) Get Lost

[handwritten marginalia: "it is just a reaction ... a pause ... do not have to go on ... carry on ... un..cial response"]

These reactions may "splash out" individually or in any combination of all three. When you catch these behaviors splashing out of your cup, you can know that you have jacked into a false "life" plug by valuing something on a horizontal/material rather than vertical/spiritual plane.

For instance, a friend once said to me, "I can't drive in rush hour traffic because it makes me a raging psycho."

I replied, "No you are a raging psycho; the traffic just brings it out." In other words, whether you step on a skunk or you step on a rose, when the pressure is on and stress applied, what is on the inside will come out.

Get Big

People who "get big," become angry and will fight to stay plugged in. They become competitive, protective, aggressive, and hurtful in the fight to keep their "life" cord supply going. The young, on-fire sales executive can be intimidating and pushy because he gets "life" from his performance — from his passion to be the best. He fights to excel and show up his competition.

A wife gets loud, talking over and interrupting her husband to win her point. A parent uses the "I'm-your-father/mother-do-what-you're-told card.

This is an ORPHAN way of controlling one's world. ORPHANS tend to be intensely competitive. They don't realize what unrealistic benchmarks they set for coworkers who make family a priority over work-related goals.

Some examples of "Get Big" behavior are:

+ **Escalation** Being quick to argue, raising one's voice, using unpredictable outbursts of anger, raging at others, intimidating others by harsh uncaring responses and over-exaggeration. The desired result is that others back off; so the one who escalates the loudest "wins."

+ **Exaggeration** Making overstatements or enlarging explanations beyond boundaries or truth. Using catastrophic statements, building mountains from molehills, using danger and fear as a way to control others.

+ **Aggression or Abuse** Defaulting to anger to conceal one's true emotions or to control others. Reacting when another person threatens to take away the thing one has plugged into for "life." Turning fear-based anger into verbal or physical aggression, and, in some cases, abuse. Some aggressors/abusers are easy to spot by the words they use, the anger they express. More reserved abusers cause greater pain, inflicting emotional scars that take years to heal.

+ **Negativity** Projecting and believing the other person is far worse than is really the case, shaping others in a negative light. Telling others how they have failed or crossed one or let one down. Instead of giving thanks for another person in one's life, criticizing him or her, even having imaginary dialogues with that person when he or she isn't there.

+ **Polarizing** Transferring negative motives by characterizing others as enemies. When someone disappoints, crosses, or fails to live up to a polarizer's expectations, the polarizer starts broadcasting all of the other's faults and issues.

I could see how I polarized my relationships when I started to examine my own heart with the *Principle of Splash*. Everyone who stood in my way was an enemy I had to deal with. In my thinking, either they didn't have their head screwed on straight or they didn't understand God and His Word. I actually felt proud when someone said, "Whenever we try to talk to Jim, he just brings out the Bible and we never win." Now I look back and wish I had been much better at listening and loving people rather than trying to win my agenda with an encyclopedic knowledge of the Bible.

+ **Blaming** Placing responsibility on others as the problem, the one who has to change, the one with the issues that have to be dealt with. Not asking God to change oneself first or examining one's own cup, or allowing the splash to show how selfish one is. Even Christians may exhibit this "Get Big" behavior by not accepting fault, convinced that someone else is always to blame.

Before Father showed me how to plug into the true source of LIFE, my ORPHAN spirit quickly transferred blame to others. All conflict had to be the other person's fault. If they would just submit to my authority or do things the way I wanted them done, then everything would be fine.

+ **Fix-it Mode** Focusing exclusively on problem solving, and never hearing the feelings of others. Here's a typical example:

Sara (up to her elbows in 2-year-old Wesley's diarrhea diapers): Oh, I am so sick of all these poopy Pampers! When is Wesley's diarrhea going to clear up? I'm so worried about his rash. And he's still running a fever.

Michael (his eyes never leaving "Monday Night Football"): Well, Sara, didn't you hear what Dr. Smith said? It might take 48 hours, and kids get rashes and diarrhea all the time. I'm sure Wes will be fine. You should just stop worrying. But you could probably put more Desitin on his bottom.

Needless to say, Sara heard the pediatrician's advice just as well as Michael did. She knows what to do; she just wants to share her concerns, vent her feelings and be comforted and supported by her husband.

+ **Denial** Inability to receive and accept the truth about oneself. By refusing to admit the truth, people in denial make it hard for others to tell them their true feelings.

Get Little

On the other hand, when some people can't fight and win, they will "Get Little." They shrink inwardly and become submissive. They try not to make anyone angry or upset with them. They become compliant, doing whatever they believe is expected of them in their job — working longer hours, sacrificing their family, putting up with insults. Why? Because they do whatever seems necessary to hang on to what gives them "life."

Some "Get Little" behaviors are:

+ **Apathy, Loss of Care** Becoming devoid of emotion, and having no regard for anyone. The person may decide to reject others before they can reject him or her.

- ✦ **Complaining** Expressing unhappiness, making accusations, often criticizing and creating lists of others' faults.
- ✦ **Withdrawal** Avoiding others, or alienating oneself without resolution.
- ✦ **Defensiveness** Defending oneself and providing an explanation of one's actions, instead of listening to others.
- ✦ **Clinginess** Developing a strong emotional attachment or dependence on the other person (co-dependency).
- ✦ **Care-taking (vs. Care-giving)** Being responsible for the other person, doing things for the other that he or she should be doing.
- ✦ **Humor** Making jokes to laugh one's way out of painful situations, in order to avoid dealing with the issues.
- ✦ **Sarcasm** Using negative, pointed humor; hurtful, exaggerated, belittling or cutting comments, demeaning statements.
- ✦ **Rationalization** Attempting to make one's actions seem reasonable by explaining why one has done things.
- ✦ **Rabbit Trails** Throwing people off course by overloading them with huge amounts of information or distractions, picking on other issues and insisting on discussing them.
- ✦ **Abdication** Giving away self-respect or responsibilities.
- ✦ **Indifference** Becoming cold, impassive, and showing no concern about others.
- ✦ **Passive Aggression** Displaying negative emotions, resentment, and aggression in passive ways (for example, making cutting remarks in a soft, calm voice or pretending to cooperate while, in fact, doing nothing to help another).
- ✦ **Invalidation** Devaluing the other person; not appreciating what he or she feels or thinks or does.

Get Lost

The third reaction to getting bumped is to "Get Lost." When someone or something threatens their "life" cord, these people physically and emotionally leave. They walk away, stop trying, and stop caring. Their philosophy of life is built on apathy and cynicism.

Bars and clubs are full of people who have given up. They feel no need to try harder to work through painful circumstances and relationships; instead they leave. Why? They have tried to "Get Big" and were beaten up. They tried "Getting Little" to let others win, in hopes they might win, too. But there was no win/win for them. So they've given up, walked away and developed the "Get Lost, get out, get away" attitude.

"Getting Lost" may have been their pattern of reacting to a person or group or family member or authority figure growing up. Perhaps current circumstances have overwhelmed them and they're just following the escape route, saying, "That is not going to hurt me again, because I am out of here." Some people have perfected this pattern as a lifestyle; out of reflex they reject others before they can be rejected themselves.

Deep down inside, both the "Get Little" and the "Get Lost" group may be boiling with anger. Although they appear quiet in spirit, all of a sudden, as they're walking through life, someone crosses them and bam! They explode!

"Get Lost" behaviors include:

+ **Acting Out (Hard Addictions)** Obvious hard addictions: engaging in negative behaviors, drug, alcohol, sex, extramarital affairs; anything to anesthetize the pain of not being in control.

+ **Acting Out (Soft Addictions)** More hidden addictions: excessive shopping, spending, overeating, and other obsessive behaviors that serve to isolate the person and build walls to keep others out.

+ **Manipulating** Controlling other people for one's own advantage. Using rejection and polarization, to get others to do what one wants.

+ **Wearing a Mask** Building protective defenses around one's emotional attachments, keeping other people from seeing one's true self and genuine emotions. Using the world as a stage, where one is both actor and audience, watching oneself play one's role. Other people are potentially hurtful and can never be let in.

ORPHANS, dependent on the world value-system for "life" and fulfillment, don't see their actions and words as indicators of what they are plugged into.

SONS, who are maturing in their faith walk, learn to review their recent words and actions in order to clearly identify the false "life" vines they are plugged into.

See False Vines As Idolatry

The Bible has a name for seeking to get life from a created thing rather than from the Creator: idolatry. Before realizing this, I would never have thought of myself as an idolater. Idolatry was practiced by uneducated, Third World tribal people in the depths of dark jungles. It certainly did not characterize a 21st Century thinker like me. Yet I was shocked to see how much the false vine was my source of "life," and realized idolatry was a big part of my life.

Wikipedia defines Biblical idolatry as, "an act of worship toward any created thing...."[37] Webster's online dictionary defines worship as, "...a derivative of the old English word, 'worthship,' meaning, 'an attitude or action that gives worth or value to something.'"[38] Clearly, then, idolatry is the act or attitude of giving worth to any created thing.

When someone gives excessive value to a created thing by trying to protect it or control it or achieve it or make himself look good by it, he is practicing idolatry. He is giving it a place of worth equal to God.

Whenever you plug into a world vine and get "life" from it, you engage in an idolatrous relationship with it. This is clearly seen in Paul's indictment of those who "exchanged the truth of God for a lie, and worshiped and served the creature rather than the Creator, who is blessed forever."[39]

The Power Behind the False Vine — the Law

Genesis 3:5-10 describes the following destiny-changing drama:

The serpent said to the woman, "You surely will not die! For God knows that in the day you eat from it your eyes will be opened and you will be like God, knowing good and evil." When the woman saw that the tree was good for food, and that it was a delight to the eyes, and that the tree was desirable to make one wise, she took from its fruit and ate; and she gave also to her husband with her, and he ate. Then the eyes of both of them were opened, and they knew that they were naked; and they sewed fig leaves together and made themselves loin coverings.

They heard the sound of the LORD God walking in the garden in the cool of the day, and the man and his wife hid themselves from the presence of the LORD God among the trees of the garden. Then the LORD God called to the man, and said to him, "Where are you?"

He said, "I heard the sound of You in the garden, and I was afraid because I was naked; so I hid myself."

Satan promises something very interesting here: "The day you eat from it your eyes will be opened and you will be like God." (Emphasis mine.) The truth is they were already like God. God had said so Himself in Genesis 1:26-17:

"Let Us make man in Our image, according to Our likeness; and let them rule over the fish of the sea and over the birds of the sky and over the cattle and over all the earth, and over every creeping thing that creeps on the earth." God created man in His own image, in the image of God He created him; male and female He created them."

Adam and Eve were created in the image of God and were also created in His *likeness*; they were already *like God*. That does not mean they were *equal* to God or *were* God, but that they were created *like* God. That's how God made them.

So what actually was Satan's offer? That by *their own* action, through *their own* self-effort, on *their own* terms, they would gain *what they already possessed*. They would be God-like. Since that dramatic event, our entire horizontal world value-system has been based on this principle: Man can — by his own effort apart from depending on God — be *like God*.

Even more sinister (and often overlooked), was Satan's promise: "In the day you eat you will be like God, *knowing good and evil*." What does that mean and why is it such a bad thing?

I pondered this question as I was driving on the freeway one day. *What determines the difference between something that is good and something that is evil? Why would the Holy Spirit, as the author of Genesis, tell us the name of the Tree of the Knowledge of Good and Evil unless it had some importance?* I wondered. Just then I passed a Speed Limit sign, instinctively looked at my speedometer, and slowed down because I was going too fast. How did I know that I was going too fast? Because a motor vehicle law judges my performance! The speed limit law gives me the knowledge of right and wrong, good and not good.

So if the tree Adam and Eve ate from was "the knowledge of good and evil," then it was the tree of the Law! The *moment* they sinned, they subjected themselves (and all humankind) to the Law — the law of performance, the law of looking good, power over people and things, possessions, popularity and praise. *The Law is the power behind the world value-system.*

The Law judges performance and appearance. The Law controls and rates who has the best stuff. Laws judge and rank materials according to systems of weights and measures and quality control. Societies judge actions as good or bad, right or wrong according to civil laws.

But people also judge other people as too fat or too skinny, pretty or ugly, rich or poor, strong or weak, successful or failing, above or below their social station. Most of these world value-systems feed on the Law of the knowledge of what is "good" and what is "evil." The Law is the power behind the world's system.

The entire world value-system is based on Law not GRACE. The Law of good and evil is the foundation for the entertainment industry, sports, academics, social and cultural pursuits, politics, business, advertising, and sales. This model permeates relationship arenas we expect to be safe and some we hold sacred: friendships, marriages, families. Even churches are affected by "Consumer Christianity" — whose church provides the best programs, has the most attendance, rakes in the most offerings, presents the most professional-looking productions.

The Law was never meant to be the Tree of LIFE. The Law cannot give LIFE — it was never meant to do so. In fact, Galatians 3:21 specifically says exactly that: "Is the Law then contrary to the promises of God? May it never be! For if a law had been given which was able to impart life, then righteousness would indeed have been based on law."

LIFE *cannot result from meeting the requirements of any law. The Law's purpose was never to provide an opportunity for people to show God how good they look. It was never intended to provide* LIFE. *There is nothing created that can provide what only the Creator can provide.*

Efforts to Gain Value Through the World's Value-system Result in Emptiness

According to God's Word, people who make idols and live by those idols become like their idols.[40] Those idols are no more powerful than the people who fashion them: "The idols of the nations are but silver and gold, the work of man's hands. They have mouths, but they do not speak; they have eyes, but they do not see; they have ears, but they do not hear, nor is there any breath at all in their mouths. Those who make them will be like them; yes, everyone who trusts in them."[41]

Sooner or later, all earthly things decay or lose their value; only what's done out of a relationship with Christ can last forever. People who build on a horizontal world value-system will one day discover it's all going to be burned up. According to 2 Peter 3:10, that day will sneak up on us "like a thief, in which the heavens will pass away with a roar and the elements will be destroyed with intense heat, and the earth and its works will be burned up."

Every bridge, skyscraper, limousine, trophy and diamond-studded crown will melt into oblivion. Three times the Bible records Jesus saying, "Heaven and earth will pass away, but My words will not pass away."[42] No matter how well something is built to last, if it is of this world, it will pass away. Why? Because it is built on a foundation of things of this world.

The Addiction of the Law

Unfortunately, the short-term satisfaction derived from performing, owning, controlling and looking good works like a drug in people's minds and hearts. And as with drugs, the following comparisons are true:

1. **A drug makes the user feel good**. So does the world value-system, providing short-term effects, it becomes a drug that gives people a high.

2. **A drug is consumable, it is never enough, never completely satisfies, leaves the user wanting more**. No matter how hard one works, competes or pushes, it will never completely satisfy. Only Jesus completely satisfies, and anything short of Him is a counterfeit affection.

3. **A drug numbs the user's mind, masking the truth that the drug itself is clouding the user's reality**. One of the worst results of operating in the world system is the numbing nature of worldly affection. The more accolades one receives for performance, the more one wants and the less capable one becomes of seeing reality.

This blindness is like the tale of how to kill a wolf: On a freezing-cold day, dip a sharp double-bladed knife in blood, and let it freeze. The wolf will smell the blood and start licking the knife. Because of the numbing cold, it won't realize that it is shredding its own tongue and will bleed to death. That harsh depiction is the true image of counterfeit horizontal world-system affections.

4. **A drug will also create dependency through the "cycle of addiction."** Picture a graph with point zero as the place a person starts before ever using a drug. The first drug use results in a high point of 10. This person thinks this drug is the best thing that ever was. However, the next time, the person won't get that high, because his or her body and mind start adapting, so all he/she gets is a 9. The next high rates only an 8 and requires more of the drug.

Oh, but it gets worse! Instead of coming off the drug and returning to a zero, where the person started, he/she now drops to -1. Now that this person is feeling bad, he/she uses the drug again. This time he/she starts from -1 and goes up 9 steps to an 8. The problem is that when the drug wears off, the person's low point drops again, and now down to -2.

The progression is ever downward. Even worse, the high from the drug cycle begins to plummet at an even greater speed; -2 plus 8 equals 6, drops back 10 to a -4. Re-use of the drug brings the person up 7, which gets him/her only to a 3, then dropping back 10, which results in a new low starting point of -7.

Before long, the person exists in the minus column, and nothing, absolutely nothing he/she does, makes it better. More drugs are needed, but the original high is never again attained. *More, more,*

more is demanded. Welcome to addictive behavior. Every time this person takes the drug, he/she must take more to get the same high, but soon that doesn't work, so now he/she is maximizing the drug in order to get the "high" which is always lower. The low gets lower and lower. This phenomenon is described by Eric Nestler and Robert Malenka in their article for *Scientific American*:

For many users, the sight of a drug or its associated paraphernalia can elicit shudders of anticipatory pleasure. Then, with the fix, comes the real rush: the warmth, the clarity, the vision, the relief, the sensation of being at the center of the universe. For a brief period, everything feels right. But something happens after repeated exposure to drugs of abuse — whether heroin or cocaine, whiskey or speed. The amount that once produced euphoria doesn't work as well, and users come to need a shot or a snort just to feel normal; without it, they become depressed and, often, physically ill. Then they begin to use the drug compulsively. At this point, they are addicted, losing control over their use and suffering powerful cravings even after the thrill is gone and their habit begins to harm their health, finances and personal relationships. [43]

+ That's what alcohol does

+ That's what sexual perversion does

+ That's what porn does

+ That's what excessive eating does (and here comes the absolute shock)

+ That is exactly what the world value-system does.

    A person gets an A, achieves, performs then has to do it again and again and again. Only the high isn't as high and the low is much lower. A person succeeds at business and gets a massive financial boost, repeatedly. Soon this person has more money than he/she needs, yet continues pouring his/her life into the system. The athlete succeeds, but where does he go from there? The world value drug is the most powerful of all. And sadly, the workaholic addict is praised and rewarded and held up as a model for others.

5. **When the person stops using the drug, he/she experiences physical or emotional withdrawal**, which can include symp-

toms like irritability, anxiety, shakes, headaches, sweats, nausea, or vomiting. That is what a drug does.

Have you ever noticed a similar phenomenon occurs in the world value-system? A woman may starve herself because she doesn't think she looks thin enough. Or a workaholic slaves at his job till he has a stroke because "it's never enough." *I believe this false vine, this world value-system, may be far more addictive than cocaine or heroin because there is no negative social stigma. There is little to caution the addict away. It's more acceptable and wider spread.*

6. **A drug fuels the denial of its actual consequences**. It gives the user a euphoric rush while numbing him or her to the actual consequences of being a user. This is not a side effect from the drug. It's a side effect of the world value-system. People don't blame the value-system when they're pushing harder to perform or to present themselves worthy. Or when they're striving for the praise of men, or searching for that one special person to fulfill their fantasies. The tendency is to blame something else.

We might say, "That person let me down." Instead, the problem lies in our determination to will another person into providing "life" for us. Or we complain, "No one likes me," when in reality we don't like ourselves enough to not care if someone doesn't praise us. The problem is, some of us feel liked only if we're receiving praise.

Get God! Abide in Christ the Vine!

So how do we proceed beyond the three choices of Get Big, Get Little and Get Lost? Let's look at one other "Get" option. I call it, "Get God." Get God intermixed in your life. Get God and get Him in first place. Draw your LIFE from your vertical relationship with Him.

I'll never forget the time Phil approached me after a service. Despite major health issues, he overworked to meet his wife's material demands. Yet the marriage ended with divorce, betrayal, loss of his children and ongoing financial injury. He felt isolated and alone. Bitterness and unforgiveness had him in a vice-like grip.

I felt Phil's sadness and asked God what I should say to him. Father said simply, "Ask him, 'Is My Love enough, or do you need more?'" So after carefully listening, I said, "Phil, I want you to ask yourself this question every day this next week: 'Is God's Love enough for me, or do I need more?' Do that all this week and then come back to me."

A week went by and Phil wasn't at the next service. The following week, Phil came to me again after the service. He went back to the same story. (It's what we do when we're hurt; we nurse it, curse it and re-hearse it). Again I listened then asked him, "What was the question I gave you to work on?" He continued reciting his hurts and tragedies.

"Phil."

"What?"

"Phil, I'm not diminishing your pain, but what was the question I gave you to work on?"

He started again. (Sometimes people need to know what you tell them is important enough to keep them accountable).

"Phil," I said a third time.

"What?"

"Phil, what was the question I asked you when we last spoke?"

Knowing I wasn't giving up, he looked down and said, "I forgot."

One of the things that impresses me above all else is honesty, period. I told Phil I was blessed by his honest heart, and it was OK that he forgot. Most people don't get it the first time. I told him I loved him. (People desperately need to know God's Love.) Then I said, "OK, here it is again. This week, every day, I want you to simply ask yourself this question: 'Is God's Love enough for me, or do I need more?' Write it down. Will you do that?"

We parted and he set off again, question in hand, promising he would do as I asked. This time he followed through. He took his faith and met a Loving Father at the corner of Praise Street and Thanksgiving Avenue. Over the next week and the weeks to come, Phil's attitude, face and heart changed radically. He came back with stories of God working in his life as Love took root and faith was rejuvenated. He grabbed God and refused to let go. The change in this man was amazing! He "got God"!

I call it "living vertically." Instead of being horizontally controlled by circumstances and other people, you can start learning to get LIFE from God and God alone. Is God enough for you? Or do you demand more? You can live horizontally, controlled by circumstances and people, living like an ORPHAN, or you can ask yourself Phil's question, "Is God's Love enough for me, or do I need more?" Continually evaluate the condition of your heart. *Live Life Vertically* is the name of the game. Watch your heart to see if you are living vertically.

One of my mentors, Dr. Fred Barshaw, had a favorite illustration he used: "If we are walking through the forest together and decide we want to make a cross how many sticks do we need?"

This is not a trick question. The answer is two (and maybe some string). Dr. Fred would say, "Which stick has to be in place first?" The obvious answer is the vertical one. If you try to build a cross by placing the horizontal stick first, it falls to the ground because it has no support, no foundation, and no stability. The horizontal stick depends on the vertical stick to stay off the ground. The vertical must be used first, because without it everything falls. The same principle holds true in our vertical relationship to God and the horizontals of the world in which we live.

Your horizontal world relationships — whether they're awesome or keeping you awake at night — are simply horizontals. They are composed of people and circumstances. If you try to gain "life" by hanging on, fixing, controlling, looking good, living in the horizontals, you are in for the roller-coaster ride of instability. You will keep falling down. Nothing supports you.

So you must learn to put the vertical beam in place then hang all of your horizontal relationships on it. Jesus said it this way: "Seek first the Kingdom of God ... and all these things will be added to you."[44] Put God first; seek Him first. His Love for you and your response to it are more important than anything or anyone else. That does not completely devalue other things and people. But they are not first in importance. "Is My Love enough for you, or do you need more?"

The Psalmist referred to horizontal living this way: "*Whom have I* in heaven but *Thee and besides Thee I desire nothing on this earth.*" You must come to that place where you refuse to be dependent on, defined by, get "life" from a false vine.

The *vine* of John 15 is Christ, and the *vinedresser* is Father God. These roles define the relationship God longs to have with you. Jesus said this happens only when you learn to abide in Him. The English word "abide" is the Greek word MENO. It means to abide, remain, dwell in, take up residence, be connected to, to be held, to be kept, to endure.[45]

As Jesus describes this abiding relationship in John 15, He uses the word "if" five times: "If a man abides," "If anyone does not abide," "If you abide," "If you obey My commands," "If you do what I command." This relationship requires your participation. *You* choose to abide, to remain, to live in the vine.

How does someone abide in Christ? By obeying His Word more? Praying more? Producing more fruit? Often even Bible teachers answer with a formula of work, work, work, and try harder. Are you ready for the surprise of the passage? Jesus tells us straight out, "Just as the Father has loved Me, I have also loved you; abide in My love."[46]

How many times did I read this passage and never see it? How many times did I go through this passage concentrating on fruit, bearing fruit, more fruit, much fruit? I became a human *doing* not a human *being*.

Abide in My Love! John defines "abide" in 1 John 4:16: "And we have come to know and have believed the love which God has for us. God is love, and the one who abides in love abides in God, and God abides in him." God *abides* in you when you *abide* in Him; not in the works, not in the performance, not in the value system of the world. He *abides* in you when you simply walk into His court and *sit down* in Christ. You run HOME to Father's embrace. God doesn't need you to be great at your job. He doesn't need you to be a great anything. God wants you *just for who you are.* He wants *you!* He wants you to abide in Him, to live in His relationship with you.

When you abide, things happen — you bear fruit, more fruit, *much* fruit. The flesh, the ORPHAN, will constantly put the world value-system of performance before the joy of simply being loved. Living in Christ becomes a duty instead of a delight, a job instead of joy.

Jesus is the LIFE vine. Father is the vinedresser. What does a vine-dresser do? The person who tends the vineyard doesn't just rake it a bit and go home. Vineyards take a lifetime commitment of care to produce. The vinedresser doesn't casually decide, "Time to prune the vines and throw away the pieces." He tends the vineyard and will give his life to protect it.

This commitment can be seen in John 15:2: "Every branch in Me that does not bear fruit, He takes away; and every branch that bears fruit, He prunes it so that it may bear more fruit." Some commentators interpret this to mean, if you don't perform you get cut off and thrown out. But no vinedresser would just throw away a branch, and for a very good reason. Branches are much too valuable. The Greek word AIEREO translated "take away" may also mean to raise up from the ground, or elevate. A vine grower will tell you that if the vines have fallen and are covered with insects, mulch or debris, the branches are gingerly lifted up and tied off in the sunlight. The bad leaves are pruned away and, often, the dresser will tie the branches to other branches as well, to help them stay up.[47]

Why would you prune a branch you cut off and cast away?

Father God never casts His children away. He lovingly cares for us and lifts us back into the light, off of the moldy ground, where mildew and sickness exist. He prunes us so that we draw our LIFE from the vine. He teaches us to live life vertically in His Presence instead of living on the horizontal roller coaster of the world's drug. It's a process where we realize the immense value of God's Love that far surpasses any possible counterfeit the world might give us. Pruning is not fun; Father comes to take those things out of our lives that are not conducive to drawing LIFE from His Son. He clips away some performance issue; He allows certain possessions to be lost; He removes a significant person from our life — all part of the pruning process.

Living life vertically is like swinging from one trapeze to another. You cannot move forward until you release your hold on the swing you are on. Father God will go to great lengths to get you to release that swing, to risk free fall only to find yourself caught in His hands *every time.*

This process begins as you understand the Love God has for you, when you step into the discovery of what is so amazing about GRACE.

My daughter, Kristin, had an outdated cell phone that dropped calls and had horrible reception. The day came when we went together and replaced it with a top-of-the-line touch-screen phone. The phone worked great and lasted a whole week. Carrying her groceries in from the car, Kristin had the phone cradled in her arm. As she reached for her keys, the phone slipped out and hit the sidewalk. The screen spider-webbed into a thousand pieces.

When she picked up the phone and saw the screen, the first thing that went through her mind was, "Is God's Love enough or do you need more?" Immediately she felt a peace about the whole thing. She used the phone for some time, and then a daddy's heart (that loves her much) did the upgrade thing and got her a new phone. A heart just like our heavenly Father's.

APPLICATION: LEARNING TO HEAR FATHER'S HEART

Note that with this chapter, and from this point on, our "Application" section will be titled "Learning to Hear *Father's* Heart" (rather than the Shepherd's Heart). Many of us relate to the image of Jesus as the Good Shepherd, gentle and kind. But the Father is the one whose heart is reflected in Jesus. It's time for you to transition into hearing the Father's heart directly. Even as Jesus spoke to His disciples in John 16 just before His arrest in the Garden of Gethsemane, "In that day you will ask in My name. I am not saying that I will ask the Father on your behalf. No, the Father Himself loves you because you have loved Me and have believed that I came from God."

Check Your "Life" Cord

Looking back at your week, can you see what your "life" cord is plugged into? What thrilled you? What caused sadness, depression or fear? What caused you to Get Big, Get Little, or Get Lost? Visualize your relationships with family members and ask yourself, "What would they say I'm plugged into?" That's how you can tell what you're plugged into for "life."

If you're in a small group, help other group members honestly evaluate their week. Ask one another the tough questions. Help keep one another accountable.

1. GET SERIOUS: "I will stand and station myself ..." to wait on God.

Take some time and step to the side of everyday life. Don't skip over this APPLICATION section; it is the most important thing you can do to glean lasting results from this book. Stand before the Lord and show Him you are intentional about hearing from Him. The Psalmist wrote in Psalm 46:10, "Be still and know that I am God."

2. BE FOCUSED: "and I will keep watch to see what He will speak to me."

Deeply inhale God's Word as a swimmer gulps for air. Ask yourself seriously, "Am I watching to see what God will say, or just going through the motions with my quiet times?"

3. PRACTICE AUTHENTIC HUMILITY: "how I may reply when I am reproved."

The essence of sin is self-dependence. Remember the flow of God's GRACE comes to the humble heart. "'For My hand made all these things, thus all these things came into being,' declares the LORD. 'But to this one I will look, to him who is humble and contrite of spirit, and who trembles at My word.'"[48] Breathe in His Word and exhale self-stuff. Write out what splashed from your cup this week. It's tough, because we don't like to admit our anger, irritation, frustration, unforgiveness, and hasty words. Recognize that God's Love is enough and let Him love you through it.

4. WRITE IT, CHECK IT, RUN IT: "Record the vision and inscribe it."

Learn to journal your conversations with God. Remember who God is, listen quietly and let Him speak or lead however He chooses. Write what He places on your heart and then learn to check what He shows you by sharing it with at least three trusted advisors. Then run in the power of God's Word to you.

SECTION TWO: THE PRODIGAL FATHER

CHAPTER 6: THE FACE OF GRACE

"Amazing GRACE, how sweet the sound, that saved a wretch like me…"
— John Newton

"My cup was full of sin and selfishness; He drank it — drank it all — that's called mercy. My cup was empty, nothing left; and He filled it — filled it full with Himself — that's called Grace."
—Jeff Chariker, Worship Pastor, Faith Bible Church (September 18, 2011)

I HAVE heard many people say they understand the meaning of GRACE. Yet they cannot explain it adequately. In "Christianese" sayings, GRACE is usually focused on the death of Christ. I've heard it summed up as God's "Unconditional Love." What does that mean? An acrostic GRACE — standing for God's Riches At Christ's Expense — while very true, carries little meaning to motivate change in the believer's life.

Imagine you're watching a romantic movie featuring a tropical sunset, painted against an open sea and unending sky by a loving Heavenly Father, just for two of His awestruck children. They stroll together — a thirty-something couple on a well-deserved vacation. They feel the cool, wet sand beneath their feet; hear the rhythmic waves lapping against the shore. The sun, a magnificent ball of brilliant orange against the horizon, sinks into the sea. Clouds set on fire by the sun's final moments dance against gray cotton-y backgrounds, licked by flames within a fireplace of panoramic proportions.

Broken only by a sail, a paper blown by a gentle breeze, the distant horizon meets the sky. The couple stand entwined, alone, together, their faces to the sunset. She, blinded by a past accident, depends on him to be her eyes, to unlock her memories of color. His words are brushes that paint the canvas of her imagination with what she feels in the warmth of that sunset.

"Describe it for me, please," she says. "What do you see? What colors are there and how do they paint the sky?"

"Sweetheart," he kindly replies, "what I see is GRACE, plain and simple. It is GRACE, a life-changing moment we'll never forget."

"What does that mean — GRACE?" she asks. "What does it look like? How does it feel? What is in your heart? Please tell me, because I can't see it, though I know it's there. What do you mean by GRACE? What does GRACE mean?"

"It's GRACE," he says. "Just the grandness of GRACE." He speaks softly now. Surely, now she'll get it, he thinks as he explains, "Honey, it's Geometric Rotation Acquiescing Coronal Effluence."

Another pause. Only now, the pause is yours. What did he say? What did he mean? How could he be so unromantic, so unfeeling to not describe this scene to his blind wife? Surely, that is not in the script! CUT!

Obviously, this scenario is absurd. But can you picture Leo DiCaprio holding Kate Winslet on the prow of the *Titanic*? Shouldn't this guy at least TRY to capture the magnificence of that sunset for the love of his life? Then he could have ended his description with "But there is nothing here as beautiful as you!" That's the way it's supposed to go.

Yet I, as a pastor, teacher, counselor and life coach, witnessed similar scenes with disturbing regularity through thirty-plus years of ministry. I listened to and counseled numerous people who desperately needed to hear the brilliant colors of God's Love. They wanted to experience that Love — climaxed in the death of His Son — spoken by Him through the ages. They wanted to feel the Love that set the colors of the sky afire. Instead I gave them only worn-out phrases and empty words: "It's GRACE, just GRACE, **G**od's **R**iches **A**t **C**hrist's **E**xpense."

Where is the passion in that answer? How does God's Love reach someone, and how does it set one's life on fire? What does GRACE mean? What does it look like? How does it feel? People are blind; they can't see. They want to know what is on God's heart. They are asking,

"What do you know of this God, and why would His Love be extended to me? Tell me, how can His GRACE change my life, and why would I want it to?"

I want to paint for you in words the splendor of His Love until the canvas of your life is covered with all that He wants you to know of Himself.

Jesus — The Introduction to GRACE

This may shock you: The Bible calls the agonizing death of Christ just an introduction to the GRACE of God. Read Paul's words to the Romans:

> *Therefore having been justified by faith, we have peace with God through our Lord Jesus Christ, through whom also we have obtained our **introduction** by faith into this Grace in which we stand; and we exult in hope of the glory of God.* [49] (Emphasis mine.)

When I first saw this, I couldn't believe it. If we read correctly, this passage teaches that the death of Christ — infinite in its scope, providing our justification with God — was just an *introduction* into GRACE. Is reading the introduction to a literary masterpiece a substitute for reading the book itself? Similarly, a movie trailer is meant as an introduction to the movie itself. The trailer is not the movie; its purpose is to whet your appetite, challenge you to want more. But still, it is just the *introduction*.

Romans 5 says that the death of Christ was just the "trailer" to GRACE. Most Christians treat the death of our Lord Jesus Christ as the *introduction, beginning, middle and end* of GRACE, as though there is nothing more to talk about. Well-intentioned preachers give the impression that everything they need to know is in the death of Christ. But according to the Bible, Jesus' death was just the *beginning* of the redemption story.

As I began to understand God's GRACE, I discovered a Presence so amazing, a power so strong that a transformation began in my life. This was not a momentary high from attending a conference or a "wow" from reading the latest book, but a transformation that finally stuck. I came back to peace, joy, rest, freedom and truth. I began thinking through this concept and looking at God's Love with the eyes of my heart. I saw the infinite cross of Christ as only the *introduction* to GRACE, and began searching its meaning. The more I saw the height and depth and width and length of God loving me, the more my life changed. I became utterly amazed by GRACE.

I define GRACE as ***acting in the best interest of another without any pre-condition or expectation of return, based in the character of the one doing the loving, not in the behavior of the one being loved.***

GRACE started displacing my ORPHAN thinking in many ways. I stopped thinking so much about me and started thinking so much more about Him. I saw that when I got burdened and confused, it was usually because I was focused on "all about me." When I stopped and stood in GRACE, then peace, joy, rest, freedom, and truth returned.

Dwight L. Moody of Chicago, was a seasoned preacher who helped found the YMCA in the last century. He was in New York City when he experienced God's Love falling on him in a way he later could barely even speak of. Moody had been listening to a preacher talk about the Love of God. The next day Moody was walking down Wall Street, meditating on this truth, when the Holy Spirit's power came upon him and he was filled with the Holy Spirit. "Oh what a day! I cannot describe it. ... I seldom refer to it. ... .I can only say that God was revealed to me, and I had such an experience of his love that I had to ask him to stay his hand," he wrote.[50]

Has this happened to you? Have you ever been so overwhelmed with the splendor of the sunset of GRACE that you have asked God to stay His Hand? I can tell you His Presence is just that indescribably overwhelming, and it will displace your "me" heart with a Christ-focused heart.

In *We Would See Jesus*, Roy and Revel Hession write:

> *The whole essence of Grace is that it is undeserved. The moment we have to do something to make ourselves more acceptable to God ... to be blessed of God, then Grace is no more Grace. ... If what we receive from God is dependent, even to a small extent, on what we are or do, then the most we can expect is but an intermittent trickle of blessing. But if what we are to receive is to be measured by the Grace of God quite apart from works, then there is only one word that adequately describes what He pours upon us ... "abundance!" The struggle ... is to believe it and to be willing to be but empty sinners to the end of our days, that Grace may continue to match our needs.*[51]

In John 14:6, Jesus says, "I am the way, the truth, and the life. No one comes to the Father except through Me." Regarding this verse, international Bible teacher Derek Prince wrote, "I believe that many of us have only apprehended the first half of that verse. A way only has meaning if it leads to a destination. Jesus is the way, but the Father is the destination."

Our goal as believers is to move through the *introduction* of Christ to a Father's Love and see if we can drink in deeply what GRACE really means.

A Missing Link

Knowing and understanding God's Love is the most important thing, the first and foremost among many important things that Christians need to know and believe. We must see that without God's Love, the rest of what we call the Gospel is meaningless. This is what John was communicating when he wrote in 1 John 4:16, "We have come to know and have believed the love which God has for us. God is love, and the one who abides in love abides in God, and God abides in him."

We know about God's Love. We have read books, newsletters, devotionals and papers on GRACE. We speak in awe of it; we sing about it. But do we believe it? Does GRACE touch our hearts every single day of our lives? Do we wake up realizing the GRACE of God in creation, in our breath, in our relationships?

I know you know God, but are you *experiencing Him* as your loving Father every day? If so, then you have moved beyond "the introduction."

My lack of understanding of GRACE was pinpointed when a friend asked me to help him understand Ephesians 3:14-21. I began to examine the passage's principles. Paul spends three chapters discussing our adoption in Christ. He covers who we are in Him, how we are saved by faith and how we are unified with others.

Then he comes to the apex of his letter in this powerful passage:

> *For this reason I bow my knees before the Father, from whom every family in heaven and on earth derives its name, that He would grant you, according to the riches of His glory, to be strengthened with power through His Spirit in the inner man, so that Christ may dwell in your hearts through faith; and that you, being rooted and grounded in love, may be able to comprehend with all the saints what is the breadth and length and height and depth, and*

apex → the top or highest part of something, especially forming a point.

to know the love of Christ which surpasses knowledge, that you may be filled up to all the fullness of God. Now to Him who is able to do far more abundantly beyond all that we ask or think, according to the power that works within us, to Him be the glory in the church and in Christ Jesus to all generations forever and ever. Amen.

I wrote out the passage, read it in parallel translations, diagrammed it, and applied the principles of good Bible study learned from my years in seminary and pastoral ministry. I looked at it grammatically, contextually and historically. I read reputable commentaries. I thought I had pretty well covered the passage. I gave the results to my friend, *and put the study back on my shelf.*

But something kept nagging at me. It troubled me a lot, in fact. It was as though God's Spirit was nudging me hard, saying, "You're not done; there is something more." Here is my journal entry from that day:

This passage, Christ dwelling in me, comprehending God's Love, living filled with the fullness of God, this isn't the characteristic ongoing flavor of my life. My life doesn't exhibit the power of God like this. ... I just need to discipline myself more to get this done. It's all by faith, so I need to surrender more, discipline more, work more, try harder, pick up my cross more, deny myself more, push harder, make it happen. But honestly, faith is a struggle for me. It is a constant effort to surrender to the Lord again, conquer the flesh, crucify myself, deny myself, follow Christ and pick up my cross. ... I talk about it, I want it, but my spiritual life is a series of ups and downs. I'm in with God for a while and we seem really close, then it all falls away, and pretty soon I'm struggling again. ... This has been my Christian life for 30 years. ... I'm exhausted with trying harder, God. I just can't do this anymore.

I returned to the passage, because God was bugging me about it. And these words in their original Greek, "rooted" (ERRIDZOMENOI) and "grounded" (TETHEMELIOMENOI) in Love, jumped out. Their tense implies something that an outside influence has done and continues to do in and to us. Simply, the passage says that as believers we have been rooted and grounded *by God* (not ourselves) in Love. It is a past act that has *continuing ongoing importance.*

"Having been rooted and grounded (in the past) in Love" — *OK, I get that.* "GRACE was on the cross" — *Got a seminary degree in that, so what?* But wait! And "continuing to be rooted and grounded in" — *Whatever that means. What does that mean?* And then, "rooted and grounded — *in what? —* IN LOVE. I kept digging.

I realized that Paul was stating an assumption: "I am assuming going forward as I construct a model for the Christian walk, that you understand this foundational truth — you *know* and *believe* that *you have been rooted and grounded by God in His Love.*"

Then the meaning of this phrase jumped out at me because of the word order in Greek.[52] The priority emphasis of the language used here is "*in Love*" — "In Love being rooted and grounded." I journaled:

> *I'm making an assumption that God loved me when He died on the cross. Jesus died for millions of people, and I'm told, theologically, that He would have died for one, but, seriously? God? You love me? Quite honestly, I DON'T EVEN THINK YOU REALLY LIKE ME. ... Sometimes You seem close, and if I work hard at prayer, You speak to my heart, but, I can't say that You like me much. ... Frankly, I think that when I got saved, You had a sense of "not much to work with here." I feel like you tolerate me, I'm never good enough, can't do it right, never succeeded much, not very important to You.*

Have you experienced a similar conversation with God? I encounter many people who think God is angry with them. At best, He's not very happy with them. They think if it weren't for a loving Jesus, we would all be experiencing God's anger all the time.

I ask them, "When you picture yourself coming to Father God, is He smiling or is He frowning?" Many of the people I minister to answer, "I see a frown." If that's how you feel, I'd like to change that perception.

What Do Roots Do?

Plants can't grow without good dirt. When the ground is sickly, unfertilized or nourishment deficient, the plant will be the same way, sickly, lacking vibrancy, undersized, stunted, shriveled, unfruitful. The soil is the primary determinant of how the plant will survive, grow and bear fruit. Roots in good soil are the source of the life of that plant. Roots provide the system to get the soil's nourishment to the plant.

I acquired first-hand experience with roots when I decided to remove a crabapple tree in our front yard. After hours and hours of chopping, sawing, cutting and pulling, even connecting my car to the stump to pull

— an effort that nearly ripped out my car's bumper — I realized that the root system of a tree is an astoundingly intricate and enormous mass of material. There are easily many more roots than there are branches, and they spread out everywhere. This is how a plant or tree lives, drawing nourishment from the ground.

The question is, what type of ground is nourishing you? Do you live in and abide in the world's value-system? Or are you planted in God's Love? Do you draw your LIFE from knowing that He loves you? The Bible says we should be rooted in God's Love — Is that your only source of LIFE?

I learned to ask this test question in everything: "*Is God's Love enough for me, or do I need more?*" This powerful question will change your whole life if you let it.

Psalm 73:25 says, "Whom have I in Heaven but Thee and besides Thee I desire *nothing* on this earth." *Rooted* means getting one's LIFE from God and God alone. Rooted in *Love* means getting one's LIFE cup filled *by God only*, depending on Him. When the horizontals (job, marriage, kids, friendships, the false vines of "life") go bad, you can know and rely on your Father's Love for you.

What Does Grounded Mean?

Webster's defines "grounded" as "mentally and emotionally stable, admirably sensible, realistic, and unpretentious." God tells us we must be daily grounded in His Love. Our mental and emotional stability must not be determined by the horizontal ups and downs of life but by the question, "Is God's Love enough for me?" No matter what happens, one thing will never ever change —Father's Love for us.

The greatest battle most believers face is in the area of *fear*. Christians are often told that to defeat fear, we need to believe in God. On the surface, that advice seems sound. But the core of our faith in God is not just His greatness, but *His desire to protect us and guard us against all the evil in this world*. Our God is not only Almighty God, He is also *the One who has loved us with an everlasting Love*.

Even though I repeated the words "Do not fear" over and over, fear was not defeated in my life until I began to deeply trust that God loves me. This is precisely what the Apostle John was driving at in his first epistle when he said:

> *We have come to know and have believed the love which God has for us. God is love, and the one who abides in love abides in God, and God abides in him. By this, love is perfected with us, so that we may have confidence in the day of judgment; because as He is, so also are we in this world. There is no fear in love; but perfect love casts out fear, because fear involves punishment, and the one who fears is not perfected in love.*[53]

Personally, fear is one of my weakest areas. Despite 35 years of Bible study, a seminary education, hundreds of conferences and seminars, and thousands of hours of listening to sermons, tapes and messages, I struggle more with fear than I care to admit. Especially regarding finances. It is not because I don't believe in a great God. I do with all my heart. *But what changed my life was the realization that this Almighty God is also my dear Father. He loves me.*

As a father, I would never withhold provision for my son or daughter. By comparison, there is no comparison; God loves me far more than I can love my children. I must repeatedly return to my grounding when my *fears* start to eclipse my *faith*. His Love for me is the ground I stand on.

In their book *The Blessing*, Gary Smalley and John Trent describe what a father's love should bring into the life of a child. They use the acrostic B.L.E.S.S. to state five things parents should be giving to their children:

- ✦ Being committed to them,
- ✦ Loving touch,
- ✦ Expressing value,
- ✦ Seeing potential in them, and
- ✦ Saying it often.[54]

Children desperately cry out for affirmation in each of these areas. They especially need to hear the words "I love you" from their fathers. If a child hears his father say "I love you" only once during the first ten years of his life, he'll buy into the message of rejection from the silence of the other nine years and 364 days.

This acrostic, B.L.E.S.S., is a picture of our heavenly Father. God, the perfect Father, uses His GRACE to show us He will provide what we need consistently if we let Him. He wants to B.L.E.S.S. us, but we must choose to come to Him and depend on Him and get our LIFE from Him. This is what it means to be rooted and grounded in Love.

Fear is defeated by our faith in a great God who loves us dearly. When we learn to *truly believe* that God loves us, then we *know* that not one thing can come our way that God does not see, cannot get us through, cannot handle.

How do you respond when you get blindsided by adversity? Do you try to work it out on your own? Or do you *ground* yourself in Him? God promises that whatever you go through is for your best and will glorify Him if you give your situation to Him. Whatever you endure — even consequences of your own actions — can be used for good in the long run. God is your Father Who loves you; nothing can come your way that will be a surprise to Him. Your Father will always get you HOME.

What's So Amazing about Grace?

The word we know as GRACE, historically, has a double meaning. The Greek word CHARIS refers to the emotional expression of kindness, favor, friendliness, and humility in giving to another without expectation of anything in return. In ancient Greece, CHARIS meant giving to another out of love and generosity, making the other person glad by the gift. But in Paul's day, Greeks were not expressively sentimental; they viewed CHARIS as a weakness. So the word CHARIS was not often used in their vocabulary, and was more or less despised as a character trait.

The early believers borrowed and transformed this seldom used term, giving it a brand new meaning. It became associated with their Christian belief alone. Think of how computer technology has morphed the meanings of words like "use your mouse," "download the file," "key in your password," and "access the Net." So it was with GRACE. It became pregnant with meaning and passion. James Moffatt explains that because the word was not used often, "All that Paul had to do was to fill it with fresh content."[55]

Within the New Testament, CHARIS was adopted to uniquely refer to the explosively new revelation of the heart of God expressed through the death of Christ. The apostles took this ordinary Greek word and invested it with a distinctive Christian application. They stamped it with new meaning as they identified GRACE with God's unconditional Love and kindness toward us.

This concept of GRACE was unique; there was no Old Testament word to compare to it. What the New Testament writers were attempting to explain was something *"new"* — a *"new and living way,"* a *"new covenant"* and *"newness of life"* in Christ Jesus. Paul's word CHARIS for GRACE became the code word for a revolutionary concept.

God in Christ had amazed them. He took their breath away. John Piper captured this feeling in one of his papers when he wrote a description about the birth of Christ:

> *It's dangerous to try to put the ocean in a raindrop. In essence, putting God's righteousness and His Love in something so small. God did it once. He put His infinite self in a single human being, Jesus Christ. This was far more amazing than putting the ocean in a raindrop. And it was the first expression of Love.* [56]

Father's Love acts in a way that demonstrates to us that we 1) belong to Him, 2) are significant or important to Him, 3) have great worth and value to Him, 4) are accepted and approved of by Him, 5) are protected from harm by Him, without regard for how well we measure up. We bring nothing to the table to benefit the giver of GRACE.

As this Truth soaked in and displaced my toxic ORPHAN thinking, it changed my life. Suddenly, it hit me. God likes me! The message I had studied for so many years, preached in so many sermons yet somehow had not seen, started jumping off the pages of Scripture. *Father's Love for me is not based on my ability to impress Him. He loves me because it is His desire to do so.* Like the "prodigal son," I have a HOME I can go to, to live in His intimacy, no matter what I have done or how bad I smell.

This was the captivating thought of the early Christians. They could hardly speak of it. I can only imagine their wonderment as they said the word … "GRACE." It was all about GRACE. "And the Word became flesh, and dwelt among us," wrote an enraptured Apostle John in 1 John 1:14, "and we saw His glory, glory as of the only begotten from the Father, full of GRACE and truth."

The Old Testament concluded with Malachi's warning of God's curse. But Jesus preached, "Blessed are the poor in spirit for theirs in the kingdom of heaven," and invited "all who are weary and heavy laden" to come to Him for rest.[57]

John saw, touched, heard then testified in his first epistle, "Here was Life." Here was GRACE and Truth. God's Love is more than a book on your shelf, more than a Sunday school study, more than a concept; it's personal. His name is Jesus, and He provides the means for a Love relationship with Father God.

GRACE means God values you. Not because you meet His expectations, but because it is in His character to love, and He loves you.

Max Lucado said that if God had a refrigerator, your finger paintings would be on it; if God had a wallet, your picture would be in it. Of all the places in the universe He could have picked to build a home, He picked your heart. Face it; He is crazy about you.[58]

For the ORPHAN a relationship with God cannot be very personal. The relationship always has to do with knowledge and performance, trying to impress God in hopes that He will bless their efforts.

SONS learn that a relationship with God is about abiding in His Presence, coming to Him not for what they can get, but for intimacy, connection and Love.

In Search of A New God

In order to understand more about GRACE, I had to change what I thought was or wasn't true about God. The "upside-down" glasses had to come off.

During this season of my life, I was greatly influenced by the Bible teaching of author and speaker Jack Frost, founder of Shiloh Place Ministries. In one of his messages, he described his visit to missionaries in Tibet. They took him to some Buddhist temples, where people were afraid, anxious and hopeless. Children cried out in fear, while their parents prostrated themselves before their terrible Tibetan gods.

All Frost could think was, *these people need a new God.* Later, in ministering to the missionaries, he realized their lives were full of similar fear and uncertainty. The Tibetan gods were aloof, remote, apathetic, demanding and harsh. He realized that these Christian missionaries needed a new God as well.

Coming from my background, I viewed Father God as anything but loving and forgiving. He seemed unreachable, judgmental and uncaring about any of my concerns. That kind of image of God as Father taints everything about how one sees himself.

Most Christians need a new image of God as well. They may have dozens of descriptors for Jesus as their Lord and Savior, Son of God, Lamb of God, and so on. But when it comes to describing God the Father, even the most mature believers are often left scratching their heads after five or six words.

But let's face it: Most pulpits preach a lot more on Jesus than they do on the Father. The systematic theology books used in our seminaries are stocked with chapters on Jesus and the Holy Spirit. But none have more than a page about God as our Father. Few popular Christian writers even refer to Father God's Love for us. The point is, most pastors, professors and theologians who are teaching and training upcoming pastors, professors and theologians don't see the depth of the Face of GRACE at all.

One of the most powerful teachings of Jesus about the character of God is inappropriately called the "Parable of the Prodigal Son."[59] A better title would be "The Prodigal Father." The word "prodigal" means *extravagant* or *exorbitant.* In the story, the reckless sinfulness of the wayward son is eclipsed by the extravagant love of the father who never gives up on him.

In its Biblical context, this story is the third in a series Jesus tells on the theme of the extravagant Love of God, rejoicing over the lost then found. First He tells of a lost sheep that is found by a shepherd. Second, a lost coin is found by its owner. Finally, this passage describes a father's extravagant, extraordinary, and exorbitant love for his sons in the context of the younger son's selfishness. It's not about the selfishness of the son at all.

The action begins when the younger son approaches his father demanding his share of the inheritance prior to the old man's death. This selfish son wants not just the money but also complete control over his destiny. He knows that to be accepted in a foreign country among a foreign people he will have to give expensive gifts and host lavish parties. So he asks his dad for the money. He doesn't want the responsibility and obligations of managing the property. Imagine how his father must have felt. The son's request in that culture is the equivalent of wanting his father dead and out of the way. *important WOW*

Thus begins Jesus' process of tearing down the image of an aloof, uncaring, angry Father. This young man, in his selfishness, cannot wait for his father to die before he snatches his inheritance. He relocates to a foreign land (which is so typical of people who cut themselves off from intimacy and connectedness with God). He is living in a land filled with strangers. He spends all of his money on self-indulgences. When the money runs out, he finds himself in a place where no Jewish young man should be. With the toss of his last shekel, he experiences total and complete rejection.

He finds the only place left for him in this foreign land is at the hogs' trough, slopping hogs in abject misery; and they eat better than he does. He has hit rock bottom. Jews abhor these unclean animals. But he has been forced to renounce all that he was in order to herd pigs. This son, who plugged into the wrong vine for "life," and pursued the counterfeit affections of the world, now finds himself in the dumpster of Jewish culture — not just a lowly shepherd, but worse, a pig herder. As a net result of that counterfeit affection and hitting rock bottom, he is stripped of the very thing he has made his god.

Eventually, he remembers that his father's servants have more than enough to eat, and here he is, perishing with hunger. So he picks himself up and decides to go to his father and say to him, "Father, I have sinned against heaven, and in your sight; I am no longer worthy to be called your son; make me as one of your hired men."

This is one of the most beautiful portions of Scripture because we see the story from the father's point of view, told by Jesus, who has been a first-hand witness to our heavenly Father's joyous reaction when one of His children returns home. Even while the son is a long way off, says Jesus, the father sees him, has compassion on him, and runs and embraces him and kisses him. What an amazing picture of GRACE!

The father must have been staring down the road. How else could he have seen his son a long way off? How many days has he stood there, misty-eyed, watching that road, longing to see his son coming home?

My friend Evi Fulford, who has spent years researching the culture of Israel shared, "It is well known historically that as a man grew older, it was a sign of dignity and respect that he walked slowly and deliberately. For an older man, a respected elder, to be seen running would be extremely undignified and a huge embarrassment for him. Yet, this father did not care what others thought because his son was coming home! What an incredible picture of God and His Father Love for us. How many of us would ever have seen our father reject the care of what others thought and run to us in our failures?"

Do you think of God that way? When you consider this passage — first the rejoicing over the found coin and sheep, then the father running with joy to the child, embracing and kissing him again and again — do you recognize these as true pictures of Father God? Most people, even Christians, don't conceive of God in this fashion. Their thoughts of God involve feelings of condemnation and fear, and a sense of being looked down on. That is the picture of our Heavenly Father most believers hold.

Men and religion focus on people's sins and selfishness rather than on the amazing nature of the Father's Love. Religion would highlight the son and his sin, because that is what religion does. It focuses on the performance and failure of the one who doesn't measure up.

No wonder we live our lives in fear! No wonder we try to attach ourselves to counterfeits. Who would want to worship a Heavenly Father who is aloof, distant, condescending, angry, and not very interested in having us around? Children growing up with that kind of image assume that they are the problem. Thankfully, according to this passage, that is not the God we serve.

I heard a young woman I'll call "Gracie" share her story at a Celebrate Recovery® support group. "I got straight A's in high school," she said, "but I didn't know how to handle all the freedom of life away from home in college. I tried all the wrong stuff and ended up feeling empty. I thought marriage would fill the emptiness inside, so I married 'Mr. Right.' But the luster quickly wore off."

Lost and alone, without LIFE, Gracie turned to the dumpsters of counterfeit affection. Taking advantage of her vulnerability, a professor told her she was special and loved, and soon this straight-A Christian girl was embroiled in a terrible, adulterous relationship. After the affair surfaced, it took years to heal the pain — not just her husband's, but also that of her own wounded heart. She discovered what was fueling her severed heart — performance, pretending, praise of men, and power issues.

"Could my husband ever forgive me?" she asked. "Would God?"

The journey was difficult, but ultimately, Gracie found healing in her marriage and her relationship with God through the newfound blessing of knowing God as Father. She dealt with severed-heart issues, a history of family dysfunction and early trauma — all of which played a part in her warped self-image.

Concluding her story, Gracie read aloud the familiar "Love Chapter," 1 Corinthians 13, in an eye-opening way. I have often heard and taught that these words describe Jesus. But Gracie inserted another name and had her riveted audience in tears as she read:

> *If I speak with the tongues of men and of angels, but do not have love, I have become a noisy gong or a clanging cymbal. If I have the gift of prophecy, and know all mysteries and all knowledge; and if I have all faith, so as to remove mountains, but do not have Love, I am nothing. And if I give all my possessions to feed the poor, and if I surrender my body to be burned, but do not have Love, it profits me nothing.*
>
> *My Father is Love. My Father is patient, my Father is kind and my Father is not jealous; My Father does not brag and my Father is not arrogant, my Father does not act unbecomingly towards me; my Father does not seek His own, My Father is not provoked, my Father does not take into account a wrong suffered, my Father does not rejoice in unrighteousness, but my Father rejoices with the truth; my Father bears all things, my Father believes all things, my Father hopes all things, my Father endures all things.*
>
> *My Father's Love for me never fails, but if there are gifts of prophecy, they will be done away; if there are tongues, they will cease; if there is knowledge, it will be done away. For we know in part and we prophesy in part; but when the perfect comes, the partial will be done away. When I was a child, I used to speak like a child, think like a child, reason like a child; when I became a man, I did away with childish things.*

For now we see in a mirror dimly, but then I will see My Father face to face; now I know in part, but then I will know My Father fully just as I also have been fully known by Him. But now abide faith, hope, Love, these three; but the greatest of these is Love.

Then she looked up at us and added, "My Father's Love is like that."

The audience responded in absolute silence. In that moment, God had everyone's attention. *This is the Father of Luke 15.* This Father ran to His son. He embraced him smell and all. This Father rejoiced greatly, ordered the servants to bring the best robe (which would have been the Father's best robe), to get the ring (sign of authority), to get the shoes (only sons, not slaves, wore shoes) for His son who was lost was now found.

Maybe you don't need to develop a new self-image. Maybe what you need is to develop a new image of God, as your Father. Maybe instead of seeing yourself as you see you, as you think you are, maybe you need to see yourself as Father God sees you. Maybe you need a new image of God not inherited from parents or other people — letting Him show you Who He really is.

Do you understand what kind of Love that is? Have your upside-down glasses come off? What is so amazing about GRACE? This is just the tip of the iceberg.

ORPHANS are motivated by fear, and use fear to motivate others. Their image of a father is someone who is aloof, uncaring, unloving, judgmental and condescending.

SONS break through the past and see Father God for Who He really is — a Father who runs, who delights in us, who loves to spend time listening to us.

APPLICATION: LEARNING TO HEAR FATHER'S HEART

Imagine yourself walking up to God and addressing Him as "Father." What is His facial expression? Is He smiling? Frowning? Serious? Reflecting disappointment in you?

Are you digging in the world's dumpsters for counterfeit affection? Maybe you need to ask yourself, "Am I rooted and grounded in Love? Am I really seeing Father's heart? Is my image of my relationship with Him so distorted that I've never realized that my heavenly Father is also my Shepherd?"

1. GET SERIOUS: "I will stand and station myself ..." to wait on God.

Maybe you need a new image of God. Here is an experiment:

On a blank page, write at the top the name "Jesus." Beneath it, list everything you know or think about Jesus. If you have been a believer for long, the list will probably be at least half a page. It will probably contain words like Redeemer, Savior, Alpha Omega, Lion of Judah, Intercessor, Lamb of God, Lover of our Souls, Shepherd, the Great I AM, Bread of Life, etc. See how many you can write.

Now take another page and write "Holy Spirit" as a heading. Create a similar list about the Holy Spirit. You will probably be able to half fill the page with titles and characteristics like Teacher, Comforter, Another like Jesus, Indwelling God, Powerful, Guardian, Leads us to Truth, and so forth.

It's the third page that shocks most people. At the top of it, write "Father" then list everything you think or know about God as the Father. If you are like most people, you might be able to come up with 5 to 7 words. Ancient of Days, Judge, Sovereign, Controller, Creator ... umm ... and that's it.

Take some time to start focusing on God as your Heavenly Father. Clean out the movie theater in your mind; shut off the sound and pictures of distractions and simply ask God to speak to you. Stand and station yourself with intentional worship of Him by giving Him your undivided, undistracted attention.

2. BE FOCUSED: "and I will keep watch to see what He will speak to me."

Expect Him to lead you and encourage you. Keep watch as you read His Word. See yourself speaking to Him in your mind, addressing Him as your Father. Listen for what He may lead you to do and how He may speak to your heart.

3. PRACTICE AUTHENTIC HUMILITY: "how I may reply when I am reproved."

The younger son had a phrase he used: "Give to me what is mine." In following chapters, you will see that self-centered independence is the core of sin. Father God will want to take you to those selfish, severed-heart places, so He can heal you of them. Let Him, through Christ, put His arms around you and welcome you HOME. Let Him touch those areas of selfishness and self-dependence. Let Him take control of your heart and fill it with His Spirit. He is "opposed to the proud but gives Grace to the humble."

4. WRITE IT, CHECK IT, RUN IT: "Record the vision and inscribe it."

Look up Paul's prayer for the Ephesian believers in Ephesians 3:14-21. Then:

+ Write it out on a card.
+ Read it every day for thirty days.
+ Record your thoughts.
+ Share them with someone else to keep you accountable.

CHAPTER 7: GRACE UPON GRACE

"For of His fullness we have all received, and GRACE upon GRACE.
—The Apostle John in John 1:16

INCREDIBLE! In the first chapter of his Gospel, John describes everything he saw, heard, touched and experienced as Jesus Christ's personal disciple. John chose those words to encapsulate his experience of the Son of God who made the universe, yet humbled Himself to become flesh and live among His people as the man, Jesus. Awestruck and enraptured, John exclaims, "Of His fullness we have all received, and GRACE upon GRACE."

That was not my experience. I had experienced GRACE but not "GRACE upon GRACE." I knew the GRACE of coming to know Christ as my Savior, the one who guaranteed my future in heaven, and who would keep me out of hell. But that was all I knew. I knew nothing of this GRACE upon GRACE. Not until I began to know the Father better did I begin to discover all that GRACE really means. The Heavenly Father loved me enough to send His Son to suffer and die so I could have the privilege of calling Him Father. This Father I was coming to know would stop at nothing to enable me to come HOME.

Suddenly I was driven to understand what this GRACE upon GRACE really meant. I dove back into Ephesians 3:14-21, to plumb the depths of Paul's description of the power of the Christian walk. What did he mean by "being filled up to all the fullness of God" and "Christ dwelling in our hearts daily through faith"? I learned this was the overflow of being nourished and grounded in His amazing Love.

Paul describes the believer's experience as a growing understanding of the love of Christ: "So that you may be able to comprehend 'the width, and length, and depth and height, of the love of God.'"

Paul's passionate heart for each Christian is to learn how wide, how deep, how tall and how far the GRACE of God will go. He wants his readers to get their arms around this Truth, to learn and experience "GRACE upon GRACE."

Let's see if we can do that.

Adopting the Unwanted

In order to move beyond a mere introduction to GRACE, we must realize the many ways God extended Himself to us. One of the most remarkable is that we have been adopted into God's family.

A year after our dog Cola died, my wife and I went to a pet store to get some cat food, and ended up walking out with a one-year-old American pit bull terrier. We had turned the corner onto an aisle where an animal rescue group had 15 or so dogs on display. All the dogs were yelping, barking and jumping at the fence — except one. She was lying on the floor with her head between her paws, looking so lost, unloved and sad that my heart went out to her.

If dogs can feel depressed and abandoned, then this dog surely felt all that. Encircling her brown torso was a wraparound yellow nylon jacket with the words "Adopt Me" in black lettering. No one gave her attention; she was all alone. For some reason, I asked the attendant if we could see her. When they brought her out of the enclosure, she dashed into my arms. Thinking she might have obedience issues, I walked her up and down the aisle. She already understood "Heel!"

Spontaneously my wife and I decided: 1) we wanted her, 2) we were willing to pay the price for her, 3) we would take responsibility for her to live in our home, and 4) we would give her a new name. Miss Bailey Marie Sirish Crème Princess Johnson came to live with us, and we have a license to prove it.

That is the essence of adoption. Like Miss Bailey in that pen, we without God are cast away, homeless, hurt by the past, afraid of the future, wearing signs saying, "Adopt Me." And what did Father God do? He 1) made the willful decision that He wanted us, 2) paid the price of sacrificing His Son to redeem us, 3) took responsibility for us by bringing us into His family, and 4) gave us His new name.

Knowing God adopted us this way opens new windows into GRACE. We cannot really embrace God's GRACE until we understand the term "adoption." Ephesians 1:3 says that adoption was the *very purpose* of creation. According to Louo and Nida's Greek Lexicon, adoption means "to formally and legally declare that someone who is not one's own child is henceforth to be treated and cared for as one's own child, including complete rights of inheritance."

The Greek word HUIOTHESIA literally means "to place as a son." In Jesus' day, adoption involved the transfer of a child from the presence of one father to the presence of a new father. It was accomplished when the adopting father stated three times "I will" to adopt this child. That formality confirmed the adoption as complete.

With those "I wills," the legal bond between father and adopted child became *more binding than the bond between a biological father and child.* Because biological parents "got what they got" regarding their baby's sex, birthmarks, and so on, they could legally disown their natural child. However, adoptive parents knew exactly what they were getting. So legally, an adopted child could never be disowned. He or she was permanently added to the family.[60]

By using the word "adoption" in that culture, God gave the church the message that He chose the children brought into His family, and they could not be taken from it. The implications are powerful. God did not have a "ho-hum plan" about us. Father wanted us with His heart enough to pay the price of His Son. He brought us into His family by sealing us in His Spirit and putting Him inside us. Father took responsibility for us and gave us a new name, His own.

Adoption also implies another meaning: Someone who is adopted into being a son or a daughter is also *adopted out of* being an orphan. Alluding to the separation and aloneness the disciples would experience upon His departure, Jesus said, "I will not leave you as orphans." The same holds true for each of us. Apart from GRACE, we stand as ORPHANS looking in the window of His family Home hoping to be rescued. Because of GRACE, we can choose to live as adopted and free SONS of God.

Ephesians 1:5

> *"He predestined us to adoption as sons through Jesus Christ to Himself, according to the kind intention of His will. ..."*

The context of this verse describes God as our Father. The pronoun "He" points to God as Father at least 28 times in this passage. We see Father's GRACE, Father's blessing, Father's choosing, Father's will, His kind intention, purpose, glory, calling, inheritance.

And we see something I didn't realize until Father revealed it to me after 35 years of ministry: *the purpose of creation was our adoption as His* SONS *and* DAUGHTERS. Before the foundation of the world, before creation began, Father God "*IN LOVE predestined us to adoption*"! How many Christians live outside their divinely designed purpose? Our purpose for living is to be loving SONS and DAUGHTERS of God.

You can read self-help books and try to do everything right, but until you come to Father God as your Father, it's still all about you. One of the counterfeit world value-system affections is an empowered self with a self-improvement plan. Efforts at self-improvement have some value, but if you're attempting to make yourself great without being a great SON to your Heavenly Father, then you are missing out on your true purpose. You are working hard to accomplish the wrong goal.

Galatians 4:4-6

> "*But when the fullness of the time came, God sent forth His Son, born of a woman, born under the Law, so that He might redeem those who were under the Law, that we might receive the adoption as sons. Because you are sons, God has sent forth the Spirit of His Son into our hearts, crying, 'Abba! Father!' Therefore you are no longer a slave, but a son; and if a son, then an heir through God.*

Christ's purpose in redemption was two-fold. First, he bought us out of slavery. He went to the slave market, so to speak, and paid the full purchase price of us as slaves so that we were set free. By His death, Jesus bought the way out of slavery for each person, regardless of sex, nationality or past history.

But this picture is incomplete. Remember the economic chaos of the South following the Emancipation Proclamation? Where is a freed slave to go? How is he to support himself? How is she to feed and clothe her children? Galatians also emphasizes the "*from/to*" nature of redemption. Having bought us *from* slavery, Jesus didn't stop there. He redeemed us *to* adoption, *to* sonship, *to* having God as Father.

Problematically most Christian preaching and teaching emphasizes the *from's* and neglects the *to's*. We are redeemed *to* being loved as a son, *to* being embraced, *to* being wanted, belonging, important, valuable, approved of and protected. We have been redeemed *from* sin *to* HOME.

Romans 8:15

> *"For you have not received a spirit of slavery leading to fear again, but you have received a spirit of adoption as sons by which we cry out, 'Abba! Father!'"*

"Dad!" "Daddy!" "Papa!" "ABBA!" God chose this most intimate of all terms for a father from the New Testament culture as His Name for us to use for Him. *We have to get this straight because this is core drilling in the heart.* When we talk about GRACE, we have to get our arms around *the only New Testament name for God.* It wasn't the name "Jesus"; *it is the name* ABBA *Father.* This name encapsulates the amazing nature of GRACE. We have been purchased with a price, brought into a family, and adopted. We are not on the outside anymore. We have a HOME and we have a Father. His name is ABBA.

Re-identifying My Purpose

Adoption involves more than a legal decision; it is a transfer of family. In John 8:44, Jesus told the Pharisees, the Jewish religious leaders, that they were "of their father, the devil." So if God is not one's heavenly Father, then Satan is. The Bible does not present a third option. You either have God as your father or you have Satan as your father.

Dr. J.I. Packer wrote:

> *If you want to judge how well a person understands Christianity, find out how much he makes of the thought of being God's child, and having God as his Father. If this is not the thought that prompts and controls his worship and his prayers and his whole outlook on life, it means that he does not understand Christianity very well at all. For everything that Christ taught, everything that makes the New Testament new ... is summed up in the knowledge of the Fatherhood of God.* [61]

Never in all my seminary studies did I see the centrality of God as my Father. When this truth started sinking in, I experienced incredible healing in my heart and then in the hearts of my clients.

What was the purpose of Jesus' life and ministry? He said in John 14:6, "I am the way, and the truth, and the life; no one comes to the Father but through Me." The way to what? The truth about what? What life? The whole purpose of Jesus' life and ministry was to provide our way back HOME to the Father's heart.

What is the *only* New Testament name for God? You may be thinking it's "Jesus," but He actually was born under the Old Testament Law, lived under the Law and died under the Law. The New Covenant does not begin until after Jesus' death and resurrection. The Old Testament reveals at least 25 Hebrew names for God that reveal different aspects of His character, names like "God Almighty," "Everlasting God," "God Who Heals," and so on.

God's only New Testament name occurs twice, in Galatians 4:6 and Romans 8:5. According to the Apostle Paul, the Holy Spirit says that based on our adoption as God's children, we can call God by the intimate Hebrew name, "ABBA Father." *Daddy!*

As a Christian, you have the joyful right to call God "Daddy." Abraham was God's friend, David a man after His own heart, but you as a believer, are a SON or DAUGHTER. If you're like me, when you start seeing this emphasis on the Fatherhood of God in the New Testament your adoption into SONSHIP will start flying off the pages. I couldn't believe I had been so blind.

Look at the emphasis Jesus places on Father in the Sermon on the Mount.[62] He presents the ethics and mandates for Christian living in terms of a Father-child relationship. He says we are to imitate our Father: "But I say to you, love your enemies, and pray for those who persecute you in order that you may be sons of your Father who is in heaven. ... Therefore you are to be perfect, as your heavenly Father is perfect." Our way of life is to glorify our Father: "Let your light shine before men in such a way that they may see your good works, and glorify your Father who is in heaven." He says our actions, our giving, our praying and our fasting are to please and glorify our Father, not men.

Furthermore, we are to trust Him because He is our Father:

Do not be anxious then, saying, "What shall we eat?" or "What shall we drink?"' or "With what shall we clothe ourselves?" For all these things the

Gentiles eagerly seek; for your heavenly Father knows that you need all these things" (Matthew 6:31-32).

The image of God as Father holds powerful healing for the Christian. Unfortunately, it is by far the most neglected doctrine in the study of God. Theologian Diane Chen asserts that God as "father" is often neglected in theological studies. Chen contends:

Not only does the word father imply authority and mercy, ... but this familiar metaphor also underscores God's willingness to bring love, faithfulness, and generosity toward Israel, to Jesus, and Jesus' followers. In addition, within God's family, the father's relationship with his children also has implications for the relationships of God's children with one another. This communal dimension of mutual care and responsibility is not intrinsic to the images of God as Lord and Savior. [63]

Now let's go even deeper and take a look at the most shocking passage in the New Testament. Read John 13-17 because these are the last words of Jesus before going to the cross. We need to grasp the sheer importance of our Lord's final statements and instructions before His death.

Firstly, in the preceding Gospels (Matthew, Mark and Luke), "Father" is mentioned a total of 33 times. But in John's Gospel, the word "Father" is mentioned 171 times. *That is an enormous difference.* That is *fifteen times more emphasis.* Is John telling us something?

Secondly, in John 13-17, the word "Father" is specifically mentioned 54 times. *Fifty-four times in just four chapters as compared to 33 times in Matthew, Mark and Luke's 68 chapters.* John reveals that Jesus pointed to His Father 54 times in four chapters. Was Jesus trying to point us to something? It would appear He was.

Thirdly, in just these four chapters (John 13-17) describing the last hours of Jesus' life, 108 pronouns point directly to God the Father. *One hundred and eight times in four chapters?* I was shocked when I realized I had missed this emphasis (or Satan had blinded me to it) for so many years! Finally the realization hit me: In all of my Biblical learning and training, this Person of the Trinity was, in fact, an overlooked, underemphasized, unacknowledged name that I didn't even see, let alone understand.

His Name is Father! This absolutely should be a stop-you-in-your-tracks thought. *What other religion in the world says, "Come to Me and I will introduce you to My Father so that you can not only know Him, not only experience Him, but also be His* SON *or* DAUGHTER?"

Slowly reread Packer's words to absorb the importance of being God's child: "*Everything that Christ taught,* everything that makes the New Testament new … *is summed up in the knowledge of the Fatherhood of God.* 'Father' is the Christian name for God."

Re-embracing a Father's Desire

God's GRACE desires to re-embrace the lost. Who went searching for Adam after sin entered? Did Father God stand to the side and say, "Let's just see what happens"? No. God went searching for Adam with His heart and His words, "Where are you?" Jesus added that *the Father* seeks true worshipers.[64] Just as in the Garden, Father is still seeking us long before we seek Him. *Where are you?*

I always felt a certain level of intimacy with Christ as long as I was confessing sin and trying hard, but I never felt a sense of fellowship with Father God. God wants us to live in intimate fellowship with Him. Intimacy is not something people invented. We were created to bond to God and God alone. He desired intimacy with us on a daily basis.

This theme is repeated throughout the Scriptures. Isaiah wrote, "For thus says the high and exalted One Who lives forever, whose name is Holy, 'I dwell on a high and holy place, and also with the contrite and lowly of spirit'" (Isaiah 57:15). And John 17:3 reminds us that eternal life is *knowing* the only true God. Paul wrote of the "Spirit in the inner man" and "Christ dwelling in your hearts" and that the "one who joins himself to the Lord is one spirit with Him."

What does this intimate relationship that God wants to have with us look like? Here are some characteristics of intimacy:

Closeness	Oneness	Time	Transparency
Two-way	Vulnerability	Honesty	Fear (Respect)
Listening	Truthfulness	Freedom	Abandoning Self
Openness	Genuineness	Physical	Total Commitment
Humility	Shared Hearts	Mutuality	Feeling Safe, Protected

Pertinent to any discussion of intimacy is the need to understand various well-documented levels that exist in relationships. These levels may be summarized as follows:

1. **Clichés** A level of relationship that deals just in superficial communication like, "Hi, how are you, beautiful day, lovely weather." If you analyze the levels of your relationships you will find many people who fall into this category. These are people whom you would call acquaintances, or casual friends, but with whom there is no depth of relationship.

2. **Information or Facts** This relational level deals with information exchange only. You can call this the news-sports-weather relationship that you may often have with friends, where you never really get into anything serious — merely discussing the day's happenings or the facts surrounding your lives. People's parental relationships often never move beyond this level.

3. **Teamwork** The sharing of a common cause. In this relational level, you join together with another person, or a group of others, because you share a common goal. Teamwork relationship is designed to accomplish a specific task.

4. **Feelings, Opinions and Judgments** In this fourth level of relationship, people deal with the sharing of feelings and the understanding of each other's opinions. A mutual sense of judgments is shared as well.

5. **Intimacy or Connectedness** At this level, people feel connected, personal, open, safe, genuine, honest, transparent, and soul-to-soul. Relationships seldom progress to this level, because it requires so much more in terms of commitment, time, openness and trust.

I learned about these relationship levels as I was working on some of my counseling and coaching training. At one point I asked myself, "What kind of relationship do I have with God?" Is my relationship full of clichés, like rote prayers in Jesus' name where I talk a lot but never really say anything? Or is my relationship an information exchange, just talking with God to tell Him about needs and situations? Am I stuck at the level (common to many pastors) with a relationship with God that functions in the teamwork stage? Instead of true intimacy or exchange of personal feeling, there is a dedication to the Great Commission, working with God to accomplish the goal of building His church, or helping to change people's lives.

When I became brutally honest about my level of relationship with God, I realized I functioned mainly in the first three levels, and seldom in the fourth or the fifth. I began to examine those levels with God in my personal quiet time. I challenged myself to see if I could attain a deeper level of intimacy in my walk with Him.

It is apparent that God wants an intimate relationship with His children, yet how can that happen when we really don't know much about God at all? *We don't even know His name as Father*, and most of us haven't spent much time learning about Him.

Reflecting a New Father's Face?

Jesus was the exact representation of His Father. So what we see in the life of Jesus reveals the Person of God the Father and reflects the Father's face. This is an amazing view of GRACE.

We know from Hebrews 1:3 that Jesus is "the radiance of Father's glory and the exact representation of His Nature." So just as a coin bears the exact copy of the stamp, what you see in Jesus, is the exact copy of the Father. In John 14:9, Jesus told His disciple Phillip, "He who has seen Me has seen the Father," so we know what we see Jesus doing, saying, and teaching is an exact reflection of the Father's heart.

So when we see Jesus heal the leper, who was healing the leper? Jesus said, "I do nothing except I see the Father do it." It was Father God who reached out to the leper. Therefore, we know that Father is intimately concerned with our hurts, our sicknesses, our diseases and He longs to heal us.

And when we see Jesus forgiving the woman caught in adultery, who is forgiving her? Our first response is "Not God, no! God is the Judge; He is the One who is mad at her. Jesus is the One who forgives." But based on the foregoing information, who forgave her first? Father was the One who forgave her. Father is not often presented that way, is He?

When Jesus provided wine for the wedding, who was providing the wine? Father was part of the wedding, rejoicing over the couple, providing their needs. But that's not our image of God, is it?

Likewise, who healed the blind man? Father directed Jesus as his healer. Father wanted him healed. Father is not aloof, distant, apathetic, judgmental, but kind, caring, loving and compassionate.

When Jesus taught the multitudes, Father was teaching through Him. Father wants us to learn about Him; Father wants to show us Who He really is; Father wants us to understand that He loves us with all His heart. Father wants us to know that that the principles of the Word are for our good and well-being.

Let's take a larger step. When we see Jesus washing the disciples' feet, who is washing their feet? Was this the one time Jesus did His own thing? Did Jesus just break out and deviate from the script and go a bit "off the wall," or was Father behind this? *When Jesus washes the disciples' feet, Who is doing it? The Father is not often depicted this way, but it is He who is washing their feet, fleshing out His will in the Son.*

When Jesus promises us another just like Himself, who actually sends that Comforter? Who sends the Spirit of Holiness? Answer: Father God! Why? So the Holy Spirit in us would be the power and assistance and reproducer of Himself.

Here we go another step. When you get to the marriage supper of the Lamb, who will be there to greet you? Father God! Just like a proud human father, Father will be there, rejoicing for His Son and His Bride. Do you think He will be off in some room — scowling, angry and looking for someone to bury in wrath? Where do you think Father will be? Even if your past earthly image of fathers tells you He won't care or be there, that is not the Father of the New Testament, who is mentioned or named 375 times.

Pastor, theologian and author Douglas Wilson notes that the most obvious feature of the Father of Jesus Christ is His *generosity*. He is generous with His *glory*, His *protection*, His HOME and His *joy*. And the Father gives — *His Son, His Spirit and Himself*.[65]

Suddenly, our image of God as Father is starting to change. This isn't the God we have been told about. I recently heard a message by a highly respected pastor, who said repeatedly, "The Father took out His wrath on Jesus." That simply is not true. The fact is that the Law of God and the wrath of God were satisfied in the death of Christ. The Father turned His back on Jesus, forsaking His own Son as He bore our sin under the penalty of the Law.

Nowhere does the Bible teach "angry Father theology." Yet for 1,500 years the message of the Angry Father, the Father who would pour out His wrath, has been spewed from church pulpits. Father did not do that. What He did was watch when His Son was betrayed and crucified, watch Him die a criminal's death and then turn His back on His Son's cries. If you want to see amazing GRACE, then look at the Love that would drive a Father to reject His Son.

It's what the pastoral team of Bill Thrall, Bruce McNicol and John Lynch call "God's Gamble." (See appendix.) They imagine God ruminating about all the ways people misrepresent Him and His intentions toward them in their thinking. In the midst of a string of what-ifs, the authors write, "What if I tell them I'm crazy about them? What if I tell them, even if they run to the ends of the earth and do the most horrible, unthinkable things, that when they come back I'd receive them with tears and a party?"

I'm so amazed by His GRACE. This is who He really is, in His essence, not a controlling, self-exalting, aloof, indifferent tyrant with loads of rules, regulations, requirements and rituals. He is not waiting for you to step out of line so that He can point out your mistakes and give you a look of disapproval. That is not what the Bible tells us. We need a new, accurate image of God as Father — the way He has introduced Himself through His Son for 2,000 years, since the birth of Christ. And many of us have been missing it.

Paul wrote to the church at Ephesus:

> *Watch what God does, and then you do it, like children who learn proper behavior from their parents. Mostly what God does is love you. Keep close company with Him, and learn a life of love. Observe how Christ loved us. His love was not cautious but extravagant. He didn't love in order to get something from us but to give everything of Himself to us. Love like that.*[66]

Wow! I am to imitate God as a child mimics a parent. Once again, we see the concept of a loving Father. Once we belong to Him, we become the dwelling of His Spirit. We share His Nature. We are His children and have to learn to copy His essence.

How many times does the Scripture say, "God is ___?" Not often. Yet in John's first epistle, the apostle proclaims, "God is *Love*." That means God is GRACE. God wants to love you extravagantly, *prodigiously*. Remember, He is the Prodigal (extravagant) Father.

I wish I could embed here on the page a video that was created in 2001 to narrate and illustrate "Father's Love Letter." Instead I've included a link to it along with the entire text in the Appendix. Written in 1999 by Pastor Barry Adams as a sermon illustration, "FLL" opens with, "The words you are about to experience are true. They will change your life if you let them, for they come from the very heart of God. He loves you and He is the Father you have been looking for all your life. This is His Love Letter to you." What follows is a tender paraphrase of 50 Scripture verses taken from Genesis to Revelation and personalized as Father speaking directly to you, His child. Please read it with an open heart. Say the words aloud; let them soak into your heart. Let yourself comprehend the emotional power of Father's healing in your soul.

Christians are often tempted to acquire knowledge for knowledge's sake. The life of a believer is founded in the knowledge of the Word and the way of the Spirit. But they are the foundation, the basement, and not the house. Who wants to live in the basement? The foundation exists for the sake of the house. A house's beauty and appearance make it an attractive place to live. So it is with believers. Each one needs to build on the foundation of Father's Love.

But how can a believer with an ORPHAN'S heart give away what he or she has never possessed? Can someone give, from their own pain and the rejection of their own severed heart, something they do not possess, in order to fill the hole in another? The answer — missed by so many — is found in the Father whom Jesus came to introduce us to.

In the words of Bob Mumford, "As we come to know this God, the one who revealed Himself, we start feeling comfortable in His Presence. We have a wonderful Father! How I wish that when I was young and afraid, someone would have helped me to more clearly understand that Christ came to take me to His Father."[67]

Many people come from dysfunctional families. Psychologists estimate that 79-93% of us come from some kind of dysfunctional influence. Due to family-of-origin issues, the image of the Father may elicit a whole series of negative emotions in you. If that is the case for you, please put those emotions on hold for now. This topic may run the gamut of emotions including apathy, withdrawal, anger, hurt, shame, embarrassment, and a whole host of other feelings that the image of a father may generate for you.

We will explore these emotions as we progress. For now, let's just look at what the Bible says about this Person called "ABBA."

APPLICATION: LEARNING TO HEAR FATHER'S HEART

What motivates you in your Christian life?

Are you motivated by fear of punishment, or by wanting to glorify, imitate, and please God, your spiritual Father? Do you think of your relationship with God in terms of a Father-child relationship? Do you revel in what God has done, as the Apostle John did in 1 John 3:1-2? Do you allow that to be your motivation, according to 1 John 3:3?

1. GET SERIOUS: "I will stand and station myself..." to wait on God.

Print out "Father's Love Letter" and put it on index cards, carry it in your wallet or purse, meditate on it before your day begins and as you fall asleep at night. Let your Father be what He wants to be to you — so much so that He sacrificed His Son to make it happen. God wants to be regarded for Who He is, ABBA, Father, Your Dad, and Almighty God.

Close your eyes and meditate on who Father God really is. The word "meditate" in Psalm 1:1 comes from the Hebrew word meaning "to ruminate." Cattle, sheep, rabbits and other animals take in nourishment and chew it then swallow it, bring it back up again and chew some more, swallowing again and bringing the food back up until all the nutrients are pulled out. How blessed is the man whose "delight is in the Law of the Lord and in His Law he meditates day and night."

2. BE FOCUSED: "and I will keep watch to see what He will speak to me."

Listen to the living water of the Holy Spirit bubbling up within you. Let Him go heart-to-heart with you; hear what He has to say and how He is leading you. Ask Him if your image of Father God has been wrong. Ask Him to show you how and where you've made incorrect assessments of God as your Father. Ask Him to reveal what He really thinks of you.

The Father does not judge anyone! According to John 5:22, "The Father judges no one but has given all judgment to the Son." Remember the prodigal father running to embrace his son. As yourself these questions:

- ✦ "Would Father God run to embrace me?"
- ✦ "Do I matter that much to Him?"
- ✦ "Would He see me and yell out, 'My child is HOME'?"
- ✦ "What is my image of Father?"
- ✦ "What is my image of me?"

3. PRACTICE AUTHENTIC HUMILITY: "how I may reply when I am reproved."

Let Him gently rebirth humility in your heart. Inhale His Word and exhale your self-dependence. Picture Jesus as He washed the disciples' feet and realize again that we are to have the mind of Christ.

4. WRITE IT, CHECK IT, RUN IT: "Record the vision and inscribe it."

In trying to follow God's leading in your life, you will be tempted to listen to self or to the voice of the enemy. Be sure to journal your thoughts, then check them with close advisors. Then run the race in the freedom of Christ.

CHAPTER 8: THE MISSING FACE OF GRACE

You sum up the whole of New Testament teaching in a single phrase, if you speak of it as a revelation of the Fatherhood of the holy Creator. In the same way, you sum up the whole of New Testament religion if you describe it as the knowledge of God as one's Holy Father.

—J.I. Packer

THE NEW TESTAMENT reveals God's name: ABBA, Father. A close investigation of Scriptural arguments for the importance of the Fatherhood of God shows that it is the most neglected of all the primary doctrines in the Scriptures. Yet it is absolutely crucial for the maturing believer to understand the Love in which he is supposed to be rooted and grounded. The average Christian continues to struggle daily with maturity. Let's start to repaint the picture of ABBA, Father.

Father — The ONLY New Testament Name for God.

The great preacher, teacher, and well-known speaker, Rev. Haddon W. Robinson observes that the Old Testament Israelites did not individually address God as Father. Even Abraham and Moses dared not address God that way. "Yet," Robinson says, " … that is how we are instructed to speak to Him. All that a good father wants to be to his children, Jesus told us, God will be to Christians who approach Him in prayer. We can pray as children."[68]

Father Loving SONS and DAUGHTERS — The Purpose of Creation

The purpose of God in creation and the purpose for which Christ died was to present us to the Father. God was creating SONS and DAUGHTERS to His glory. He predestined us to adoption as SONS according to the kind intention of His will and to the praise of His glory. We were created to bond to this Father. The divine romance began when God as Father, Son and Spirit chose to create man and woman. Before Creation, Father purposed to predestine us to adoption.[69]

Revealing Father — The Purpose of Jesus' Life and Ministry

John 14:8-9 says that Jesus came to show us the Father — that was His life purpose. Jesus and His Spirit came *not so we would focus on Him but so that we would focus on what He focused on. He demonstrated for us how to live as a* SON, *getting our will, our words and our works all from the Father.*[70]

When teaching His disciples to pray, Jesus told them to pray directly to "Father."[71] Rather than giving them a formula to get their prayers answered, Jesus was more interested in teaching them and us to enter into relationship with the Father. Yet they didn't get it. I can practically hear Him sigh in John 14:9 when He says to Philip, "Have I been so long with you, and yet you have not come to know Me, Philip? He who has seen Me has seen the Father; how can you say, 'Show us the Father?'"

In wrapping up His last words to His disciples, He tells them basically, "No more metaphors. I'm going to *tell you plainly of the Father.*"[72] Now you must understand the impact of those words. Jesus is saying everything He has told them about the Father up to this point has been *intentionally veiled.* But soon — that is, after His Resurrection —the Spirit would be imbedded in their spirits (and in the spirits of all believers to come), and the revelation of *God as Father* would be unveiled to them. *Suddenly their knowledge of Father would be greater; He would be much more understandable, openly accessible, and intimate.*

Father as the Last Days Message

According to Bible prophecy, we are living in the "Last Days." The ministry of the Last Days centers on *the revelation of God as Father.* Historically, the Son and His sacrifice became the Church's central emphasis in the 1500s, when Martin Luther nailed his theses to the Wittenberg door. In 1850, William Booth and the Salvation Army emphasized the Holy Spirit. But where was the teaching about Father in these church movements? Not until recently, in 1980, did Vineyard church founder John Wimber emphasize the Fathering nature of God in his ministry. Then Floyd McClung published *The Father Heart of God* in 1985. Several other works have appeared in the last two decades. I believe the emphasis will continue until Christ's return.

Before John the Baptist was born, an angel announced John's upcoming ministry as a forerunner to the coming Christ "in the spirit and power of Elijah." John's ministry would be two-fold: 1) to "turn many of the sons of Israel back to the Lord their God" and 2) "to turn the hearts of the father's back to the children ... to make ready a people prepared for the Lord." [73]

John's first ministry was to put the ax to the tree and declare repentance, making a way for Jesus. But his other ministry to prepare for the coming of Christ was *to turn fathers back to children*. This, I believe, is the direction in which the Spirit of God is now moving. Fathers are to be about God's business of parenting their children, and imparting their hearts to them, just as Father God does for all His children. Preparation of the ministry of Christ includes the call for fathers to turn to their children, not in deed only, but from the heart.

Father as Misrepresented by Angry God Theology

Most religions portray the Father as the problem — He is the angry God that a loving Jesus protects us from. This concept misrepresents the Father's Love and hinders the healing of core severed-heart issues. Coming chapters will develop the need to displace such misconceptions about the Father.

Most of us need a new image of God. We tend to see God as out to either punish or bless. This misguided view drives us to law-based performance, robbing us of peace, joy and freedom. It turns us into prisoners to fear, unable to love others or to know how loved we are. This angry Father image distorts how we view ourselves, how we live life and how we view others. We demand of others what we think He demands of us.

Father — The Name that Brings True Healing

Bound up in God's role of Father is a new spiritual identity for His children. As part of His family we receive eternal significance, and a sense of value, approval and protection. *Father* is the name that brings healing to the severed, rejected, ORPHAN heart. *Father* is the only name that brings such a sense of warmth and HOME.

The injection of *Father* into our Biblical understanding of who we were created to be provides a basis for understanding our new position as His SONS and DAUGHTERS. With this new identity we inherit the benefits of SONSHIP: a new Father, a new nature, a new name, a new access, a new life purpose and perspective, a new responsibility, a new mission, and a new enemy.

Father Speaks to Pride, the True Issue of Sin

Father introduces a sense of intimacy that reaches into the prideful depths of the human heart, attacking the core stronghold of sin — self-dependency, self-sufficiency, and the pride of life. The sacrificial death of Christ focused on bringing us to salvation, rescuing us, and reconciling us to God. But problems occur when we don't move on.

The cross introduces Christians to a relationship with God. But there's more! A believer may stubbornly withhold or keep an area of his or her heart private, untouched. This willful choice to exclude God from having authority over all of one's life keeps the believer from progressing into SONSHIP and learning to relate to Him as a loving Father. By failing to move forward in a Father-child relationship, Christians may arrive at and leave the cross with much of their pride intact. An intimate relationship with a loving Father requires humility on the believer's part.

A believer who has no intimate communication with God will remain cocooned in self-sufficiency. With no impetus to release pride, a person will actually end up nurturing it. So it's possible for a Christian to trust in God for salvation but not move into the exposure, vulnerability, and transparency necessary to connect intimately with Him. As long as the relationship is not rooted and grounded in Love — which requires obedience — it produces rebellion. The Christian walk becomes a job, not a joy — a duty, not a delight. And it leaves self-dependence, i.e. pride, intact.

When people bow to Jesus from a sense of duty or obligation, it's because they haven't been wooed by Father's divine Love. They don't know that the kindness of God leads them to repentance.[74] So many who have accepted Christ arrive at the cross with all their aggressive striving, their competitive challenging, their critical spirit and their pushiness still intact.

I know this because that's who I was, that's who I am in my ORPHAN heart. I was in love with the Great Commission. I gave my life for it, pushed people over on my way to make it happen. I wanted to climb to the top, be the best, make it happen and get it done. I tried to come to

Father God proudly bearing all my accomplishments. But as I crossed the bridge that is paved with the blood of Christ and entered into the Father's Presence, I learned that LIFE is not about me making it happen — it's about Him making it happen, through me.

As a result, my heart came to peace and I stopped my aggressive striving and competitive pushiness. I learned to submit to His authority in everyday life — even when people confront me and circumstances arrive that unbalance me. I learned from the Father that I need to put the Great Commandment (Matthew 22:35-40) before the Great Commission (Matthew 28:16-20). *If I don't love as He loved, then I don't have a right to speak.* My pride dissolved as God became my Father, and as I practiced intimacy with Him.   /AMEN ♥ AMEN/

> ORPHANS *never get beyond self-justifying, self-defending and self-protecting. They never see themselves as they really are because their masks never come down.*
>
> SONS *have nothing to prove. Their masks are off. They become brutally honest with themselves, allowing the Holy Spirit and the Love of the Father to speak into their lives and identify the areas where they are depending upon themselves more than upon the Father.*

Father Brings Humility to the Forefront

Submission and obedience are instinctive responses to Love. We don't have to repay the Father's Love with forced submission or grudging obedience. Our willing submission and loving obedience are part of a daily intimacy that flows back toward God in a BASIC TRUST as we respond to our Father's Love. (The concept of BASIC TRUST will be further developed in later chapters.) When our responses are founded in Love, obedience and humility are a joy.

Religion, on the other hand, would have us respond to God as both Lawgiver and Judge. One's walk flows not from a relationship but from rules, rituals, restrictions, requirements and regulations. So prayer, worship, serving, giving, and so on all spring from duty rather than delight, one's job rather than one's joy.

But this Lawgiver gave us Ten Commandments that you may find surprisingly relational. The first four concern our vertical relationship with God. The next six address interpersonal, or horizontal, relationships. These two categories of relationships come together in the form of a cross.

They meet in the middle with the fifth command: "Honor your father and your mother" (Exodus 10:12). Former rabbi Michael Esses wrote:

> *God put the honoring of parents with the commandments dealing with our relationship with Him because He knew that if we did not honor our earthly parents, we could not possibly honor our heavenly Father. If we cannot show respect, reverence, awe, and fear of our mother and father, the persons who stand before us as representatives of God Himself, we cannot possibly love and honor God.*[75]

Here in America, family surnames are passed from one generation to the next through the father. The name "Father" contains a sense of submission to His authority. Jesus demonstrates this hierarchy when He tells Pilate in John 19:11, "You would have no authority over Me but such as has been given to you from above."

Do you recognize Jesus' intimate trust? He lived as a SON is meant to live according to God's design. He lived under a blanket of submission, knowing that everything came from and needed to be passed before His Father. The deep LIFE principle here says, "Father is my authority." Live your life in appreciation of His rule and His loving authority, and you will learn the joy of living just to be His SON.

> *ORPHANS do not fully give up and surrender. They have to always be in control and are unwilling to submit to the authority of others. They do not see human authority as an extension of God's. They cannot surrender because they have not learned BASIC TRUST.*

> *SONS learn through intimacy with God that He is in control. They learn to overcome fear by faith in His Love. In doing so, they develop a BASIC TRUST in Him that allows them to remain vulnerable to His will, longing to do what He desires.*

Father Begets Fathers

A father cannot give his son what he himself does not possess. From my relationship with my heavenly Father, I began to build into the lives of my children. I made mistakes, yet I cannot help but think how great the damage would have been had not Father's heart touched mine.

People — especially men — who learn to follow their Heavenly Father experience life-altering changes. A transformative healing occurs in the soul. Fathers provide their children with the five basic needs described in chapters 3 and 4: belonging, significance, value, approval, provision/protection. Fatherlessness has been called a "rot that is eating away at the modern soul."[76] We need to put the priority and importance of God as Father back in theology, not just as an afterthought, but as the directive that drives our relationship with God.

Father — The Healing Face of Grace

Smaller and lighter than most of the kids in his school, "Jimmy" endures nonstop bullying. His dad's response? "No one makes a fool of my son. Get out there and fight like a man."

Goaded by his father to join the wrestling team, Jimmy now stands on the mat face to face with an opponent more menacing than any so far. He hears Dad yell from the stands, "Kill him! Do it!" The match lasts 17 seconds. Outclassed, outweighed, pinned. Disgraced, he searches the stands for his dad. Gone. Jimmy does not doubt that his father cannot stomach the person of his son.

Do you relate emotionally to Jimmy? To his hurt, self-loathing and emptiness? This is the pain in the heart of people who know they will never be good enough to win a place in their father's heart. Yet that wound can be healed if you get your arms around the essence of GRACE.

Even after 35 years as a believer, with all my accumulated education, spiritual knowledge and pastoral experience, the message of God's Love still passed through my world value-system filter. No matter how much I heard the word GRACE, what my heart heard was "work harder, be aggressive, be the best you can be."

I never "got" what God meant by the word GRACE. GRACE never had a face. I felt duty bound. God loved me so He gave His Son — now I had to show Him how I loved Him by being obedient back. I never felt His closeness on a daily basis. Pleasing Him seemed elusive and frustrating.

Yet I never heard a preacher say, "I want to share with you how I was so overcome with the Love of God as my Father that I just couldn't describe it." Or, "I want to talk to you today as a father would his son."

It seemed no one in my life loved me for just me. Because I knew I was unloved, I was incapable of giving to others what I myself did not possess. I read the books and sang the songs on God's Love and GRACE. I heard the words "God loves you" — a lot. But the words were devoid of emotional meaning. Like "Jimmy," I was always looking into the stands after one more failure and seeing no one there.

The Fourfold Dimensions of Father's GRACE

Returning to the "rooted and grounded" concept of Ephesians 3:14-21, I want to show you more of the Holy Spirit's passion for your life. Once you learn to live in Father's GRACE, He wants you to grasp "what is the breadth and length and height and depth, and to know the love of Christ which surpasses knowledge." Imagine you're standing within a gigantic cube, pulsating with the energy and power of God. His Love and GRACE crackle electrically in the air around you. Look up, look down, to the right, to the left. What do you see?

Width — The Provision of Grace (Past)

The first time I saw the Pacific Ocean, I could not get over how it stretched ahead to the horizon and on and on to either side until it was completely out of my view. The ocean was endlessly wide!

As a Christian I learned the wide truth of Jesus' sacrifice. To express God's infinite Love, He spread His hands open wide and said, "My Love is this big." Then Man nailed those outstretched hands to a cross. Israel's Psalmist/King David wrote this testimony to the width of God's Love in Psalm 103: "So great is His lovingkindness toward those who fear Him. As far as the east is from the west, so far has He removed our transgressions from us."

Geographically speaking, East and West never end. North and South do because they each have a pole. But no matter how far you travel east you will never, ever start going west. No matter how far west you travel, you will never cross a line and be going east. A thousand years before Christ, His royal ancestor was saying, "God's Love simply has no end."

I know you know God is your Father but do you believe it every day? Do you believe it today? Have you just let Him love on you today? God's Love is unending ... FOR YOU!

Ask yourself, "Who does God love more, Jesus or me?" I'll bet you would say Jesus. But you would be wrong. That's what is so amazing about GRACE. When the Father looks at you He doesn't see sin, He sees His SON or His DAUGHTER.

> *Who is a God like You, who pardons iniquity and passes over the rebellious act of the remnant of His possession?*
>
> *He does not retain His anger forever, because He delights in unchanging love.*
>
> *He will again have compassion on us; He will tread our iniquities under foot.*
>
> *Yes, You will cast all their sins into the depths of the sea.*[77]

God's Love for you today, right now, as Your Father, has cast your sins, your failures, your breaking of His Law, your transgressions and your old natural "self" into the depths of the sea. They are gone, buried, never to be brought up again. And at that spot God has put up a sign that says, "NO FISHING ALLOWED." If He doesn't want to see your sins and failures, why do you? Why does He bury your sins? Because you're so good? No, because He is. It's not about you. It never was.

Hank Hanegraaff, radio's "Bible Answer Man," tells the story of John Griffith as an illustration of the width of God's GRACE. During the Great Depression, John tended the gears of a railroad bridge over the Mississippi River. Glad to have work during those tough economic times, John proudly brought his 8-year-old son, Greg, to work with him one day. Greg watched in wide-eyed wonder as his dad operated the levers that raised and lowered the bridge to allow trains to pass over and ships to pass beneath.

That day, John raised the bridge according to schedule, and took Greg for his lunch break. Caught up in telling stories about working along the river, John barely heard the whistle of an approaching train. Snapped back to reality, he remembered that he'd left the bridge in its raised position. As Hanegraaff puts it:

> *In the calmest tone he could muster he instructed his son, "Stay put." ... As the precious seconds flew by, he ran at full-tilt to ... the control house. ... And then, as he had been trained to do, he looked straight down beneath the*

bridge to make certain nothing was below. As his eyes moved downward, he saw something so horrifying that his heart froze in his chest. For there, below him in the massive gearbox that housed the colossal gears that moved the gigantic bridge, was his beloved son. [78]

John realized his son must have tried to follow him but had slipped off the catwalk and was now wedged in the cogs of the gearbox. Lowering the bridge to allow the train to pass would require crushing his son in the gears. The panicked bridge operator searched his mind for ways to save the day — grabbing a rope, clambering down the ladder, pulling his son to safety, rushing back in time to lower the bridge.

But he knew he didn't have the time to save his son as well as the 400 people on the train roaring down the track toward the bridge. Hanegraaf continues:

He knew in a moment there was only one thing he could do. ... And so, burying his face under his left arm, he plunged down the lever. The cries of his son were quickly drowned out by the relentless sound of the bridge as it ground slowly into position. With only seconds to spare, the Memphis Express — with its 400 passengers — roared out of the trees and across the mighty bridge.

John Griffith lifted his tear-stained face and looked into the windows of the passing train. A businessman was reading the morning newspaper. A uniformed conductor was glancing nonchalantly at his large vest pocket watch. Ladies were already sipping their afternoon tea in the dining cars. ... No one even looked his way. No one even cast a glance at the giant gearbox that housed the mangled remains of his hopes and his dreams.

According to plan, Jesus stepped into the gears and Father pushed the lever. How can a human mind begin to comprehend this love? "God made Him who had no sin to be sin for us, so that in Him we might be called the righteousness of God." [79] And why would we ever doubt that the Love that sacrificed this much would not also provide everything else we need to be whole? Here is Father's healing for each of us.

Length — The Presence of Grace (Present)

Paul challenges us to know the "length" of God's love, and I think again of my experience with the ocean. During the Vietnam War, I flew to Turkey. Uncertainty blanketed our nation. I felt fear about the future. Sleepless through the long, moonlit night, I looked out the aircraft window and could see nothing below but ocean. Hour after hour, the scenery never changed: thousands of miles of dark, empty water. I felt lonely, isolated. Then, about mid-flight, I saw something in that vast water — a huge iceberg, floating there, all alone. Then I remembered my Father and knew that He knew the iceberg was there, and I realized, "God knows where I am. He knows where I am going. He will be with me every step of the way. He is the One who said 'I will never leave you nor forsake you.'"

The Father was, and is, there. He saw — and sees — me in the midst of the ocean of time and space and emptiness and aloneness. He can find me. He can walk with me. The length of His GRACE lasts a lifetime.

I have learned that in the times of my life that seemed the darkest and most confusing, when the things I trusted in were taken away, when I lost possessions or was betrayed by trusted friends, still God's Love surrounded me every step along the length of life's highway.

Nothing can prepare you for some of life's moments. One day in May 2011, my wife, Cheryl, said to me, "We need to talk."

"Sure, honey," I said. "What's up?"

"I have cancer," she replied.

In spite of all my training and years of walking with God, I felt like the rug had been pulled out from under me. We gathered the facts. I remained strong and mission-oriented. Then we drove to a salad-bar restaurant. Standing in the food line Cheryl asked me, "Are you okay?"

Only then did I allow the emotions I was feeling to find words. "No, I'm not," I said. "I'm confused, I'm angry, I'm a bit scared and I'm uncertain, and I feel very alone against life." Even as I spoke, Father was assuring us He would guard us with His GRACE. He would walk the length of this ordeal with us because that is what GRACE does.

As it turned out, Cheryl came through uterine cancer surgery just fine and remains cancer free to this day. But the fears and uncertainty were there for us, and GRACE walked the length of the process with us.

GRACE isn't just about hard times, though. God wants to walk the length of life with us every day, fellowshipping with us, talking with us, showing us His power over sin and circumstances as we lay things before Him. Every day of our lives, from His point of view, is simply about having a constant relationship with us.

God loves to walk with you. His GRACE goes the length of life.

Height — The Perspective of Grace (Future)

Paul hopes believers will learn the height of God's Love. Again the ocean's vastness comes to mind. Standing on an eighth-story balcony, I watched the sun setting in the west. High clouds dotted the sky like leopard spots, and I could measure the sky in relationship to the ocean's expanse. Looking up, I realized the heavens' expanse. The sky touched the ocean then kept going straight up overhead. There was too much sky to comprehend.

And so is the height of Father's Love for us. As we grow in maturity, we begin to understand that His GRACE extends all the way into the highest heaven. We have been promised not just heaven as our end, but an unimaginably rich inheritance as well: "Eye has not seen nor has ear heard nor has it entered into the heart of man all that God has prepared for those that love Him."[80] According to 1 Peter 1:4, our inheritance can never decay or lose any of its beauty — it will be unspoiled forever. The Father Himself "qualified us to share in the inheritance," says Colossians 1:12. And its riches are beyond any the wildest imagination can envision.

Paul knew we needed to discover the value of this "GRACE in which we stand." And Jesus said in John 14:2, "I go to prepare a place for you that where I am you may also be." Can you imagine where Jesus is at this moment in eternity? That's where we are, too!

But Father's Love extends far beyond what we gain as heavenly possessions. His Love is really the gift of all He is — His Presence. He is that place you can call HOME, where you can daily re-center in Father's Love. He Himself is the place to which you can always return and hear, "You are the child I love and in whom I am well pleased." That is, after all, what He said to Jesus, and you have the wonderful righteousness of Jesus in Father's Presence.

You can go HOME. You can live in His embrace, in the center of the Creator's heart, the center of universe. He is where you can go to get your LIFE nourishment and grounding. He is your true vine. He is where you abide. The Father Himself is the HOME where you can find your security, comfort, provision, protection, rest, affirmation, acceptance, belonging, inheritance and identity … forever. His Heart is where you can abide — a place of light and warmth.

That is the height of God's GRACE. You'll never know it until you practice living in it on a daily basis. Read the Word then meditate on it. Stop the busy life stuff. Close your eyes, let earth fall away and just dwell in your Father's Presence. Let His Word live in you and through you.

My dear friend, Jeff Gilbert, says, "Just Look Up." In fact, he named his catering company "Just Look Up Catering." Pretty cool! When you're looking up at God's Love for you, remembering that your Father has His inheritance for you, suddenly you're filled with His Presence again. You are unplugging from the false vine and plugging into the true vine.

The Depth of Grace (Pressures)

After exploring the dimensions of God's Love in its infinite width, length, and height, Paul leads us to consider the depth of God's Love.

I first saw the ocean in San Diego on a Christmas Day. I was able to run and play in it without fear because the water along the shore was shallow. But I would later learn that much of the ocean is treacherous and mysteriously deep.

The highest elevation on Planet Earth is about 5 miles above sea level. But the deepest point in the Pacific Ocean is nearly 7 miles down. The weight of the water even a mile under the surface is so great that it crushes anyone who ventures that deep. At that depth, the pressure is the equivalent of having 50 jumbo jets on one's shoulders (33,000 pounds per square inch).

When scientists finally were capable of exploring those depths, they made an amazing discovery. Where man could not go without sophisticated equipment, there were fish — transparent, fragile, small, seemingly insignificant creatures able to do what man could not. They exist in the depths of the sea. How could that be possible? The answer is simple. The pressure inside the fish's body is the same as the pressure on the outside. They exist where others cannot because the pressures are balanced.

That is what GRACE does for us in the midst of the pressures and extreme weight of life. The GRACE of God (Father's Love for us) within us is equal to the pressure of the trials we experience on the outside.

This was Paul's point when he said he had learned the secret, that he could do all things through Christ who strengthened him. *The truth that Paul knew was that no matter what the pressure is on the outside, God's Love never stopped loving Him.* Father's heart never lost track of him or didn't care. No matter what depths of trouble or pain you undergo, the pressure of God's GRACE within you, His assurance that He loves you and will never let you go is greater than or equal to any pressure that pushes you down.

APPLICATION: LEARNING TO HEAR FATHER'S HEART

Reflect on your relationship with God. Does it lack the intimacy of knowing Him as your Father? I know that, as a believer, you know God. But the real question is, Are you experiencing Him as Father on a daily basis? You may never have heard Him speak to your heart as Father. Yet, it was this Father who created you and this very same Father who has been seeking you from the beginning in the Garden with the words, "Where are you?"

1. GET SERIOUS: "I will stand and station myself ..." to wait on God.

Think about John Griffith, the father forced to choose between his son and the 400 people on the train. Maybe you're like me, one of those people on the train, unaware of the father's great sacrifice. Perhaps it's time to look again at the great cost of Grace paid by the Father to welcome you HOME to His outstretched arms.

2. BE FOCUSED: "and I will keep watch to see what He will speak to me."

Take up your watch for Father's words to you. Others may leave you in your failures or times of struggle, but He never does. Let Him speak to you through the bubbling brook of living water in the midst of life's deserts. Don't worry about what you don't have or can't get or didn't do — just let Him talk to you.

3. PRACTICE AUTHENTIC HUMILITY: "how I may reply when I am reproved."

Walk back into humility. Allow the horizontals in life to push you back to vertical. Take ownership for your personal issues and leave those of others for God to sort out. Maybe you got hurt or falsely accused; maybe you have to pay the price for someone's actions, or someone has to pay the price for what you did. There is no place that the Father's Love can't find you when you lay down pride and clothe yourself in humility.

4. WRITE IT, CHECK IT, RUN IT: "Record the vision and inscribe it."

As God leads you, write down your insights, journal what He is telling you. Check your heart by sharing it with at least three trusted advisors. (Remember that your own heart can be exceedingly deceitful.) Then run in the power of God's Word to you.

CHAPTER 9: FIVE PROVISIONS OF GRACE

"I have never met a person whose greatest need was anything other than real, unconditional love. You can find it in a simple act of kindness toward someone who needs help. There is no mistaking love. You feel it in your heart. It is the common fiber of life, the flame of that heats our soul, energizes our spirit and supplies passion to our lives. It is our connection to God and to each other."
— Elisabeth Kübler-Ross[81]

IT IS TIME to move beyond the theoretical teaching about God the Father and into the application, the life-changing transformation of personal application. You need to see how GRACE functions in the five areas of LIFE needs discussed in Chapter 2. GRACE has to touch your heart needs and overcome your fears in each of these areas for you to feel a difference in your life. This section will show you how the Father's Love touches and meets your basic needs. By way of review, everyone has five basic areas of need. Each person functions somewhere along a scale ranging from total fear that these needs will not be met to assurance that they will be/are being met. So we can conclude that you need to have assurance that you:

1. Are protected and provided for
2. Are valued
3. Are approved of and appreciated
4. Belong
5. Are significant and important.

This is exactly what GRACE does! In His foresight and Love, God the Father has already provided specifically for you in each of these five areas. Let me show you how.

1. Provision and Protection

A good earthly father creates an environment of security and safety for his family. He demonstrates compassion when his children are hurt. He carries his toddlers when they can't keep up walking. As his kids grow, he helps them navigate through the hazards of life.

If human fathers have this innate, instinctive desire to protect their families, then how much more must our heavenly Father desire to care for us? That's what Scripture teaches. But human nature tends to look at the material world and worry about food, clothing and possessions. *Worry causes us to fear the future, rather than face it in confidence.* We imagine the worst possible outcome, and expect failure and disaster rather than trust the Father's strong hands to carry us through all circumstances.

The Fear of Insecurity — Not Being Provided For or Protected

The fear of not being protected or provided for usually originates from a sense of being left behind or abandoned in the past. Concerning this spirit of abandonment, Drs. Tim Clinton and Gary Sibcy have written:

> *The fear of abandonment is the fundamental human fear. It is so basic and so profound that it emerges even before we acquire the language to voice it. This fear is so powerful that it activates our body's autonomic nervous system; causing our hearts to race, our breathing to become shallow and rapid, our stomachs to quiver, and our hands to shake.*[82]

This spirit of fear has multiple faces. Basic life-survival issues — fearing lack of food, water, clothing, etc. —arise from having those basic necessities taken away or withheld early on. This is also one of the most powerful fears because it is actually a fear of not being safe. Frequently, people from dysfunctional family systems where power was misused will have huge issues regarding their lack of feeling protected. They are afraid to talk about their emotions. Fear of ridicule, fear of criticism, fear of being mocked, and fear of exposure run rampant in these kinds of families.

These types of fears often crowd out the assurance Jesus gave His followers when He said in the Sermon on the Mount (Matthew 6:25-34):

> *"For this reason I say to you, do not be worried about your life, as to what you will eat or what you will drink; nor for your body, as to what you will put on. Is not life more than food, and the body more than clothing? Look at the birds of the air, that they do not sow, nor reap nor gather into barns, and yet your heavenly Father feeds them. Are you not worth much more than they? And who of you by being worried can add a single hour to his life? And why are you worried about clothing? Observe how the lilies of the field*

grow; they do not toil nor do they spin; yet I say to you that not even Solomon in all his glory clothed himself like one of these. But if God so clothes the grass of the field, which is alive today and tomorrow is thrown into the furnace, will He not much more clothe you? You of little faith! Do not worry then, saying, 'What will we eat?' or 'What will we drink?' or 'What will we wear for clothing?' For the Gentiles eagerly seek all these things; for your heavenly Father knows that you need all these things. But seek first His kingdom and His righteousness, and all these things will be added to you. So do not worry about tomorrow; for tomorrow will care for itself. Each day has enough trouble of its own."

Worry comes from *fear* of the future. In the Garden of Eden, Adam and Eve had no foreknowledge of the next day or even the next hour. They simply depended on the Lord, day by day. Like them, you need to stop heeding your worrisome thoughts and start telling your mind what to be thinking. You have the power to tell your mind to live here and now, so tell yourself the truth. Say to yourself, "Don't worry, God has it under control." Why? Because you have a relationship with your Heavenly Father! *He does have it all under control.*

God is providing for everything you need. The trust-level of your relationship with your Heavenly Father determines the level of your worry.

You can know you are provided for and safe in His Presence because He says:

- ✦ You have your needs provided for as you seek Him first. (Matthew 6:33)
- ✦ All your needs will be supplied according to His riches in Christ. (Philippians 4:19)
- ✦ Nothing can separate you from God's Love. (Romans 8:35-39)
- ✦ You are established, anointed and sealed by God. (2 Corinthians 1:21-22)
- ✦ You have total access to God through the Holy Spirit. (Ephesians 2:18)
- ✦ You can approach God with freedom and confidence. (Ephesians 3:12)
- ✦ You will never be abandoned. (Hebrews 13:5)

✦ You have a Father who wants to meet all your needs. (Luke 15:31)

For ORPHANS, life is thinking and worrying about the future, wondering what could possibly happen, painfully full of anxiety and fear.

SONS learn to live by faith, planning for the future while not living there. Sons choose to live life in the moment and trust their Father to meet their needs.

STOP and Examine Your Life

In the sphere of Provision and Protection, do you see yourself as an ORPHAN or a SON?

Rate yourself for the following eight questions, using the scale below:

1 = I can never trust God to provide for and protect me.

2 = I know God can provide for me, but I don't think He wants to.

3 = I'm trying, but it's hard for me to not worry about the future.

4 = God helps those who help themselves. Sometimes He helps me; sometimes I help myself.

5 = I've experienced His provision in the past, and I pray about the future, but I'm not sure I can give it all over to Him.

6 = I'm telling myself the truth, but catch myself falling into old habits of worry.

7 = I give over this area of my life on a daily basis, trusting God as my loving Provider and Protector.

Ask yourself the following questions, rating yourself on a scale of 1 to 7, according to the above scale, and answer honestly:

1. Do I live my life as though God is providing for all my needs as I seek Him first?

1   2   3   4   5   6   7

2. Do I live my life as though God is richly providing for all my needs?

1   2   3   4   5   6   7

3. Do I live my life as though nothing can separate me from God's Love?

1	2	3	4	5	6	7

4. Do I live my life as though I am established, anointed and sealed by God?

1	2	3	4	5	6	7

5. Do I live in my total access to God through the Holy Spirit?

1	2	3	4	5	6	7

6. Do I approach God with freedom and confidence?

1	2	3	4	5	6	7

7. Do I live in confidence that God will never abandon me?

1	2	3	4	5	6	7

8. Do I feel assured that my Father wants to meet all my needs?

1	2	3	4	5	6	7

What Did You See?

As you assess your recent past, do you see yourself as confident that God is going to provide or do you see yourself as fearful and worried about your future provision? You may be tempted to start bashing yourself, but I urge you to refrain. Simply total your numbers and rate yourself somewhere along the scale from 8 (I live like an ORPHAN in the area of Provision and Protection) to 56 (I live fully as a SON in the area of Provision and Protection). Your "score" here is not meant to measure your "success" or your "failure" as a Christian, but to reflect back to you your own view of yourself in relationship to Father God as your Provider and Protector. You need to start with where you *are*, not with where you *think* you should be, in order to eradicate ORPHAN thinking in your life and live like the SON you are.

Tell Yourself the Truth

Speak these simple truths aloud to yourself daily:

1. I am provided for because Matthew 6:33 says God is supplying all my needs as I seek Him first.
2. I am provided for abundantly because Philippians 4:19 says God gives to me out of His riches in glory.
3. I am inseparable from God's Love because Romans 8:35-39 says nothing can ever separate us.
4. I am established, anointed and sealed by God because 2 Corinthians 1:21-22 says the Holy Spirit is my guarantee.
5. I am fully able to approach God because Ephesians 2:18 says the Holy Spirit gives me total access to Him.
6. I am able to approach God with freedom and confidence because Ephesians 3:12 says our faith in Him makes us bold.
7. I am confident that God will never abandon me because Hebrews 13:5 promises that He will never leave or forsake me.
8. I am assured that God wants to meet all my needs because Luke 15:31 shows me the Father's prodigious Love.

2. Worth and Value

God the Father placed an infinite value on you when He gave up His SON as a sacrifice for you. The natural ORPHAN spirit within is all about proving yourself worthy, making yourself seem valuable to others. But that is not the case in your loving Father's family. He wants you. Period.

The Fear of Insufficiency — Having No Value or Worth

Words of encouragement, acts of affection and attitudes of affirmation, especially by a father figure, have enormous power. Several family counselors have presented a formula similar to this:

+ The value of praise in the life of a child or adult is worth 1 point.
+ The value of a praise that reaches into the depth of the person is worth 10 points.
+ The cost of a general criticism is minus 10 points.
+ The cost of a criticism that reaches to the depth of a person's self-image is minus 100 points.

Remember Gary Smalley and John Trent's acrostic from *The Bless-ing?* It describes the antithesis of the dysfunctional parent:

B — Be Committed to Your Child

L — Loving Touch

E — Express Value

S — See Potential

S — Say It Often.

From a child's perspective, meaningful, loving touch requires being hugged consistently and often. A spoken expressed value is hearing the words "I love you" consistently and often. Children need to know they matter and are worth being loved. Parents bless their children by letting them see that they envision a special future for them, that they have po-tential — unique gifts and capabilities God will use to bless others.

Proverbs 27:5 says, "Better is open rebuke than love that is con-cealed." How many have received the message verbally or through body language, "You've been a pain since you were born," or "You again, why are you taking so much of my time"? Parents show their kids they have no value or worth by avoiding them, being uninterested in them, criticizing them, interrupting them, talking over them and not giving them attention and time.

This lack of valuing ties directly into the one fear more deeply felt than all the rest: the *fear of insufficiency,* or the *fear of not being good enough.* Historically, some of the world's most notorious criminals grew out of homes where they were constantly berated and reminded they had no value. Such infamous fatherless figures include Billy the Kid, Saddam Hussein, Adolf Hitler, Jack the Ripper, Lee Harvey Oswald, John Wilkes Booth, Jeffrey Dahmer and Charles Manson.

Personally, I was deeply wounded in this area. I have very few memories of growing up, but I was a hyperactive child and frequently found myself in trouble. While my sister was great at "being good," I seemed to have a knack for being the family mistake. Milk spilling was one of my specialties. I remember spilling my milk and being hit in the back of the head, seeing sparks flicker in my eyes. The message was

"You are a filthy milk spiller. You will probably grow up as nothing more than a milk spiller and you will end up in jail as a milk spiller."

Such constant criticisms and putdowns take a huge toll in a child's heart. The resulting adult seldom and maybe never grows out of earshot of the message "You are wrong." It goes beyond guilt (you made a mistake) and becomes deep shame (you *are* a mistake). → MY MOM

This mindset is what I brought into my walk with God. God was another parent I couldn't please. I gave up on my original parents only to find — in my mental image — the Parent of the Universe looking for someone He could find fault with (and hit when needed). It is said that 80 percent of our identity comes from our fathers and their opinion of us. We derive our worth and value from them.[83]

God made a statement in sacrificing His Son, Jesus. Do you want to see how valuable you are? Look at the crucifixion, at the beating and betrayal Christ endured. Why did He endure? Hebrews 12:2 says that because of "the joy set before Him, He endured the cross and despised the shame." What joy? YOU! *You are His joy.* Remember, the cross of Christ was just the *introduction* to GRACE!

The bloodied cross portrays Christ's excruciating death as a statement of the *unconditional acceptance, value and worth* that our Heavenly Father places on believers. Did you ever think of your Heavenly Father as One who dedicates His time to you, shows His interest in you, and gives Himself and all His fullness to you? Think of it this way: Your Father calls you by name; He wants to know you intimately; He listens and values your thoughts; and He loves to share in your ideas and opinions. This is the meaning of fellowship. You are worth everything to Him.

You can know you have worth and value because your Heavenly Father's Word says:

- You are worth so much to Him that at His infinite cost He allowed His Son to die and purchase you out of sin and slavery to the Law. (John 3:16)

- You are worth the price He paid to redeem you from slavery. (1 Corinthians 6:19-20)

- You are worth being chosen and adopted as His very own child. (Ephesians 1:4-5)

+ You are made righteous, not just declared righteous. God is not angry with you. (Romans 8:1)

+ You were given His Grace and He loves you as much as He loves Jesus. (Romans 5:1-8)

+ You were chosen, justified and redeemed so He could adopt you, seal you and put His Spirit inside you. (Ephesians 1:3-14)

+ You can come to Him using His New Testament Name, ABBA Father. (Galatians 4:4-6)

+ You were given GRACE *according to* His riches and mercy, not just *from* His riches and mercy. (Ephesians 3:14-21)

The ORPHAN *spirit constantly sends the message that the* ORPHAN *has no worth and no value, so life becomes all about striving and controlling to find value in one's job, relationships, marriage, children, religious efforts, endeavors, and dreams.*

SONS *learn over time to base their value in God's Love for them. They constantly reject the counterfeit affection of the world's offers, refusing to be defined by what they do, who they know, how they look and what they have.*

STOP *and Examine Your Life*

In the sphere of Worth and Value, do you see yourself as an orphan or a son?

Rate yourself for the following eight questions, using the scale below:

1 = I can never trust God to value and place worth on me.

2 = I know God values me, but I don't think He wants to.

3 = I'm trying, but it's hard for me to imagine God as really counting me as valuable or worth anything to Him.

4 = I know God's Word says He loves me enough to send Jesus to die for me, but I still feel His disapproval when I make mistakes.

5 = God declared me righteous, and I work really hard to stay that way so He won't remove His blessing from me.

6 = I know lots of verses about the price God paid for me, but I still don't feel valued or worthy of His Love.

7 = I give over this area of my life on a daily basis, trusting that God values me and gives me worth as His child.

Ask yourself the following questions, rating yourself on a scale of 1 to 7, according to the above scale, and answer honestly:

1. Do I live my life as though I am worth so much to Him that at His infinite cost He allowed His SON to die and purchase me out of sin and slavery to the Law?

   1   2   3   4   5   6   7

2. Do I live my life as though I am worth the price He paid to redeem me from slavery?

   1   2   3   4   5   6   7

3. Do I live my life as though I am worth being chosen and adopted as His very own child?

   1   2   3   4   5   6   7

4. Do I live my life as though I am *made righteous,* not just *declared righteous*, and that God is *not angry* with me?

   1   2   3   4   5   6   7

5. Do I live my life as though I have been given His GRACE and He loves me as much as He loves Jesus?

   1   2   3   4   5   6   7

6. Do I fully live as one chosen, justified and redeemed so He could adopt me, seal me and put His Spirit inside me?

   1   2   3   4   5   6   7

7. Do I come to Him using His New Testament Name, ABBA Father?

   1   2   3   4   5   6   7

8. Do I live as one given GRACE *according to* His riches and mercy, not just *from* His riches and mercy?

   1   2   3   4   5   6   7

What Did You See?

As you assess your recent past, do you see yourself as someone whom God highly values? Do you see how much you believe you are worth to the One who sent His SON to die for your salvation?

Total your numbers and rate yourself somewhere along the scale from 8 (I live like an ORPHAN in the area of Worth and Value) to 56 (I live fully as a SON in the area of Worth and Value). A low "score" here may indicate a fear of insufficiency in your walk with the Lord. This does not mean you are "failing" as a Christian, but it should reflect back to you your own view of yourself in relationship to Father God as one valued and counted worthy of SONSHIP by Him. You need to start with where you are, not with where you think you should be, in order to eradicate ORPHAN thinking in your life.

Tell Yourself the Truth

Speak these simple truths aloud to yourself daily:

1. I am valuable and have infinite worth to God because John 3:16 says that He allowed His Son to die for me and purchase me out of sin and slavery to the Law.
2. I am worth the price God paid to redeem me from slavery because 1 Corinthians 6:19-20 says my body is a temple of the Holy Spirit and I do not belong to myself.
3. I am worth being chosen and adopted as God's very own child because Ephesians 1:4-5 says it pleased Him to predestine me for adoption into His family.
4. I am made righteous, not just declared righteous, and God is not angry with me because Romans 8:1 says that there is no condemnation for those who are in Christ Jesus.
5. I have been given God's GRACE and He loves me as much as He loves Jesus because Romans 5:1-8 says that while I was still a sinner, Christ died for me, and through Him I have gained access into the GRACE in which I stand.
6. I am chosen, justified and redeemed so God could adopt me, seal me and put His Spirit inside me because Ephesians 1:3-14 says God chose me before the foundation of the world to be holy and blameless in His sight.

7. I can come to God using His New Testament Name, ABBA Father, because Galatians 4:4-6 says that the Spirit of His Son who lives within me calls out, "ABBA, Father," and I am no longer a slave, but His child.

8. I have been given GRACE according to God's riches and mercy, not just from His riches and mercy, because Ephesians 3:14-21 says I am strengthened with power through God's Spirit in my inner being out of Christ's glorious riches, that His Love for me surpasses knowledge, and that He wants me to be filled to the measure of all the fullness of God, immeasurably more than all I ask or imagine.

3. Approval and Appreciation

Everyone needs to feel appreciated and approved of. I am the type of person who would die for it. In my earlier years, I felt as if the last person in the world who approved of me was God. I pictured Him consistently frowning and scowling at me. He was a Person to Whom I had to report, and no matter what I did, it wasn't enough.

The Fear of Inadequacy — Not Approved of; Never Good Enough

People with an inordinate need for acceptance carry within them a spirit of judgment and inadequacy. They think, "I can never measure up; I'll never be good enough." They strive for a sense of approval, believing that their value is based on measuring up to a real or perceived standard. Their past experiences and relationships have made them hypersensitive and trained them to be on guard so as not lose someone's approval. Fear of inadequacy makes them susceptible to hurt when others make negative comments or express judgmental thoughts. Criticism devastates them.

Hypersensitive to "the look" of disappointment by others, they work ever harder to please and be judged approved. This striving transfers into their walk with God. Rather than pleasing Him by daily trust, people who fear inadequacy try ever harder to prove they are worthy of approval. Unfortunately, the proof they seek can be found only through comparison, which is the rocket fuel of shame. They are constantly observing and sizing up others — usually with ample doses of criticism — comparing themselves to others to see how they measure up. They keep a mental ledger of past offenses, and are as critical of others as they are of themselves, frowning upon and avoiding those who fall short of their standards. They cannot forgive themselves or others, and tend to spurn others in the same way they imagine themselves spurned. For those who struggle with this fear, any praise or encouragement or blessing falls on parched ground that thirsts for affection. They are like the soil in Jesus' parable that cannot sustain life for the sower's seeds.

God Approves and Appreciates

But the Word reveals a Father Who nods approvingly. The Bible says He doesn't even judge us! He has given all judgment to the Son.

He is excited when His children enter the room. He tells us to "draw near with confidence to the throne of GRACE, so that we may receive mercy and find GRACE to help in time of need." He doesn't glance up from His desk and frown, giving us a disappointed look, but rather He says, "Come in! The door is open; find all the mercy and GRACE you need right here in My Presence." That picture makes me smile.

In his short story "The Capital of the World," Ernest Hemingway told of a Spanish father who wanted to reconcile with his son who had run away to Madrid. The father placed an ad in the newspaper, El Liberal: "PACO MEET ME AT HOTEL MONTANA NOON TUESDAY ALL IS FORGIVEN PAPA."

Paco is a common name in Spain; when the father showed up at noon on Tuesday there were 800 Pacos looking for their all-forgiving Papa.

HOME is a place to belong; a place where Father says all is forgiven, and welcomes us in with open arms of joy and excitement. Proverbs tells us He takes His delight in people: "Rejoicing in the world, His earth, and having My delight in the sons of men."

You can know you are approved of because your Heavenly Father says:

- ✦ You are His child. (John 1:12)
- ✦ You are His friend. (John 15:15)
- ✦ You are free forever of being under condemnation. (Romans 8:1)
- ✦ You can draw near to Him with great confidence. (Hebrews 4:16)

- ✦ You have been made righteous and seated beside His Son. (Ephesians 2:6-7)
- ✦ He has desired to make His HOME in your heart. (John 14:16-21)
- ✦ He desires to dwell in you. (Isaiah 57:15; 66.1-2)

The ORPHAN feels an inner pain of not being approved of, not being appreciated, a hurt that drives the ORPHAN to push harder for the approval that comes through externals.

The SON learns to find approval not from others but from God Himself; he learns to live in the understanding of Father's GRACE, and that the SON is beloved beyond words.

STOP and Examine Your Life

In the sphere of Approval and Appreciation, do you see yourself as an ORPHAN or a SON?

Rate yourself for the following eight questions, using the scale below:

1 = I can never trust God to approve of and appreciate me.

2 = I know God can approve of me, but I don't think He wants to.

3 = I'm trying, but it's hard for me to not picture God looking at me disapprovingly.

4 = I know I am His child, but I think He loves His other children a lot more than He loves me.

5 = I am gaining confidence in drawing near to Him.

6 = I'm telling myself the truth, but catch myself thinking I need to work harder to earn His love and approval.

7 = I give over this area of my life on a daily basis, trusting God as my loving, approving and appreciating Father.

Ask yourself the following questions, rating yourself on a scale of 1 to 7, according to the above scale, and answer honestly:

1. Do I live my life as though I am God's child?

   1   2   3   4   5   6   7

2. Do I live my life as though I am God's friend?

1   2   3   4   5   6   7

3. Do I live my life as though I am free forever of being under condemnation?

1   2   3   4   5   6   7

4. Do I live my life as though I can draw near to God with great confidence?

1   2   3   4   5   6   7

5. Do I live my life as though I am righteous and seated beside His Son?

1   2   3   4   5   6   7

6. Do I live my life as though God has made His Home in my heart?

1   2   3   4   5   6   7

7. Do I live in confidence that God desires to dwell in me?

1   2   3   4   5   6   7

What Did You See?

As you assess your recent past, do you see yourself as trusting in God's acceptance and approval of you or as fearful of proving to be inadequate? Total your numbers and rate yourself somewhere along the scale from 7 (I live like an ORPHAN in the area of Approval and Appreciation) to 49 (I live fully as a SON in the area of Approval and Appreciation). Remember not to judge yourself according to where you land on this continuum, but recognize how you relate to Father God as One who *approves of and appreciates you.* Change your ORPHAN thinking by assessing yourself honestly and accepting that as your starting point.

Tell Yourself the Truth

Speak these simple truths aloud to yourself daily:

1. I am God's child because John 1:12 says that everyone who receives Jesus Christ as his or her Savior becomes a child of God.
2. I am God's friend because John 15:15 says that Jesus calls me friend and He tells me what Father God has said to Him.
3. I am free forever of being under condemnation because Romans 8:1 says there is no condemnation for those who are in Christ, and I am in Christ.
4. I can draw near to God with great confidence because Hebrews 4:16 says that at His throne I will receive mercy and find GRACE to help me in my times of need.
5. I have been made righteous and am seated beside God's SON because Ephesians 2:6-7 says that I have been raised up with Him and seated with Christ in heavenly places.
6. My heart is God's HOME because John 14:16-21 says His Spirit dwells with me and in me.
7. My heart is a place where God wants to dwell because Isaiah 57:15 says He dwells in high and holy places, and also with people who have humble and contrite spirits.

4. Belonging to His Family

By nature, human beings long to be part of a larger group, to be accepted by peers, to be approved of by others and to be anticipated upon returning home from a journey. In his 1943 paper, "A Theory of Human Motivation," Abraham Maslow cited "belonging" as the third most important human need on his hierarchy of human needs, after only physiological and safety needs.

A quick Internet search reveals the value of belonging and, more importantly, what happens when belonging doesn't occur: depression, hopelessness and despair.

As a child, I was the smallest of all my peers. Starting school early made matters worse. I was always the last chosen for team games. Even the girls were picked ahead of me, and when the captains got down to the last person (ME), they seemed to look behind me for someone else.

Once, when a teacher made me the captain, my classmates screamed and ran over to the other captain … humiliating! But when God my

Father saw me, He said, "I chose you from the foundation of the world and predestined you to be a SON." Woohoo! It doesn't get better than that!

The Fear of Isolation/Rejection — Not Belonging

"You are going to be rejected because you are not good enough … you don't perform well enough … you don't look right, dress right, wear your hair right … you don't earn enough money, own the right stuff." That's what the spirit of rejection says. Rejection feels like being on the outside looking in, not having a place, not being connected, not being part of something that gives value — and it is extremely powerful. Rejection ranges from the silent treatment (often used in families) to outright refusal to acknowledge the existence of a person at all. It also includes legally disowning someone or refusing to be seen in public with him or her. Some people are subjected to guilt trips; others get "the look" — that stare that communicates major disappointment with a person.

This sense of rejection goes beyond healthy disagreement. Some people are reared in an environment of life-and-death issues. Even the possibility of minor infractions or honest mistakes leads to dire warnings like, "If you don't get this done, don't bother coming back to see me," or, "You mess this one up, and I won't have any use for you." This powerful spirit not only plays on an overt fear of actual rejection, but also abounds in hundreds of very subtle methods that communicate rejection in other ways. The simple look of disappointment, the manipulation of a guilt trip, or words that isolate a person from the family or the organization's inner circle — all speak rejection.

God Gives Us a Home with His Family

The word "home" used to abound in negative connotations for me. At home, I was criticized, wasn't welcome, didn't fit in. It was not a place of joy and encouragement, but of other, sad things. But with God the Father, home is completely positive. The Heavenly Father's HOME is where I can get security, comfort, provision, protection, rest, affirmation, acceptance, belonging, inheritance, identity, light and warmth.

Henri Nouwen said that people will either live life as if they have a home, a place where they belong, or they will live as if they don't have a home. Being a part of God's family is the greatest blessing bestowed on believers. It should drive us to our knees in humble adoration. We can never do anything to deserve it, for it is His gift of Love, mercy and GRACE to us. We are called to become SONS and DAUGHTERS of the Living God.

God Has Placed You in His Family

The Bible says you are part of God's family; He wanted you and adopted you. What a great feeling to be wanted! When you were baptized into His Spirit, you were made part of Father's family.

You can know you are part of God's family because your Heavenly Father says:

+ He gave you the right to become His child through Christ. (John 1:12)

+ He made you His child and wants you to know it and count on it. (1 John 3:1-2)

+ He adopted you into His family and has given you an inheritance. (Galatians 4:4-7)

+ He adopted you because it pleased Him to do so. (Ephesians 1:5-6)

+ He wants you and other believers to know you are SONS of the Living God. (Romans 9:25-26)

+ He gave you His Spirit as a pledge that you will have His inheritance. (Ephesians 1:13-14)

+ Jesus returned to heaven to prepare a place for you in His Father's house because you are His family. (John 14:2)

ORPHANS always struggle to feel accepted by others, to feel welcomed into a group. Having never had a sense of family, they tend to tie in with other dysfunctional groups, looking for a place where they belong, or they reject others completely.

SONS learn that family is important. In belonging to a group and being part of a family they find the blessings of support, encouragement and comfort.

STOP and Examine Your Life

In the sphere of Belonging, do you see yourself as an ORPHAN or a SON?

Rate yourself for the following eight questions, using the scale below:

1 = I can never trust God to include me in His family.

2 = I know God says I'm part of His family, but I don't think He wants me in His HOME.

3 = I'm trying, but it's hard for me to see myself as belonging in God's family.

4 = I know I am God's child and belong in His family, but I feel left out a lot of the time. *like a stepchild*

5 = I am gaining confidence in seeing myself as part of God's family, one of His children, though maybe not loved as much as others more deserving than me.

6 = I'm telling myself the truth, but catch myself sometimes thinking I don't fit in with other believers, even though I know my feelings are deceiving me.

7 = I give over this area of my life on a daily basis, trusting that I belong in God's family, He is my loving Father and other believers are my sisters and brothers.

Ask yourself the following questions, rating yourself on a scale of 1 to 7, according to the above scale, and answer honestly:

1. Do I live my life as though God has given me the right to become His child through Christ?

  1   2   3   4   5   6   7

2. Do I live my life as though God made me His child and wants me to know it and count on it?

  1   2   3   4   5   6   7

3. Do I live my life as though God adopted me into His family and has given me an inheritance?

  1   2   3   4   5   6   7

4. Do I live my life as though God adopted me because it pleased Him to do so?

1	2	3	4	5	6	7

5. Do I live my life as though God wants me and other believers to know we are each a son of the Living God?

1	2	3	4	5	6	7

6. Do I live my life as though God gave me His Spirit as a pledge that I will have His inheritance?

1	2	3	4	5	6	7

7. Do I live my life as though Jesus returned to heaven to prepare a place for me in His Father's house because I am in His family?

1	2	3	4	5	6	7

What Did You See?

As you assess your recent past, do you see yourself as trusting that you belong in God's family or as fearful of isolation and rejection? Total your numbers and rate yourself somewhere along the scale from 7 (I live like an ORPHAN in the area of Belonging to God's family) to 49 (I live fully as a SON in the area of Belonging). No matter where you land on this continuum, do not judge yourself, but recognize how you relate to Father God as One who has accepted you into His family, the family where you BELONG. Once you have assessed yourself honestly, you can set about from that point to change your ORPHAN thinking into the thoughts of a SON.

Tell Yourself the Truth

Speak these simple truths aloud to yourself daily:

1. I can live my life as though I belong in God's family because John 1:12 says that I have the right to become His child through Jesus.
2. I can live my life as though God made me His child and wants me to know it and count on it because 1 John 3:1-2 says I am His child now, and when He appears I will be like Him.

3. I can live my life as though God adopted me into His family and has given me an inheritance because Galatians 4:4-7 says God sent His SON to buy me back from slavery to the Law, so He could adopt me and I would become a SON and heir.

4. I can live my life as though God adopted me because it pleased Him to do so because Ephesians 1:5-6 says He predestined me for adoption according to the purpose of His will, because He wanted to.

5. I can live my life as though God wants me and other believers to know I am a SON of the Living God because Romans 9:25-26 says He will call us "My people," "Beloved," and "SONS of the living God."

6. I can live my life as though God gave me His Spirit as a pledge that I will have His inheritance because Ephesians 1:13-14 says I was sealed with the promised Holy Spirit as a guarantee of my inheritance until I acquire possession of it.

7. I can live my life as though Jesus returned to heaven to prepare a place for me in His Father's House because I am His family because John 14:2 says Jesus wouldn't lie to me when He said, "In My Father's house are many rooms," and "I go to prepare a place for you."

5. Significance and Importance

Father also has the power to honor and bless us. Think of this: God can make anything significant or important just by touching it. To that end, His touch on the Christian's life makes each of us significant. He sees us as having a part to play, that we are important to Him. We don't need the world's sense of importance derived from net worth, university degrees, networking relationships, business size, career success, and so on. That is all ORPHAN thinking.

President of the National Association of Evangelicals Dr. Leith Anderson once spoke in our church and gave an illustration about the value of a pen. In the middle of a sermon, he asked if anyone in the audience of 900 people had a pen he could borrow. I had three of them. But it was just a rhetorical question.

Before I could grab her hand, my wife held up her plastic pen and said, "Sure, have mine." I sank in my chair with embarrassment. Dr. Anderson and Cheryl proceeded to discuss the price of the pen ($1.98 at Walmart) in front of all those people. Now I wanted to be *under* the chair.

Dr. Anderson collected two more pens of greater value than our dollar-ninety-eight plastic special. His point was, which pen had more value? The answer was obvious: Every pen was worth more than ours. Until he said, "By the way, there is one piece of information you need to know. This pen (our dollar-ninety-eight plastic special) was used by President Abraham Lincoln to write the Gettysburg Address."

The point was riveting. Now the one the world deemed the *least* valuable became the *most* valuable, *because of who held it*. This is what God has done with His children. Because He has touched you, your Father makes you important. Your importance is derived from the One Who holds you. It is not what you have that defines you but Who has you that determines your importance

I love to wander in my father-in-law's garden. He is a master gardener, building out his own hybrid trees, knowing the adaptability of the specific garden plants and their ability to survive Minnesota cold, heavier rain and differing soils. As we work through the plants — pinching overgrowth off some, trimming others — I am always reminded this must surely be how life with my Heavenly Father will be. As I listen to my father-in-law tell stories of this or that plant, the world and all its stupidity seem to evaporate. How I enjoy those moments! What makes it so significant is simply being in my father-in-law's presence as we do this. He is a man I greatly respect. He gives our time value, worth and importance. And we walk together in peace.

The Fear of Insignificance — Not Being Important or Significant

A spirit of insignificance may hound a person whose need for significance or importance remains unmet. The fear of being unnecessary or unimportant, of being looked down on within a family or organizational pecking order is planted in people whose parents, leaders and colleagues have not made time for them. They've received the message that they are of lesser importance as others talk over them, interrupt them, ignore them. They may not be invited to planning sessions; their opinions are not requested; they are corrected in public, intimidated, isolated and put down.

Significance is feeling that you matter in this world. You know you make a difference and are relevant, respected, considered, and valued for who you are. You sense that what you do has value to someone or toward some goal.

Yet feelings of insignificance are also real; they call into question one's entire purpose of existing. Examining, exploring, and considering the source of those feelings will reveal the true significance of one's life — of all life, as it relates to God and His greater purpose in creation. People with a high sense of significance have a high sense of confidence. People without a sense of significance often feel self-hatred and alienation, and doubt their own value and importance. They become defeated by mistakes or failures, are fearful of expressing themselves, unsure in taking appropriate risks, overcome with negative thinking and overly concerned with the opinions of others. When the feeling of insignificance is multiplied and magnified in certain personalities, it can become a major factor underlying school shootings and other public displays of erupting human volcanoes.

God Gives You Importance and Purpose

Ephesians 2:10 says that you are God's workmanship. He is continually working on you. You were created in Him for good works. You were chosen by Him to produce His fruit in the world. When you feel burdened by job responsibilities, you can stop and say, "I don't need to be a success at my job. I don't need to be a success in this world. I don't even need to be a success at being a Christian. All I need to do is be a great SON. My job is to do my Father's will."

God has called you as His ambassador. He has placed you in a foreign country (called "the world") and given you the significant job of serving as a representative of His country, His Kingdom of GRACE. As a believer, your life is essentially about being a great SON, honoring your Father, doing His will, practicing His Presence, and living in His joy. Your purpose is to receive His Love and give it away in random acts of humility. This noble life goal — this purpose — is of vital importance to the furtherance of God's Kingdom here on Earth.

You can know you are important and have purposeful significance because your Heavenly Father says:

+ He created you as His workmanship in Christ for good works. (Ephesians 2:10)

+ He chose you to bear much fruit. (John 15:12-17)

+ He will prune you to bear more fruit. (John 15:2)

+ He made you to be salt and light. (Matthew 5:13-14)

+ He made you a minister of reconciliation. (2 Corinthians 5:18)

+ He made you an ambassador for Christ. (2 Corinthians 5:17-20)

+ He strengthens you to do all things through Jesus. (Philippians 4:13)

For the ORPHAN, *being important is a driving motive and always determined by a world value-system of <u>performance</u>, <u>possessions</u>, <u>power</u> and <u>praise</u> of men.*

A SON *learns that the most menial tasks have value when they are touched by a Heavenly Father.* SONS *don't need someone to tell them they're significant; they know because they have a Heavenly Father Who says it and that settles it.*

STOP and Examine Your Life

In the sphere of Significance and Importance, do you see yourself as an ORPHAN or a SON?

Rate yourself for the following eight questions, using the scale below:

1 = I always feel insignificant and hate myself for not trusting that God thinks I'm important to Him.

2 = I know God says I play an important role as His Kingdom's ambassador, but I don't think He trusts me to represent Him well.

3 = I'm trying, but it's hard for me to see myself as a faithful ambassador for Christ.

4 = I know God's Word says I am His minister of reconciliation, but I mess up too often to be of any real value to Him.

5 = I am gaining confidence in seeing myself as significant to God, one of His ambassadors in the world, even though my results aren't very good when I try to talk to people about Christ.

6 = I'm telling myself the truth, but often think God would prefer to use someone else who would do a better job than I do at representing Him, even though I know He is using me.

7 = I give over this area of my life on a daily basis, trusting that God has chosen me for His purpose, and I look for opportunities to represent Him faithfully.

Ask yourself the following questions, rating yourself on a scale of 1 to 7, according to the above scale, and answer honestly:

1. Do I live my life as though God created me as His workmanship in Christ for good works? *try to*

    1   2   3   4   5   6   7

2. Do I live my life as though God chose me to bear much fruit?

    1   2   3   4   5   6   7

3. Do I live my life as though God will prune me to bear more fruit?

    1   2   3   4   5   6   7

4. Do I live my life as though God made me to be salt and light?

    1   2   3   4   5   6   7

5. Do I live my life as though God made me a minister of reconciliation?

    1   2   3   4   5   6   7

6. Do I live my life as though God made me an ambassador for Christ?

    1   2   3   4   5   6   7

7. Do I live my life as though God strengthens me to do all things through Jesus?

1	2	3	4	5	6	7

What Did You See?

Asking yourself questions about your recent past may disclose issues to you of which you might not be consciously aware. Do your answers reveal that you see your life as purposeful, significant and important to God or as fearful of insignificance and not mattering to God? Total your numbers and rate yourself somewhere along the scale from 7 (I live like an ORPHAN in the area of Significance and Importance) to 49 (I live fully as a SON in the area of Significance and Importance). Even if your numbers reflect a fear of insignificance or feelings of unimportance to God, do not judge yourself, but recognize how you relate to Father God as One *who has given you importance and significance in His Kingdom as His ambassador for Christ and minister of reconciliation in the world and in His church.* Once you have assessed yourself honestly, you can set about from that point to change your ORPHAN thinking into the thoughts of a SON.

Tell Yourself the Truth

Speak these simple truths aloud to yourself daily:
1. I can live as God's workmanship in Christ, created for good works because Ephesians 2:10 says that before I was even born, God prepared good works for me to do in my life.
2. I can bear much fruit in my life because John 15:12-17 says that God appointed me to go and bear fruit that will abide, and He will give me whatever I ask the Father in Jesus' name.
3. I can live my life expecting God to prune me to bear more fruit because John 15:1-2 says that God is like a Gardener who trims His grapevines to produce the most grapes, and I am a fruit-bearing branch on the "Jesus vine."
4. I can season and preserve my world like salt and shed God's light on those around me because Matthew 5:13-14 says God made me the salt of the earth and the light of the world.
5. I can be a minister of reconciliation within all my relationships and to those around me in the world because 2 Corinthians 5:18

says God reconciled me to Himself and gave me the ministry of reconciliation.

6. I can act as an ambassador for Christ because 2 Corinthians 5:17-20 says that God entrusted the message of reconciliation to me so I can be Christ's ambassador to the world.

7. I have the strength to fulfill God's important purposes for me on earth because Philippians 4:13 says that God strengthens me to do all things through Jesus.

APPLICATION: LEARNING TO HEAR FATHER'S HEART

This chapter has been full of application. Reflect on what you've learned about yourself and your relationship with God. Are you living in the fullness God intends for you as His child? Can you speak of yourself what God's Word says is true of you in the five basic areas of life, or do you live in some degree of fear associated with one or more of these areas? Are you living as a SON experiencing God as your Father on a daily basis? This Father created you and has been seeking you from the beginning, calling, "Where are you?"

1. GET SERIOUS: "I will stand and station myself ..." to wait on God.

Stand and station yourself to see you as God sees you — as a SON or DAUGHTER. Stand on that; don't falter; don't look at your past. Stand and station yourself as at a guard post. Pray in His Presence. Father's room is a room of GRACE. You stand not because of who you are, but because He is your Father, and He wants you to stand before Him.

2. BE FOCUSED: "and I will keep watch to see what He will speak to me."

Father told His SON, "You are my beloved SON in whom I am well pleased." Because you are in Christ, those words are also spoken to you. Father bends to welcome you HOME. Let His arms pick you off your feet. That is what Love does. Let Him tell you, "I have loved you with an everlasting Love … and I am so glad you're Home."

3. PRACTICE AUTHENTIC HUMILITY: "how I may reply when I am reproved."

Let Father put his arm around you; tell Him where you may have failed (Hint: He already knows). Let Him bind up your heart, and reply to

Him with thanksgiving and praise. Let Him speak what He wants you to hear.

4. WRITE IT, CHECK IT, RUN IT: "Record the vision and inscribe it."

Don't forget to journal your conversations with Him. Write down your thoughts and His, and remember to check your journal by sharing it with at least three trusted advisors. Then run in the power of God's Word to you as His SON or DAUGHTER.

Seeking my Abba God?,
where can I stand & station
myself ... to wait on God

SECTION THREE: THE POWER OF DISPLACEMENT THINKING

CHAPTER 10: THE HEART OF GRACE — BASIC TRUST

"Truly I say to you, whoever does not receive the kingdom of God like a child will not enter it at all."
—Jesus (Luke 18:17, Mark 10:18)

THE FIRST nine chapters of this book have covered GRACE and my discoveries of God as Father. These are huge components of healing. But what follows is *far more significant.*

Throughout my years as a pastor, I searched for GRACE and significance but couldn't seem to hold on to my understanding of either. My performance orientation and fear of failure and rejection kept me in a constant state of stress.

I was like the plate-spinner on *The Ed Sullivan Show* from the early days of television. He set up a row of tall spindles and started spinning glass plates on top. As he worked his way down the row, the first ones would slow down and wobble. So he had to keep running back and forth, starting new and speeding up the old, until there were too many and he couldn't work fast enough to keep plates from crashing and breaking.

In my ministry efforts, I was that man — exhausted by my efforts to keep all my "plates" spinning. Finally, emotionally spent, I simply stopped.

And there I stood with the "broken dishes" of damaged ministry and relationships scattered at my feet.

"But God"

In my thickest darkness, God showed His great GRACE. Father brought me in my failure back to those words He spoke to me on a gravel road years earlier: "If you can love Me so much, why do you find it so hard to understand that I love you so much more?"

"I'm just a loser, Lord." (A lie from Satan.) "I don't understand anything at all." (Well, that was probably true.) It was a bright morning on a snow-packed Iowa road. The sun shone on my face as Father reached in through my broken heart and said, "Then maybe we can build My Way." And all I could say was, "Okay."

There He showed me a deeper heart issue that needed healing. Externally, I had trusted God with my mind and commitments, but *deep inside — in the foundational level below my belief system — dwelt a horrible inability to attach to God (or others) in a basic level of trust.*

What Is BASIC TRUST?

The solution came in understanding BASIC TRUST and how it relates to God, especially as Father. For me, trusting God encapsulated the words Master and Lord and Good Shepherd and King. I would not hesitate to take a knee before such a beautiful, gracious, and forgiving Jesus. But inside was the gnawing feeling He didn't like me very much. I had to learn to trust God at such a primary, emotional, intimate Fathering level that no matter what happened, I wasn't concerned anymore. He was my peace and joy and rest; He loved me and liked me and wanted me. I needed to be totally convinced and completely abandoned to His will in BASIC TRUST. I knew how much I as a father unquestioningly love my son Jeremiah. So my Father, deeply and emotionally, loves me, His child.

BASIC TRUST *is the ability to hold one's self open and vulnerable to another, dropping all defensiveness and guard, without questioning the other's motives.* BASIC TRUST is the *hidden core of emotional conviction* where a person 1) becomes *absolutely convinced of the good intentions of another person,* 2) has *no doubt that the other person's motives are pure and free of malice,* and 3) becomes *willing and vulnerable to hold one's self open to another, even in the face of circumstances that seem questionable.*

It is a *deep-seated primary emotional response of conviction that your Heavenly Father always seeks your very best* so that *you remain completely vulnerable to His choices for your life.* It is the gut-level belief that His Will is perfect and complete and lacking in no good thing for you. Nothing that happens to you is beyond the scope of His Father's heart. And He protects and provides for you, approves of you, values you, makes you part of His family, makes you significant and gives you purpose (*even if that purpose includes suffering pain, disease, or loss of loved ones*).

Over time, this basic, rooted-and-grounded trust (or lack of it) affects one's behavior, actions, and reactions. When you live in a state of BASIC TRUST in Him, His LIFE works through you and changes you. If trust is damaged, all of one's life becomes filled with anxiety and hopelessness followed by fear, aggressive striving, competition, inability to socially related, worry, depression and a host of other things.

Understanding Basic Trust

The term "BASIC TRUST" comes from child developmental work by Erik Erikson who used it to identify the early developmental months in infancy. These early months are *fundamental to the development of one's ability to trust others* and *to have confidence in oneself.* In fact, damage often occurs to children's BASIC TRUST level *in the first two years,* then *the next four years* of life. Such breaches spew out all sorts of ugly, unwanted behaviors.

So powerful is this BASIC TRUST core that founder of Life Skills International Dr. Paul Hegstrom has written:

> *If emotional growth has been arrested, inner character will not develop normally. Instead, a child can create a pseudopersonality that becomes a mask to protect from rejection. In this process the child is trying to meet the expectations from the people who are important in life, but in the process his or her own development is sacrificed. Crucial areas of relationships and personal life management are hindered.* [84]

Hegstrom continues:

> *The most obvious result is a loss of self-respect. This will manifest itself in many ways. I will 1. lose my sense of security, 2. not develop an ability to trust, 3. doubt truth, 4. fear knowledge.* [85]

What incredible struggles many believers face every single day, trying harder to be trusting and faithful and good, pleasing and acceptable to

God! Yet if BASIC TRUST is damaged, as Hegstrom says, *"the inner character will not develop normally."* Read that again! Without BASIC TRUST there is a loss of self-respect (self-image), no sense of security, no ability to trust or embrace truth, and a fear of being discovered. Damaged BASIC TRUST may affect every area of your life. Yet you may be oblivious to it. You try harder to believe more and be better and somehow show God you have arrived. Yet deep inside, you believe you are not wanted, not approved of, not acceptable, not important, not protected, and, frankly, you just don't belong.

BASIC TRUST as a Reflex

Here is an illustration of how BASIC TRUST becomes damaged. Let's say we are building a wall and you are holding a nail for me to hammer. Though I have been accurate several times, one time I miss the nail and hammer your finger. The next time I go to hammer a nail you are holding, what happens? You instinctively jump back. That instinct to protect yourself is motivated by a broken BASIC TRUST. You *know* I didn't mean it, but still your *natural reflex* is to protect.

At the foundational level, deep in your heart, trust has been injured. And to protect against re-injury, a reflexive action takes over. So you flinch or pull back, do not trust fully. Your *mind* says I am trustworthy, but *in your heart — deeply tucked away in the core of your thinking — the reflexive part says, "Pull back!"* This is what many believers do with their faith in God.

Many who serve God and diligently study the Word cannot comprehend that God loves them. Their *reflexive* faith won't allow Him in. They see Him as Lord and Master; they bow before His royal rules, and rightfully so. Outwardly, they look godly, but the inward struggle is intense. Intellectually, they *know* they are God's children, *but* that just means they must *work harder, do it better, get the grade, achieve the goal, comply with demands, make sacrifices, and gain status.*

They don't talk about their successes; that would be pride. They do what they are told to do: surrendering their will, being broken, living as overcomers, committing themselves to being ever more obedient, disciplining themselves for the purpose of godliness, speaking faith, proclaiming victory, confessing sin. All scriptural pursuits, and vital to the

believer's walk. *But* **at the BASIC TRUST core level,** *these sincere believers —
like me — **may not believe God even likes them, let alone loves them**.*

To live in GRACE, one must understand that *God's Presence is accessed
with the trusting heart of a child.* Jesus said that in the Scriptures quoted
above.

What Happens When a Christian's BASIC TRUST Is Damaged?

Many Christians who serve God and diligently study the Word still can't
comprehend that God loves them, because they have a reflexive faith
that won't allow Him too far in. Though they look godly outwardly,
their inward struggle is intense. They know they are God's children, but
that just means they must work harder, do it better, make the grade. All
of life is viewed as a constant struggle. There is little peace and joy and
rest, because they think God doesn't even like having them around. As a
result, they have little ability to rest in His will or believe He is actively
engaged in their lives.

When I was in seminary, my wife and I lived way below the poverty
level. Every dime had to be managed, every dollar accounted for. Imagine the excitement when one day in the mail I received a donation from
an anonymous person for fifty dollars! I compiled a list of everything I
hoped to do with that money. I was going to tithe $5 of it — because
that's what you do. Then I would use the remaining $45 for some things
that my wife and I really wanted to do. But within a few days, it became
obvious that my car needed a new muffler or we were going to be pulled
over. So I took my car to the muffler shop. The bill was $37.50. I'll never
forget the amount. I was really irritated with God. "It was nice of You
to provide the money, but then You took it back right away. That doesn't
seem right!"

My irritation acted out my level of trust. I could have beaten it into
submission by telling myself what a lousy, unfaithful Christian I was. I
could have reviewed my notes on submission and confession and speaking words of faith, or attended another conference or listened to another
tape, or read another book on how bad I was, which is exactly what I
used to do.

Without BASIC TRUST, you live in your own strength because you
lack trust in God's Fatherly care for you, and the results are devastating:

+ anxiety or fear

+ hopelessness or depression

+ constant striving for reward, for the praise of men

+ competition and comparison against others

+ critical attitude, judgmental, not seeing how God can reward others

+ bitterness and resentment

+ burnout from not running in the Spirit but in the flesh

+ high need to achieve and perform and be approved of

+ constant grab for value, questioning what a particular thing adds to one's self or one's agenda.

As I began to research the consequences of damaged trust, I found hundreds of examples of the devastation — injuries during early emotional development far beyond what I dealt with:

+ According to attachment theory experiments in Rhesus monkeys, when BASIC TRUST was damaged, subjects were constantly anxious, fearful, depressed, angry, unable to adapt to a group when introduced to others, antisocial behaviors, all the way to extreme schizophrenia and aggressive sexual aberrancies including rape and homosexuality. (See appendix F.)

+ In other studies, animals separated from parents through natural or human causes become competitive, angry, depressed, cannibalistic, sexually aberrant and killers.

+ Babies deprived of touch during early years exhibit numerous emotional damages, and physical as well.

+ As adults, these children later exhibit self-grasping, total lack of gregariousness or interest in exploring their environment, withdrawal, aversion to contact with others, hyper-aggression, inability to nurture, and abusive behavior.

+ They also display symptoms of depression, anger and aggression, impulsiveness.

+ They avoid closeness or emotional connection; they are distant, critical, rigid, anxious and insecure, not physically nurturing; they are controlling, blaming, erratic, unpredictable; sometimes charming, sometimes chaotic; insensitive, explosive, abusive, untrusting even while craving security.

+ One study showed that lack of relationship with parents at an early age became the common denominator in mental illness, hypertension, malignant tumors, coronary heart disease, and suicide.

+ Another study showed incidence of suicide jumps 300 to 400 percent in teens related to lack of parental relationship.

+ Another author documents moderate to severe mental health issues, depression, anxiety, suicidal thoughts, addictions, bullying, harassing others, love-hate relationships, inordinate amounts of time invested in television, video games, surfing the internet, listening to music, lacking social interaction, feeling angry, anxious, depressed, isolated, paranoia, and so on.

Many of these will be referenced in the next chapter as we begin to look at how BASIC TRUST is damaged. But the point is this:

Ungodly fruit is often rooted in damaged trust.

And no matter how hard we try to change, an inner drift exists within, pulling us toward worldly solutions.

BASIC TRUST — an Absolute to Understanding GRACE

BASIC TRUST sits at the heart of GRACE. It allows you to receive God's Love without doubt. Basic Trust is the core of emotional healing whereby a person 1) becomes absolutely convinced of the good intentions of a Heavenly Father God, 2) has no doubt that the Father's motives are pure and free of disappointment or condition, and 3) becomes willing and vulnerable to and holds him- or herself open to Father's Spirit, even in the face of circumstances that seem questionable. Over time, this basic, rooted-and-grounded trust infects the upper "fruit" of one's behavior, actions, and reactions.

One of Christianity's top five books of recent decades is J.I. Packer's *Knowing God*, quoted earlier. I remind you of Packer's words:

If you want to judge how well a person understands Christianity, find out how much he makes of the thought of being God's child, and having God as his Father. If this is not the thought that prompts and controls his worship and prayers and his whole outlook on life, it means that he does not under-stand Christianity very well at all."[86]

Read that five times out loud.

If you learn to live like this with God — to see Him as the amazing Father He really is — every single belief and every single behavior of your life will be affected. The teachings of author and founder of Shiloh Place Ministries, Jack Frost, profoundly affected my understanding of the concepts in this book. Yet Frost's wife, Trisha, said, "Forty-five minutes in the arms of Father God did more to change my husband than getting saved, four years of Bible school, fifteen years of ministry and the baptism of the Holy Spirit."[87]

Loving and trusting Father God transformed all my relationships, how I view my surroundings, how I view myself and how I deal with others. I came to understand the meaning of HOME in my Father's Presence. This understanding infected others to whom I could now be open and vulnerable, in my family and even in the business world, because I "caught it" from my Heavenly Father. I learned that because my Father is my Peace, and my Father loves me, I can listen to my family or my business associates tell me I messed up. I can correct those things my Father directs, and others know they have been heard.

I can sit, unrattled, in the middle of an angry mediation or arbitration, because my Dad is right there with me. It's His business not mine. I have spent time with Him; I am on His assignment, and this is His stuff, not mine. I can have people in my face in anger, yelling at me and putting me down, (it's part of what I do in negotiation) and be just fine with it. As Father touched my inner soul, healing my heart, peace and rest and joy became the standard, not the exception in my demeanor.

In the early days of flying, without electronic guidance systems and weather radar, storms could be life-threatening events. A pastor on such a flight noted terrified people crying out in fear as the plane bucked in gale-force winds. All were obviously scared with one exception — a little nine-year-old girl who sat in one of the front seats. During the entire turbulent flight, the pastor watched this little girl's reactions. Despite the plane's buffeting, she continued to color in her coloring book.

When extreme shaking scattered her crayons, she simply gathered them up and continued with her picture. The plane finally landed, and the relieved passengers gathered their bags and belongings, thankful to be safely on the ground. The pastor held back to stop beside the little girl. "Young lady," he said, "I couldn't help but notice that in the midst of the storm you never seemed to be upset, even when everyone else was so scared. I was wondering if you could tell me why."

She replied, "It's easy. My daddy is the pilot and I know no matter how bad it gets, he will always get me safely home."

That little girl's statement encapsulates what it means to live in BASIC TRUST of God as your Father — a child's trust that her daddy will get her safely home. Conceivably a pilot father could make a mistake; but your Heavenly Father can never make a mistake. His will for you is as Romans 12 says, "...good, acceptable, perfect." As a believer walking with your Father, you need to be so rooted and grounded in Father God's Love that nothing shakes you. Your roots get LIFE only from Him. You are grounded in the assurance that His Love will never fail, never falter and never leave you hanging. He will not drop you; He will not ask you to do more than you are capable of doing; and He has promised to get you HOME.

Perhaps it is the gift of being a grandfather now ("Poppa J" to toddler Jaxon), but how I long to look into the eyes of my little one! I tear up when I hear him cry because he must stay behind when I go somewhere. My heart melts when his little hand reaches out for me to help. How I long for the day when I'll hear him speak his thoughts. I love watching him learn and grow.

And who created this relationship? A Father who was Father God before He was Creator. A Father who established this primary relationship as His own to reveal Himself to us. My roles as father and grandfather mirror His heart for me.

Little Jaxon and I don't usually exchange kisses — that's a girl thing, and he gets those in abundance from Mama and Grammy. But guy-to-guy, when we hug each other, often you will see us touch forehead to forehead, where an incredible exchange occurs: "I love you, Son, you are my heart, we are together."

Let Father God touch His forehead to yours. Let Him be Father and you be SON. Let Him tell you "I love you, SON, as much as I love my Jesus." Isn't that weird to think that He loves me as much as Jesus? No … it's GRACE. Amazing GRACE. Transforming us from ORPHANS to SONS.

APPLICATION: Learning to Hear Father's Heart

1. GET SERIOUS: "I will stand and station myself …" to wait on God.

Quiet the noise. Your lack of trust gives so many voices validity in your thinking; quiet the noise. Let every voice diminish to mute. Let your heart relax in waiting on Him. Stand and station yourself at peace waiting for Father to move in your heart. Read J.I. Packer's quote out loud again.

2. BE FOCUSED: "and I will keep watch to see what He will speak to me."

Focus on God as Father. Look at Him not as Lord or Master or even King — though He is all this and more. Sit beside Him as a child with Daddy. Focus on walking with Him as two walk together in Love. Feel His hand on your shoulder, hear His Fatherly heart. Let Him assure you of His Love. "I have loved you with an everlasting love" (Jeremiah 31:3). Read it aloud. This is a time to focus in on Him as a Person, His feelings, His heart, His thoughts about you. Take a literally verbal stand against the Five Basic Fears:

+ The Fear of Insecurity — Not Being Provided For or Protected
+ The Fear of Insufficiency — Having No Value or Worth
+ The Fear of Inadequacy — Not Approved of; Never Good Enough
+ The Fear of Isolation/Rejection — Not Belonging
+ The Fear of Insignificance — Not Being Important or Significant

3. PRACTICE AUTHENTIC HUMILITY: "how I may reply when I am reproved."

And reproof will come. Not because of what you have done, but deeper inside as He walks through your heart; the gentle reproof that says so easily, "I miss you a lot. I miss our time together. I miss our fellowship. I created you to rejoice in you and over you and through you."

Then you reply, sometimes just a smile, because in that gentle discipline you know, "I'm loved, I belong here, I am important to Him, I'm valuable in His Presence, I'm affirmed in His sight, and I'm protected by His provision."

And then you feel that gentle nudge and respond, "How could I have ever doubted You, dear Father?"

4. WRITE IT, CHECK IT, RUN IT: "Record the vision and inscribe it."

Write it down. I tell many, "I know you know God, but are you *experiencing Him* as your Father on a daily basis?"

When you start to see this response in yourself, write it. Write it all out and then come back and read it again and again to remind yourself how you got here. The key turned the lock; the door opened; you are HOME. Do you trust Him and His Love for you enough to say with your heart, "YOU are my Portion, YOU are my Strength, YOU are my Song, YOU are my Source, YOU are my Direction, YOU are my Perspective, YOU are my EVERYTHING"? The words of the Psalmist from Psalm 73:25, "Whom have I in heaven but Thee, and besides Thee I desire nothing on the earth," describe this kind of trust. ***This is what it means to live life vertically.***

CHAPTER 11: WOUNDED TRUST

"Yet, You are He who brought me forth from the womb; You made me trust when upon my mother's breasts."

David (Psalm 22.9)

SEEING my own damaged BASIC TRUST and my ORPHAN spirit mindset triggered a revelation that I was not rooted and grounded in Father's Love. Aha! That was why I couldn't access the life-changing power in my Christian walk on a long-term basis. I could make short spurts and dashes, but the marathon walk was always evasive. Because I didn't trust God at the *basic* level, I struggled to see myself as loved by God. Everything was a duty instead of a delight, a job instead of joy.

Outwardly, my attitudes and words projected total trust in Him. But underneath, a desperate struggle for control hindered my primary emotional response. I trusted God because it was the "right thing" to do, yet like an addict I ran back to the counterfeit affections of performance, pretending, possessions, power, people, praise, personal agenda and pursuit of pleasures. This obsessive behavior was largely due to my damaged BASIC TRUST.

So how is BASIC TRUST damaged? The rips and tears start early, primarily within early original-family systems. John Townsend writes, "The first and most fundamental human need the family should meet is the need for forming deep and loving attachments, the need to develop the feeling of being close to someone 'with skin on.'"[88]

The umbrella over this line of study is called "Attachment Theory." According to John Bowlby, "Attachment can be defined as the strong bond that develops first between parent and child, and later in peer and romantic relationships." Statistical research findings over the last fifty years represent volumes of information and go much deeper than the scope of this book. But the research undeniably shows that parental shaping, starting with early development and continuing through the teenage years, not only impacts human relationships, but also dramatically affects a child's view of God as Father. Yet in most typical coaching and counseling, this statistically significant impact is rarely mentioned.

In *Why You Do the Things You Do,* Drs. Tim Clinton and Gary Sibcy address the concepts of intimacy, attachment, original family issues and how these lead to good or problem relationships with others. They write, "The underlying reason why we do the things we do is our relationship style or, to use a word we counselors often use, *our attachment style.*"

According to Clinton, *at a subliminal level, we behave, react and interact relationally mainly due to our attachment style, as learned during family-of-origin development.* The gravity of that statement is overwhelming! If the underlying reasons we do or don't do things are buried deep in our childhood development, we must learn to deal with them, especially if these issues currently cause us anxiety or hopelessness.

BASIC TRUST and God's Image: Damaged by Original-Family Dysfunction

I believe that the biggest injury to our image of a loving Father and our BASIC TRUST in Him comes from original-family dysfunction. Psychologists say 83 percent of us were raised in dysfunctional homes. Counting just addictive behavior, The American Medical Association places the number of dysfunctional family systems at 73 percent. Dr. John Bradshaw, a leading expert on family co-dependency, states his estimate is 96 percent, basically everyone. Others reference 80 to 83 percent, but believe the incidence to be much higher. My experience as a coach and counselor places original family dysfunction and its impact at about 9 out of 10 or 90 percent. And it is my personal belief the impact reaches far into adulthood and to the fourth through the tenth generations. I believe this

I first heard of the impact of BASIC TRUST from Jack Frost of Shiloh Place Ministries.[89] His recounting of his daughter Sarah's issues got my attention. Sarah had been born in a time of great trauma — hospital trips for their older son and then her mother's multiple bouts of depression. Sarah was damaged in the area of BASIC TRUST at an early age.

According to Frost, "By the age of 2, Sarah would beat up any 4 year old she could find. Essentially she did not 'get along well with others.'" As she grew older, she rejected all forms of affection, was antisocial, and was defiant of her parents or anyone who tried to tell her what to do.

Although she performed well in school, receiving straight A's most of the time, her attitude toward relationships and authority left something to be desired. Sarah was also a tomboy; she never had girlfriends in grade school, but she could whip most of the boys in any sport. She denied her femininity (bonding) and embraced only masculinity (performing). She had not allowed her femininity to be nurtured when she perceived rejection coming from her mother.

The Frosts discovered the root of Sarah's problems when they started talking to her about her sense of being welcomed to life, of being a child who was loved. Sarah recounted an event that occurred when she was 5 years old. She had run across the living room and landed on Jack's (ouch!) crotch. Jack reflexively picked up his daughter, and as he was collapsing to the floor, quickly pushed her over to the couch. He noticed a different cry in her voice, as she sobbed uncontrollably.

> *Although I was rolling on the floor almost nauseous from the pain, my young daughter, while having suffered no physical injury, was experiencing a much deeper pain than I was. She had come running to enjoy her father's embrace only to be thrown away because she had failed to perform or act in the right way. She had risked opening up her heart to me ... only to have it slammed shut.*

At age 17, amidst multiple problems at school, Sarah's buried issues boiled to the surface. Frost recounts Sarah's emotional remembrance:

> *That night, as we prayed with Sarah, we didn't pray over the 17 year old; we prayed over the 5 year old. Something inside her burst loose in wailing, agonizing groans, and she wept and wept. For about 30 minutes, she lay cradled in my arms as we poured out love and comfort to her. It was a defining moment in Sarah's life — the beginning of realizing, "If my father, as broken a man as he, could comfort me at 17 years old, how much more does Father God want me to run to Him in every moment of crisis?"*

The behavior of the 17-year-old teenager was rooted in the pain of a moment in a little 5-year-old girl. Through Frost's work, I began wondering if there could be a connection between this BASIC TRUST issue and how it relates to God. I researched as many books as I could find on how a child's trust could affect his or her relationship to God as Father.

Could family of origin actually affect one's ability to believe and trust God — especially as a Father? I found that, similar to Maslow's pyramid of needs, all children must receive from their parents five specific affirmations: 1) They belong to the family, 2) They are important, having a purpose to contribute, 3) They are worthy of being loved, 4) They are approved of, and 5) They feel protected.

I realized Father God wants to meet those needs in His relationship with us, His children. How amazing is the change in people when they allow Father God to welcome them to life and say these words: *"You are my beloved child in whom I am well pleased"*!

Yet I had to ask myself, "Do the injuries of childhood and early-adulthood development affect one's ability to have a healthy relationship with one's self and others, including God? Do they deafen people to the tender voice of God?"

The evidence mounts that early childhood issues, family-of-origin dysfunction, abuse, neglect and later peer relationships have a definitive negative impact on our ability to change behavior and maintain relationships. How much more our walk with God?

In 1945, Rene Spitz found discouraging results in orphaned human babies placed in non-nurturing environments such as nursing homes. Although their physical needs were adequately met, more than a third died. Twenty-one were still living in institutions after 40 years. Most were physically, mentally, and socially retarded.

In the 1950s Harry Harlow and others experimented with Rhesus monkeys, substituting cloth-wrapped wire-mesh forms for their real mothers. The monkeys bonded or attached to these forms. For those who had the wire mothers, there was no attachment and into adulthood, these monkeys exhibited all sorts of deviant and aberrant, aggressive, antisocial behavior.

Vietnamese orphans taken to France manifested multiple disciplinary problems, especially around bedtime until their caregivers gave them a piece of bread to hold for the night. This is an example of an unmet need at a *root* level, causing multiple behavior issues at a *fruit* level.

Here's the point. How can one trust in a God one can't see, as one's Father, when every single relationship in one's life has distorted Father God's image?

How can you, as a believer, as His child, allow Him to change personal depression, anxiety, obsessive-compulsive behavior, lack of peace, anger, discouragement and hopelessness, when your past training tells you your Father is not there to meet needs, He doesn't care, He remains aloof, and looks to judge? What if your unchanged behaviors are caused by a severed heart, plugged into a world-value system for counterfeit affection that leaves you empty and addicted to trying harder? *What if your early experiences distorted your image of God as Father* so that your life is lived in performance, striving, pretending, possessing, protecting, concealing, and so on all to get "life"?

As noted earlier, this is not a magic wand to wave over every problem. But before heading down other roads looking for solutions to your relational and spiritual issues, try examining your early childhood experiences and damage wreaked on your heart prior to adulthood. And ask yourself, "What am I rooted and grounded in for 'life?'"

The Impact of Original Family on Trust

Regarding original family history, Clinton and Sibcy state that children in their family of origin ask four basic questions and they boil these down to questions asked of every relationship that determines a sense of well-being:

1. Are you there for me? Can I count on you?
2. Do you really care about me?
3. Am I worthy of your love and protection?
4. What do I have to do to get your attention, your affection, your heart? *Be funny*

If these questions apply to our horizontal relationships, why would we think they don't apply to our most important relationship — with God? In damaged trust, original family messages affect our interpretation of words like "love" and "intimacy" and "value/worth" and "importance," morphing them into messages of performance and world value-systems.

To demonstrate the power of early attachment, Drs. Clinton and Sibcy share Bowlby's story of 3-year-old Annie Swan, whose parents left (abandoned) her at a sanitarium in 1948 because of their fear of tuberculosis. Bowlby and his staff began immediately to document specific reactions and realized the impact this would have in Annie's later life.

They write:

> *In response to repeated abandonment Annie and many others like her developed a calloused self. Wounded emotionally again and again, they weren't about to let themselves be hurt again. So they developed a system of replacing things for relationships. Annie, for instance, realized that if she allowed herself to really want her mom, she would be deeply hurt. So she switched her desire from Mom to things – to toys, knickknacks, candy, and coloring pencils. She buried her need for trust, intimacy and closeness. Never again would she willingly reach out to anyone for emotional comfort. Instead she relied only on herself and on the material things she let herself love. Having gotten to know Annie, do you see why we believe that addiction patterns in our lives ARE ROOTED IN THIS KIND OF REPLACEMENT DEFENSE?"*

Annie's story explodes with application to later life and the development of BASIC TRUST. How can one possibly trust God and have a dynamic Christian walk with Him when there is no "rooting and grounding" in GRACE?

Clinton describes three responses that took place in Annie, representative of three progressive stages in the loss of a parent: *protest, despair and detachment.* The final *detachment cannot help but affect a person's ability to be loved by and to love others.* And more importantly, *these affect the ability to abide in a reciprocal relationship with a loving Father in Christ.* That Father, by projection, is the One who must be protested against for abandonment. An abandoned child then feels despair (which by definition occurs in the soul) and ultimately detachment from the Heavenly Father.

In my personal and professional experience, detachment seems to describe many Christians, people going through the motions, looking good on the outside, but full of emptiness on the inside. And they feel guilt-ridden by constant reminders that *they better behave right because they owe Jesus for their salvation.*[90]

If you don't think original family issues can have consequences, then consider this study identified by Josh McDowell, who himself called the doctors at Johns Hopkins Medical School who conducted the research.[91] According to McDowell, "the most significant predictor of [mental illness, hypertension, malignant tumors, coronary heart disease, and suicide] was a lack of closeness to the parents, especially the father." Additionally when there is no relationship with the father, suicide rates in 12- to 14-year-old teens is 300 percent higher. And in 15- to 16-year-olds it jumps to 400 percent higher!

The numbers in my own coaching and counseling verify McDowell's study. Ninety percent of my clients are byproducts of dysfunctional families. Fortunately, we don't wear signs.[92]

The Types of Original Family Systems that Injure

A 1997 counseling brochure from Kansas State University states in part:[93]

> *Most families have some periods of time where functioning is impaired by stressful circumstances (death in the family, a parent's serious illness, etc.). Healthy families tend to return to normal functioning after the crisis passes. In dysfunctional families, however, problems tend to be chronic and children do not consistently get their needs met. Negative patterns of parental behavior tend to be dominant in their children's lives.*

It is important to evaluate your original family structure as it impacts your basic ability to trust. From the six scenarios below, pick out the structure present in your early development and reflect on its results in your life.

1. Parents who are absent or empty

Parents of this type damage their children not so much intentionally, but by simple neglect. They may deal with chronic illness. Job stress may be a factor. They may have never received love in their own lives and just don't know how to give it out. Divorce may have occurred and left a deep, open wound that has never healed, and a child feels abandoned and doesn't understand why.

Frequently, because of the weakness of the parent in these cases, the child is forced to become the caregiver. Oftentimes the parent becomes absent because of job responsibilities, and the child is left in the hands of a grandparent or other caregiver. Sometimes it occurs by the death of the parent; the sense of abandonment is multiplied a hundredfold as the child is left alone to deal with the issues of "Why, God, would you take my _____?"

2. Parents who are passive or apathetic

The passive father/domineering mother combination often produces offspring who struggle with sexual identity issues. Without a strong father welcoming him to manhood, a son often develops anger or ambivalence toward women. A need for attention from someone of the same gender develops. Another characteristic of this system is a lack of discipline and a sense of importance that drives a motivation to achieve or improve. The system also encompasses the apathetic parent who takes little or no interest in the child. This is the parent who is there only to pass down a punishment as a frustrated reaction to the child, without a sense of invested interest. The apathetic parent is unable or unwilling to express love, touch, interest, encouragement and presence.

3. Parents with high need to control

These types of parents come in different shades of the same ORPHAN spirit. They do not view their children as developing people, but as objects that must be controlled. Whether it's from fear, overprotection, a high standard of performance, or just the desire to have power over others, these parents constantly dominate and become the driving decision makers in the life of their child. Their performance orientation allows no failure. The child who doesn't perform is devalued as a person.

Often Christian homes can be the worst in this regard with a "No child of mine is going to act like that" mentality. Outwardly nothing appears wrong, but on the inside, children are living in conflict. And, because it's a "God thing," they typically look really good on the outside, but are full of pain on the inside. Highly authoritarian parents fit into this category. Their families are all about the law and little about the love. I have observed this principle: Law produces rebellion; Love produces relationship. Statistically, prisons are full (95%) of men who hate their parents, especially their fathers. Authoritarian parents breed fear, and they also breed liars. And those kids, when they get old enough, rebel. They will run and never look back.

4. Parents who are angry or bitter at life, or abusive

An example of this parent would be a mother who views an unwanted pregnancy as destroying and controlling her life, handcuffing her to a house and lifestyle she never wanted. Parents who have anger issues are frustrated by children who behave like children. Raised with anger, these children themselves become angry. Sometimes the anger becomes abusive, whether verbal, physical or sexual. Critical, belittling words wound and scar a child's identity. Criticism of how they perform academically or athletically or at any given task, or their giftedness or intelligence or even their basic values produces kids with huge BASIC TRUST issues.

In my experience, the best definition of abuse *is the gratification of the needs of the parent at the expense of the child*. Parents are given responsibility for their children *not* to get their own needs met, but to *train the child for life*. It goes without saying that sexual abuse is the nadir of such selfishness. Here again, the parent's needs are met at the expense of the child. Emotional abuse is nearly equally devastating. Highly negative or critical homes, with parents who seldom affirm, produce kids who have huge self-image problems.

5. Parents with substance-abuse issues

The home of a child of drug abuse — or even more common, child of alcoholics — has no time for the child because of its devotion to the drug of choice. Typical dynamics are: First, the one who has the problem is allowed to continue. Second, the one who identifies the problem by his or her feelings or observations is made to feel like he/she is the problem. Third, the family is expected to keep the problem user a secret ("We don't talk about our issues.") Problematically, the child will typically think that he or she is the problem. Children don't have the objectivity, developmental security or capability to say, "These adults have a problem." Children simply assume that it is their fault. It's like a wounded muscle where all the other tissues have to take the load of the faulty one.[94]

6. Parents who deal with children with partiality.

These parents make no secret about the fact that they prefer one child over another. Parents who are partial are many times the ones who proclaim the loudest they don't treat their children with partiality. Yet, in a few short minutes of observing the family dynamics, watching the smiles and facial expressions, the pats on the back, the looks, the references in conversation, it becomes very obvious as to which of the children are "approved" of and which are not.

"This is my son, he is so successful, and we are so proud of him."

"Oh, this is my other son. We are just not sure what he is going to do; he hasn't figured that out."

"Oh, this is my other son, the musician. We are waiting for him to get a real job."

Consequences of Injurious Family Systems

Each of these systems deals a blow to the child's, and subsequently the adult's, ability to interact relationally on a horizontal basis, and vertically as well. Systems like this rob their members of the expression and understanding of love. Love is the reflection of God's character, and therefore, the system damages the perception of God. The upside-down glasses are on. According to Dr. Paul Hegstrom, the child freezes at that wounded stage of development and shuts down emotionally.

In his book *Forgiving Our Parents*, Dwight Lee Wolter lists the following effects found in children from dysfunctional families:

1. Lack of ability to be playful or childlike
2. Mature too fast or too slowly
3. Mixed modes, such as well-behaved, but unable to care for self
4. Moderate to severe mental health issues, such as depression, anxiety, and suicidal thoughts
5. Addictions (smoking, alcohol, drugs)
6. Bullying or victimized by bullying
7. Denial of severity of family problems
8. Love-hate relationships with family members
9. Tendency toward becoming sex offender
10. Difficulty forming healthy relationships with peers
11. Loner
12. Feelings of anger, depression, isolation, unlovable
13. Speech disorders
14. Distrust of others
15. Tendency toward juvenile delinquency followed by criminal adulthood
16. Tendency to drop out of school

17. Tendency to join gangs
18. Academic struggles
19. Low self-esteem
20. Rebel against parental authority, but uphold family values when confronted by peers
21. Little self-discipline (compulsive spending, procrastination)
22. Unaware of "real world" consequences (more afraid of parents)
23. Run away from home, marry young or get pregnant out of wedlock, end up in abusive relationship
24. Risk of poverty/homelessness (even if family is wealthy or middle class)
25. Self-destructive
26. Tendency to join cults or leave religious upbringing
27. Move far away from family of origin
28. Perpetuate abuses of parents as parents themselves

Gordon Dalbey provides the following illustration:

In a poignant example, Richard Rohr tells of a nun working in a men's prison. One spring, an inmate asked her to buy him a Mother's Day card to send home. She agreed, and word traveled fast; soon hundreds of inmates were asking for cards. Resourcefully, the nun contacted a greeting-card manufacturer, who obliged by shipping crates of Mother's Day cards to the prison, all of which she passed out. Soon afterward, she realized Father's Day was approaching and, thinking ahead, she again called the card manufacturer, who responded quickly with as many Father's Day cards. Years later, the nun told Rohr, she still had every one of them. Not one prisoner requested a card for his father.[95]

Mike Genung, who works almost exclusively with male sexual addicts, writes in his article titled, "Healing Father Wounds":

The reality is that many men grew up without their father's blessing — including those raised in Christian homes. The void that's left by the lack of our father's love is a set-up for a long, hard struggle with sex addiction, workaholism, gluttony or some other false coping mechanism.[96]

Dr. Ross Campbell, a former associate clinical professor of psychiatry at the University of Tennessee, College of Medicine, writes, "In all my reading and experience I have never known of one sexually disorientated person who had a warm, loving and affectionate father." Neither have I. In our support groups I ask the guys to describe their relationships with their fathers, and I can't remember one man who said his father told him "I love you" and hugged him on a consistent basis growing up.

Regarding my own life, I cannot remember ever hearing the words, "I love you," from either of my parents until I was 50 years old. I shared this memory with a group, and a man came up afterward and said, "I still haven't heard it yet." I think of the words of the Apostle John in 1 John 1:20, "For the one who does not love his brother whom he can see cannot love God whom he has not seen."

Shame from Dysfunctional Origins

Typically dysfunctional systems contain a set of common features. At their bottom line, dysfunctional families lack respectful, unconditional love. They commonly lack empathy, understanding, and sensitivity toward certain members, while concurrently over-expressing affection to one or more other members of the family. One member is marginalized while another receives inordinate amounts of attention and affection.

Characteristically these families are high in denial tactics, disrespectful of appropriate boundaries, break important promises, overreact emotionally when someone fails or a conflict occurs. They make mountains out of molehills, dole out unequal or partial treatment, offer appeasement to one who is more emotional than another, excessively use controlling behaviors, and intimidate or induce fear in others to speak what they really think.

Other characteristics include ridicule, conditional love, disrespect, contempt, isolation, intolerance, stifling free speech, being overly protective, discipline based in emotional frustration rather than in healthy avenues. Boundaries or rules that are designed to control another rather than bless them may be present. Value systems are often expressed one way in public and another way at home. Additional evidence is unpredictable emotional anger levels without any explainable cause; blaming one child for the actions of another child; and using children as tools or objects.

Children in dysfunctional homes hear statements like, "You never do anything right," "I could care less," "You didn't just make a mistake, you are a mistake," "You should never have been born," "Do as I say, not as I do," "Just because you say you're sorry doesn't fix anything," "You're a cheater, you're a liar, you're a mess." Another common form emotional abuse opposite of making mountains out of molehills is trying to maintain peace at any price. Some families "play" a "game" with the following rules:

1. You must always be right.
2. You can never be wrong.
3. If you are wrong and have to admit it, blame others.
4. If you are wrong, you didn't just make a mistake, you ARE a mistake and must be rejected, isolated and intimidated.

Beyond all this comes a sense of shame fostered in original family dysfunctional structures. *Shame is internalized guilt. Guilt says I did something wrong, shame says I am something wrong.* Guilt says I made a mistake but shame says I am a mistake. Shame is an acidic emotion that is driven by guilt but in a self-deprecating way.

Imagine getting pulled over by a police officer for a traffic violation. Guilt says, "You broke the law; here is a ticket." Shame says, "You broke the law, and you deserve the death penalty."

Shame is an over-exaggerated emotion of worthlessness. Shame-based people appear outwardly to be very full, but they are empty on the inside. These people find themselves constantly pursuing idols in the world value-system to gain counterfeit affection to fill the emptiness inside. Typically, they are very performance- or presentation-conscious and are exceptionally down on themselves because they feel inadequate and don't measure up.

Shame-based people are typically out of touch with what they really feel. Often they cannot remember much of their childhood, and when they do, it comes in snapshots. These individuals stuff their feelings because they have been taught that it's wrong to express their emotions. Sitting in a room full of people or attending a conference, they feel totally alone and sad. They have a hard time trusting people because people are not safe. For them normal is abnormal and abnormal is normal

— they will even choose abnormal hurtful situations or relationships because it's the only "normal" they have ever known. They are constantly afraid of relationships because of fear of abandonment.

Dysfunctional family systems destroy BASIC TRUST and fill the heart with fear-based responses. They destroy the ability to function or exist in healthy relationships horizontally and vertically. They deeply affect the ability to relate to God intimately. They do so by warping or damaging the meaning of the words GRACE and Love. GRACE has little meaning when assessed through a filter of shame. When one says, "I love you," to another within a dysfunctional belief system, the words mean a multitude of things:

+ There are strings attached
+ There are goals to be achieved
+ There's a performance level to maintain
+ There is an inability to internalize the feeling
+ Emptiness will be momentarily filled but with cravings to follow
+ And a host of other things.

Typically and unfortunately, these shame-based dysfunctional feelings and beliefs are ultimately transferred to one's idea of God. The result is a rollercoaster of addiction to world value-systems and a grossly distorted BASIC TRUST.

But What If ...?

What if we *started* healing our hearts here? This vertical relationship with God as Father brings supernatural healing to our hearts as we start hearing the words, "You are my beloved CHILD in whom I am well pleased." The intimacy of the very word "ABBA" speaks of the Father's desire to hold us in His heart. In Father's Presence we lay down the ORPHAN heart, leave the dysfunctional behavior patterns we learned from struggling parents and grow into what a SON of a Heavenly Father really means.

APPLICATION: LEARNING TO HEAR FATHER'S HEART

Whose picture are you imposing on God? Whose voice do you hear over the sound of His Word? Do you avoid intimate relationships because your parents were unpredictable and explosive? Did you feel out of control as a child?

1. GET SERIOUS: "I will stand and station myself ..." to wait on God.

Consider the following consequences of and responses to your family of origin:

- ✦ First, original family greatly determined your ability as a child to understand, receive and comprehend a personal and healthy sense of self.

- ✦ Second, original family has greatly determined your ability as an adult to build and maintain normal horizontal healthy relationships.

- ✦ Third, by way of response and to bring healing to your heart, you must correctly evaluate your BASIC TRUST level and then make nurturing it a priority in your personal growth plan.

- ✦ Fourth, remember no other relationship is more important than the vertical. Ultimately, good parenting was to be a "skin on" representation of God as our Parent. The parent-child relationship is where unconditional love, respect and support were meant to be modeled for every child.

2. BE FOCUSED: "and I will keep watch to see what He will speak to me."

Imagine yourself sitting across your kitchen table from God, your ultimate Parent. You finally have a chance to ask Him these four family-of-origin questions. How do your think He answers them regarding His feelings for you? Consider how you "hear" Him answer these questions in terms of your perception of Him and how He relates to you.

- ✦ Are You there for me? Can I count on You?
- ✦ Do You really care about me?
- ✦ Am I worthy of Your love and protection?
- ✦ What do I have to do to get Your attention, You affection, Your heart?

3. PRACTICE AUTHENTIC HUMILITY: "how I may reply when I am reproved."

Think of the attachment issues that occurred in those Rhesus monkeys because of the deprivation they experienced. Their early deprivation snowballed into so much bad behavior. Is early deprivation likewise instigating such bad behavior in our society?

Consider your own heart. Has early deprivation arrested your development and caused you to fixate on certain issues? Do early wounds cause a reflexive mistrust of God despite your faith in Him? Remember that BASIC TRUST is the very heart of GRACE. Let Father God lovingly work Himself in your heart. Allow His Peace, the same Peace that Jesus gave us when He said, "My peace I give to you not as the world gives…" Let Father God lean into you and start to heal the injuries and trust issues you have.

4. WRITE IT, CHECK IT, RUN IT: "Record the vision and inscribe it."

Don't forget to journal your conversations with Him. Write down your thoughts and His, and remember to check your journal by sharing it with at least three trusted advisors. Then run in the power of God's Word to you as His SON or DAUGHTER.

CHAPTER 12: SHUTTING OFF TOXIC WASTE

"Do not love the world nor the things in the world. If anyone loves the world, the love of the Father is not in him. For all that is in the world ... is not from the Father but is of the world."

—1 John 2:15-16

SO *how do you do it?* The next chapters explore specific steps to stay centered in the Presence of Father God, allowing His Love to transform you.

Imagine you've just purchased your "dream home," located on acreage with a large pond in the center. You bought the house in winter, and have looked forward to a warming spring to enjoy the lawn and garden, fruit trees, grapevines, flowers, birds and crystalline water. Spring arrives and new life abounds. But soon the trees begin to wither, the vineyard is dying, flowers are yellowing and a stench rises from the pond. Dead fish float to the surface. Something is very wrong.

You test the water and learn it is toxic with poison and is killing everything around it. A report cites four contributing factors:

✦ The fresh-water spring feeding the pond has been blocked by rocks and fill.

✦ Local factory discharge pipes are dumping toxic sludge into your pond.

✦ Your pond was built over an old landfill that leaks into the bottom.

✦ A beaver dam blocks the outflow of water, so the water doesn't drain and remains stagnant.

This pond is a picture of you. Before accepting Christ, you had no LIFE; winter's cold and death filled your spirit. When you accepted Christ as Savior, spring arrived, melting the ice. Your garden came to life. But before long, something apparently went wrong, and your life (i.e. garden) reflected it. Relationships soured, dreams were frustrated, and something below the surface seemed to drift you in wrong directions. Now your life feels yellow, dry and stagnant.

Can it be fixed? The good news is *yes*! *It happens by re-centering in Father's Love, daily getting Life from abiding in the Vine of Christ.* This process *does not happen automatically*; you have to *commit yourself to learn it* as a skill and *choose to make it a daily practice*. But it is very doable. *It is affecting change by transforming from the inside out. And it happens by displacement thinking.* The process looks like this:

+ Recognize that the problem is not the fruit (your behavior); the problem is what the roots are feeding on.

+ So the source of your problem is your source of "life."

+ You can't affect real change by painting the brown fruit to look good.

+ The garden will naturally change when the water becomes clean.

+ Likewise, the garden of your life changes when you displace toxic ORPHAN world value-system thinking with God's Love.

There are two methods of changing human behavior. One is by *conforming* to rituals, religion, requirements, rules, rites, and regulations. This method, based in the Law, is all about *fear* and *reward*. Changes occur from the outside in. Problematically, *the outward man may change, but the inner heart does not.* I call this plastic Christianity. You replace the brown grass with plastic AstroTurf, hang plastic fruit from trees, stock the pond with plastic gold fish, hang plastic grapes, stick plastic flowers in the garden and then start feeling proud about how "godly" you look. You're the same person, except now you're just covered in plastic. People might comment, "What a beautiful garden!" But its beauty is fake, having only the outward appearance of true "life." *The Real*

The best method is inside out, found in the *power verse* of human behavior change: *apple only*

Therefore, I urge you, brothers, in view of God's mercy (God's Love), to offer your bodies as living sacrifices (give Him control), holy (separated from world) and pleasing to God (ultimate goal, not primary) — this is your spiritual act of worship (valuing Him). Do not be conformed (forcing behavior by outside laws) any longer to the pattern of this world, (horizontal value-

*system) but be transformed (changed from the inside out) by the renewing of
your mind (Displacement Thinking) that you may prove (demonstrate
through your life) what the will of God is, good acceptable and perfect. (Par-
enthetical comments mine.)[97]*

Transformation (not conforming to rules) is God's plan for us. The
word *transformation* is derived from the Greek word "metamorphosis"
from two words, META, "change," and MORPHE, "form." Metamorphosis is the process a caterpillar undergoes to become a butterfly. The DNA
of the butterfly is written in the caterpillar. The DNA of Christ is in us.
In Christ, we are already equipped for good works.

Transformation is the process whereby we morph into who we are in
Christ by RENEWING OUR MIND. Beating fear into a caterpillar,
assigning performance rules, creating a list of positive formulas, rewarding with food, etc. will not cause metamorphosis. You can glue wings to
it, send it to butterfly seminars and flight school, and assign reading on
cocoon spinning. You can scream rules at it, but you do very little except
hurt its little ears. None of this will change caterpillars into butterflies.

Every single follower of Christ, born again by God's Spirit, has the
DNA of Father God's Spirit and nature inside him or her. Like the
Prego advertisement of the '60s, "It's in there."

John Lynch, co-author of *Truefaced*, has said, "Because a caterpillar
is a butterfly in essence, it will one day display the behavior and attitudes
and attributes of a butterfly. The caterpillar matures into what is already
true about it."[98]

So what do we do to turn loose that essence within us? In Romans
12:1-2, Paul explains how transformation occurs: 1) *"Do not be conformed
to this world, but …"* 2) "Be transformed *by the renewing of your mind.*"

First, rid yourself of the ORPHAN thinking that longs to be conformed to the world value-system feel-good feelings and, second, renew
the water in the stagnant pond of your thinking. Displace the old with
the new *and you will change.* Picture your mind as that stagnant, stinking
pond. The water is rancid, and nothing healthy grows in the garden of
your horizontal relationships. *Displacement* is the process of pouring in
clean water while draining the toxic water until the pond looks and
smells beautiful, flowers and crops grow, and trees bear delicious fruit.

In your spiritual life, *displacement thinking* (renewing your mind) requires:

1. Shutting off the toxic world value-system appeal and recognizing its counterfeit affections. Identifying the garbage landfill called "sin nature" beneath your garden and breaking its influence. (*Chapter 12*)

2. Re-centering your heart daily in the clear water of Father's Love, learning to abide in Him and live in Him, and renewing your mindset in the knowledge you are a son or daughter. This is where BASIC TRUST will heal and restore. (*Chapter 13*)

3. Pulling weeds (of sin) and breaking rocks (of strongholds) in the springs of God's Word and the flow of His Spirit. (*Chapter 14*)

4. Tearing out the dam and pouring your life into the lives of others. (*Chapter 15*)

Getting started

I want to mention one sidebar regarding trying to change: *chemical imbalance*. The "mind" and the "brain" are two different things. Your brain is an organ in which your mind dwells. How you feel physically influences how you think and how you behave mentally. Your brain is affected by chemicals that influence your behavior — no matter how strongly you may try to change. Just as drinking alcohol impairs your ability to drive a car, naturally occurring chemical imbalances in the brain can do the same. Depressed people often try to overcome their illness by praying more, reading more, serving more, and so on, when the cause is the chemistry of the physical brain.

For years, I suffered with severe migraines and depression. Through fasting, I discovered that corn, rye, blueberries, mushrooms, onions, molds and a few other foods were non-negotiable for me. Perfumes, fragrances, and highly scented soaps also trigger headaches. If I don't want a migraine, then I don't eat corn.

Coffee and caffeine reset our biological clocks, as does sugar with its associated lows and highs. Sleep, diet and exercise influence how we feel. No one can have a life-changing walk with God from the dark fog of a migraine. If you deal with such body-chemistry issues, please consult a qualified physician.[99] I require medical assessments of all my clients before I work with them.

Shutting Off Pipes

You must recognize the ORPHAN-thinking lies you cling to based on the world value-system. As you grow in Christ, you begin to realize that a chemical factory called "The World Value-System Company" is using eight sewer pipes to dump pollutants, toxins and bad chemicals into the "pond" of your mind. And — get this — it's self-deceiving. Not only does the WVS Company pump the toxic stuff into your mind, but the company reps tell you it's OK because you will be able to achieve your dreams.

Those toxic-water pipes are the world's values you embrace. You can't shut down the WVF factory, but you can turn off the valves. So look for the eight world value-system lies splashing from your cup: 1) performance, 2) pretending, 3) possessions, 4) power, 5) praise of men, 6) popularity, 7) priority "me," and 8) people codependency. Call them out for what they are: Idolatry. I am not talking about bowing down to graven images here, but rather the much more common 21st-Century practices of depending on something or someone other than God for "life," valuing the creation over the Creator.

Remember, your task is not to change the pond or the lawn and garden of your life; your job is to cut off the toxic waste being dumped into your mind. You have to stop being defined by the world's values. You do not belong there anymore. The world is not what makes you important. You will never find your value in horizontal relationships. Ultimately, *the world cannot protect you or provide for you.*

The ORPHAN spirit lives to be praised by men. Fiercely competitive, the ORPHAN spirit strives to win at everything. It wants to be stroked. It looks to answer, "What will this do for me?" The ORPHAN spirit longs to be accepted by a significant person. It likes being regarded as special or important. It exaggerates achievements; it maneuvers to get someone's pat on the shoulder; it uses people to get things. It needs to control others to remain copacetic. It desires to, it *must*, control.

Listen to God's Word from Romans 8:6: "The mind set on the flesh is death, but the mind set on the things of the Spirit is life and peace."

Here is one of the primary questions I learned to ask; I call it the WARNING QUESTION: "*Where is that sense of peace and joy and rest that you had?*" If you start using that loss of peace and joy as an alarm system, you will recognize every time the ORPHAN spirit starts grabbing control. The self-exposure is tough, but it's worth it.

We've already examined the "Prodigal Father" of Luke 15:11-32 in Chapter 6. Now, watch these principles come to life in the "Prodigal Son" of the same story. This young, foolish son (we'll call him Younger for short) embraced a set of lies about the world. He "gathered every-thing together and went on a journey into a distant country, and there he squandered his estate with loose living." In such a short statement, we see how the counterfeit affections and their addictive allure had captured Younger's thinking.

First, his ORPHAN spirit — Although he lived in his father's house, he never connected to his father's love. His only desire was to use his father for his own agenda, getting money. Second, his ORPHAN spirit believed he could spend this wealth on himself, his friends and his lifestyle with-out having to work to replace what he was spending. Third, he believed he could live his life in the world without any concerns for conse-quences. Fourth, he believed that his friendships and lifestyle were more secure, fulfilling and rewarding than the love of his father. And lastly, he believed nothing could shake his security.

Unfortunately, "what goes around comes around," and he discovered the consequences of the false vine when "there arose a famine in that land." Famines are inevitable in life. Hard times force us to see the toxic pipelines the WVS Factory is dumping into our hearts. When hard times hit Younger like a tsunami of trouble, all of the eight systems dumped him. Like the addict he was, he ended up feeding pigs, and became so desperate he wanted to eat their swill.

For a proud young Jewish man, this station in life was lower than a rabbit hole in Death Valley. He had chosen the world with all its allure … and then came a famine, and it all withered like grass in desert heat.

The point is: Don't let the world deceive you. Learn to recognize the toxic messages coming in. Feel them inside you. See your own reliance on how well you perform, how good you look, how much you have, how in control you are. Running from good time to good time, compiling a list of friends as shallow as you. Start shutting down the toxic pipes. They are killing the garden of your mind.

To shut off the valves, you have to develop a *Must See It* attitude. Examine what comes out of your cup when you're bumped. Look for every opportunity to discover what makes you Get Big, Get Little, or Get Lost. Become passionate about being brutally honest with yourself.

Start asking the DIAGNOSTIC QUESTION: "*What am I getting 'life' from; what's splashing from my cup?*" When you see something that causes you to Get Big, identify it and realize it's just the world's value-system — not God's. When you see yourself getting irritated by circumstances or by other people, call it out for what it is. Maybe you're running so fast that anyone who gets in your way is blown off the road — call it out. Maybe you are short with your spouse or family because you think your boss has to be pleased — call that out. Maybe you're irritated with how your kids behaved in church because they made you look bad — call that out.

Stop letting such WVS attitudes define you. Father's Love is what you need. Worldly substitutes may stroke your ego, but you can't rely on them. Maybe you think your professional status makes you special, or conversely, your lack of success at work causes you to feel like a failure in every area of your life. Look hard at your life. What worries you? What irritates you? What makes you want to escape? Where do you act in false submission?

Shut off the valves that poison your thinking with WVS lies, or the following principles will be meaningless. Any further steps you take won't shut off the living sewage the world is dumping in. Your pond may look outwardly presentable, yet be full of rottenness. And you and your Father and your family will all know it.[100]

APPLICATION: LEARNING TO HEAR FATHER'S HEART

Dialog with Father for several moments about the pond and garden of your thinking. Are you painting flowers on withered stalks?

1. GET SERIOUS: "I will stand and station myself ..." to wait on God.

Start by shutting off all the outside messages that try to get your attention. When you start looking for the toxic lies, the enemy spirits get very nervous and try to distract constantly. Refuse to heed them, stay in the Word and listen for God's voice. Ask the WARNING QUESTION, *"Have I lost my peace and joy and rest?"* Then ask the DIAGNOSTIC QUESTION, *"What am I getting 'life' from?"*

2. BE FOCUSED: "and I will keep watch to see what He will speak to me."

The ORPHAN spirit infects everything we do. So inhale God's Word, then exhale self-dependence, and ask Father to send His Spirit to open your eyes to your world-based thinking. Look for situations in which you Get Big, Get Little, or Get Lost. Think back over the past week, the last few days and even the last few hours. Make this a practice. Note when you were angry, upset, irritated, sad, depressed. What "life" vine was being threatened? Stand and watch to see the toxins in your life God's Spirit reveals to you.

Once you start seeing the ORPHAN spirit in yourself, you'll see it everywhere. One of my clients called me one day and said, "Jim do you think I have an ORPHAN spirit?"

I wanted to laugh but simply said, "Do you think you don't?"

A week later, he called, dismayed. "I see it in me," he said. "It's all about me, the ORPHAN spirit is in everything I do."

3. PRACTICE AUTHENTIC HUMILITY: "how I may reply when I am reproved."

Take out a piece of writing paper, and ask the Holy Spirit to show you all the areas of ORPHAN thinking evident in your life. Start with a letter to yourself, listing every way you see these eight systems in yourself ... how you have tried to influence and control outside Father's will. List those you have wronged, hurtful things you have done to others, rebellion toward your parents. Pray over each scenario and situation that comes to mind.

As soon as your Heavenly Father shows you a false vine, reply to Him. Tell Him your fears and tell Him your desire to be rid of these toxic pollutants in your life. Ask Him for His powerful help. Ask Him to do through you what you yourself cannot do. SHUT IT OFF! Get angry at those lies — they aren't real and they are addicting. Stop the world value-system thoughts. As soon as you lose peace or joy or a sense of rest, call it as soon as possible.

Dissolve your *self-dependence* into *God-dependence*. Get into the Christ Vine; abide in His Love. Let His joy flow through you and bring you back to peace and rest.

4. WRITE IT, CHECK IT, RUN IT: "Record the vision and inscribe it."

Continue journaling your time with Father God as a life practice. Write it out as He leads you then share it with trusted advisors, godly friends, life coaches, pastors or counselors. Record it so you can run in the strength of God's personal word to you. When you see the false vine and rebuke its lie, be assured of this: Satan will be back with the same lie again and again. Write out your lesson so you don't forget it.

> *ORPHANS can't cut off the toxic pipeline to the world; it's their very "life." They refuse to look at their own behaviors and analyze what makes them Get Big, Get Little, or Get Lost. They are too busy justifying and defending themselves, too plugged into getting "life" from the world.*
>
> *SONS develop an aggressive attitude toward the world. They know the end result of emptiness so they want to cut the lifelines to the false vines as quickly as possible. They learn that the toxic lies never leave a signature of peace and joy and rest, but just more of the same old stuff.*

CHAPTER 13: CLEANING THE POND

"Just as the Father has loved Me, I have also loved you; abide in My love."
—Jesus (John 5:9)

"We have come to know and have believed the love which God has for us. God is love, and the one who abides in love abides in God, and God abides in him."
— 1 John 4:16

Course-Correcting Orphan Drift

LIVING daily re-centered in Father's Love requires understanding our natural, inherent drift — a bent to the human heart — that moves us off-course and away from the center of Father's Love, away from GRACE. It happens moment by moment, day-by-day ... Often imperceptibly ... We drift away.

We must learn to live re-centered in Father's embrace to correct our drift on a regular basis. As a pilot I had to learn a very important principle practiced every day by commercial pilots. The sky can turn nasty quickly, and visibility becomes obscured. When a pilot cannot see in fog, clouds or darkness to orient to his outside surroundings, he must rely on instruments to tell him he is right-side up or upside down.

In normal everyday life, your inner ear and the fluid in it help you maintain balance. Tiny hairs in your inner ear constantly send signals to your brain so you don't lose your balance. When you spin on a bar stool, you become dizzy — a function of the inner-ear/brain connection.

When a pilot is flying blind, the inner ear becomes confused because it is not constantly updating to surroundings. When it gets confused, it convinces the brain that the plane is tilting even when it's not. This phenomenon is called "vertigo." For a pilot, vertigo can have tragic results. In a clouded sky where horizon and ground are obscured, a disoriented pilot can tilt over and crash into the ground, all while believing he or she is flying straight and level.

Many pilots have been killed because of this mistake. The tragic accident in which John Kennedy Jr. killed his wife, her sister and himself is a sad testament to this fact. Had he been trained to use his instruments, he might be alive today. Instead he lost his bearings and plummeted into the sea believing he was flying straight and level. Impact was over 400 miles per hour.

As long as pilots rely on the instruments aviation has developed to keep them flying level, they overcome the drift of their inner-ear messages to the brain. Flying remains safe, fun and profitable.

A similar phenomenon occurs in our Christian walk. We have an inner ORPHAN spirit, the world-oriented flesh, and a sin nature — self-dependence inherited from our original Garden of Eden parents. That ORPHAN spirit drifts toward the world value-system like iron shavings to a magnet. The ORPHAN spirit seeks to affirm us through counterfeit affections, and tells us we are perfectly level spiritually when, in actuality, we are not. Inevitably the ORPHAN spirit, combined with our nature to sin, will cause us to drift off-course. It pulls us toward the allure of counterfeit affections, attempting to get "life" from the world value-system vine, with devastating consequences at times.

Christians live in the world, and our minds will naturally drift off. Therein lies the basis of struggle for the passionate believer who wants to walk with God.

The Christian walk is a *dynamic* relationship with God, *not* a *static* one. We are subject always to this natural drift. "Dynamic" refers to one's ability to stay centered in Father's Love. All Christians, no matter how young or old, must recognize that "flying level" with God requires more than a one-time decision. To think one's life will be free from struggle to stay spiritually on course is sheer naïveté.

Your relationship with God is not static. Picture a marble in a bowl sitting on a table. The bowl gets bumped; the marble moves back and forth and ultimately returns to rest at the bottom. That is how a static relationship would work.

But your relationship with the Spirit is dynamic. So envision an upside-down bowl with the marble balanced on the base at the top.

When the bowl gets bumped, the marble gets jostled and usually falls over the side.

Likewise, when your life gets "bumped" by problems and trials, you don't just rock back and forth a bit and then, effortlessly, automatically re-center and return to rest, back in fellowship with Father and His Spirit. No, *you need to choose to return the marble to the base on top. That is a picture of your re-centered walk with God.*

Your heart is not static. Your ORPHAN spirit springs magnetically toward new ways of influence. Such "bumps" move you away from center. Perhaps you fall over the side — away from GRACE-based thinking and Father's Love, back into law-based thinking. This drifting off-center is dynamic, a gravitational pull away from Father's Love that affects all of us on a daily basis.

Knowing and understanding this natural dynamic drift, you can counter it like a good pilot by applying the tools at your disposal to check that drift on a daily basis.

Re-center: Home to Father's Heart

I use this as my STARTING QUESTION: "I know you *know* God, but do you *believe* He loves you, and are you *experiencing* Him as Father on a daily basis?" As you've just seen, the first step on the road HOME is to identify and shut off the world value-system toxins. Stop getting "life" from them.

The second step follows: You must allow your Heavenly Father to *touch* your heart daily, *re-center* your heart, and *know* that He loves you for who you are and not what you "should" be.

This process is called *displacement*. Shut off the toxic input, and fill your mind with what God really thinks of you, that is *displace* the lies by replacing them with TRUTH. Remember Max Lucado's words — "If God had a refrigerator, your finger paintings would be on it; if God had a wallet, your picture would be in it. Of all the places in the universe He could have picked to build a home, He picked your heart. Face it; He is crazy about you."

You have got to feel this *deep* in your BASIC TRUST: *He loves ME! He even LIKES ME!*

See the Truth about Where You Are — GET UP and GO HOME!

Younger remembered his father's house. Satan will try to keep that memory from you, by the way. He wants you to get so overwhelmed that you forget Father's house. When Younger got low enough, he remembered. Maybe, like him, you've finally hurt enough people and failed enough times to hit bottom. Maybe a failed relationship or business is staring you in the eyes. No matter what bottoms you out, Luke's gospel gives us insight: "But when he came to his senses ..."

Coming to your senses — this is where it starts. It's more than seeing the false affections of the world, it is seeing through your self-defending, self-justifying, self-vindicating denial, seeing the lie of empty counterfeit affections. Luke writes that when Younger looked around and saw the pigs eating their fill, it was a wakeup call. Typically pigs were fed carob pods, and they did not contain enough nutrition to keep a person alive no matter how much he ate!

Just like the WVS: The pigs' food looked like it might relieve his hunger, but it was an empty illusion. What's the illusion in the last straw you're clinging to? God wants you to get low enough to wake up and see through the emptiness of the false vine. But it involves a response. Like Younger, you need to make a decision: "I will get up and go to my Father's house." There it is. Younger got up and headed home, and in doing so began to clear out the springs of his life pond. You need to do the same. Right now ... no matter where you are ... GET UP and GO HOME!

Remind Yourself of the Truth about Father's Love

Jewish literature contained a similar prodigal son story that Jesus and His listeners were well aware of. Only in the version of their day, the story comes to an abrupt end when that Younger gets what he deserves. He is reduced to the low, degrading level of feeding the most unclean animals in Jewish culture and is cut off from the Jewish community and from any financial charity that would have otherwise been offered him. Jesus' Jewish audience was no doubt ready for His story to end with the harsh discipline of Younger getting his just deserts.

The on-looking crowd was expecting the hammer to fall as the story built to its climax. Imagine the shock when Jesus revealed what this

Prodigal Father actually did! They saw Father God's heart in stagger-ingly unexpected ways. Younger got up and went home, and the father he had shamed by leaving, now shames himself by running and embrac-ing him and kissing him.

What lessons are here for us about the mistruths of who God really is? *Many of us think He is mad at us most of the time.* I call it "mad Dad" theology. Listen to how the gospel is so often presented: Jesus died to save us *from the wrath of the Father.* Jesus died *because of the Law of God,* the *character of God* and our opposition to it. His sacrifice covered us in His blood *so the Law of God would not find us guilty.*

I can't find one verse in the Bible that talks about Father's wrath toward be-lievers. In fact, Jesus said in John 5:22, "For not even the Father judges anyone, but He has given all judgment to the Son." Satan would have you believe your Father is always mad at you. Satan fears that you will know the true heart of Father God. Your life pond is polluted partially because of the false images of God you believe.

These four basic mistruths rise from your family of origin and early training. This becomes the foundation beneath damaged BASIC TRUST. This is where God wants to heal you heart:

1. God isn't there for you; He's there for others but not for you. You can't count on God; He will let you down. If you want things done, you have to do them yourself.

2. God doesn't really care about you. He is aloof, apathetic, not engaged, he has no real feeling about what you are doing or go-ing through.

3. You're not really worthy of God's Love or protection. Basically you're not good enough, don't look good enough, can't do things right enough.

4. God expects you to earn His attention, His affection, and His heart for you. He doesn't really care about anything but you measuring up to His high standards and He only gives His bless-ings away sparingly and upon met conditions.

You need to know that none of these mistruths is even remotely true. Yet these are some of the rocks that commonly block the springs into our hearts. When you approach Father God in prayer, is He smiling at you, or frowning? Pleased or disappointed? Learn to see Him as He really is, as Younger's father longing for his child's return: "But while he was still a long way off, his father saw him and felt compassion for him, and ran and embraced him and kissed him."

"His Father saw him."

This says, "You belong." While this sinful son, this wasted individual who fell far short of expectations, was still a long way off, his father saw him. This father was continually looking for his son, daily staring down the road, wistfully wondering and hoping that any moment his son would appear. He might have been wondering — as all parents do — "Where is he now? What is he doing? How is he feeling?"

Is that your impression of God's feelings for you? Do you have a Father like that? Do you realize that God is staring down the road for you, longing to see you, wondering what you're feeling and thinking, hoping that you are coming HOME? Do you realize that just one step in His direction is met by His gaze — not a frown, but a longing to see you? Do you hear those words, "Adam, where are you" in your heart? He loves you; you belong to Him and He wants you back so much. Get up and go HOME.

> ORPHANS *don't realize they have a place they belong — and not just a place, but also a Person, a Father who loves them. So they often return to the pigsty of the world. It's familiar; it's what they know.*
>
> SONS *belong, and they learn to repeatedly run* HOME, *daily, to find Father's assurance and let it bubble deep in their hearts. They know that the Father who loves them IS their* HOME.

"And felt compassion."

This says, "You are approved." Most of God's people don't think He feels compassion toward them. We are convinced He is angry, upset, disappointed, irritated and a bunch of other stuff we believe from an "angry God" theology. This story shows that is not the case. When Younger came into view, his father felt compassion. This is that ache of spirit a parent knows for a child, a longing that can hardly be described. It forms the inner core of all one's other emotions.

In the Greek text it is also in "middle voice," which means *it wasn't just that the father was feeling the emotions, but the emotions themselves were driving the father's heart.* The deep hurt and love he felt for his son was gushing up inside, the pressure of his love was so great. That is God's feeling for you as your Father.

Spending time in prayer focusing on this truth will start to bring clarifying changes to a mental pool filled with the toxic lies of an "angry God" belief system. Present God with that area of your heart that's been focused on original-family abuses or injuries that cloud over His Love. And ask Him to reach in and heal it. Ask Father God to show you His Love, new every morning. Soak in His Presence — don't bring lists; just let Him speak to your heart. He is faithful. He gets you. He loves you and He approves of you. Imagine a political campaign ad from Father God: "You are My child. I love you with all My heart. My Name is ABBA Father, and I approve this message."

> ORPHANS *don't realize Father's approval of them so they spend their lives believing that God is angry, disappointed and frowning.*
>
> SONS *learn that as a child they can look back and often find a Father's smiling face full of* GRACE. *A frown only indicates that a painful experience may lie ahead.*

"He ran."

This says, "You are *important.*" As mentioned in chapter 6, in mid-Eastern culture, fathers are revered, and adult men of any social standing walk with regal stature — they simply don't run, not for any reason, under any circumstance. They must not run, for it is a grave dishonor, demeaning and unbecoming to a man of stature. Older men *never* run. Children and servants may run, but not an adult male, and not a father who has children to run for him.

Culturally, the father *should* turn away. The returning son would be brought, perhaps escorted — humiliatingly emphasizing the crime — to the father's presence, not the other way around. In no instance, would a grown Middle Eastern man take off running with his arms out to greet someone — especially not a son who had shamed him and his family as disgracefully and publicly as this one had done. Furthermore, in order to run, the father would have had to lift his clothing up above his knees held by his hands. Picture this older gentleman ridiculously trying to do that while reaching out with his arms at the same time. Few things could look less dignified than this. Yet, that's what the father in this parable did.

Do you see Father God this way? Perhaps you see Him seated on a throne, looking across the infinity of heaven with myriads attending? He's the Ancient of Days. Can you see His other side, glimpsing you across the room, "running" to greet you? The angels' eyes are wide with wonder! Why would He do that? (Did your heart just sigh in hope?) Because Younger was important to his father — he had significance to his father's heart.

Take a moment to confront the mistruths that you may have come to believe about your Father. Speak directly to them, confess each and every one, and pour out the Love of Father God on each one. Let Father God run to you.

> ORPHANS *would never expect a father to run; for them there is no father who would risk looking bad to accept them. There is no greeting, only a stare, because the* ORPHAN *beliefs are based in past original family and injury lies.*

> SONS *have come to learn that their Father loves them more than He loves the opinions of others, more than the Law, so much so that He sacrificed His only* SON. *Father runs, He seeks, He calls.* SONS *are loved because they have value and worth.*

His father "embraced him."

It had to be one of those hugs that takes your breath away. I imagine him grabbing and hugging Younger with indescribable joy. Sometimes I tell my kids, "I'm just going to hug you right now until your head pops off your shoulders." Of course I don't, but we both laugh and they get it! And I think of how Father longs to hug me, to spend His time with me.

The spirit of lies says, "He wouldn't spend time on little you; you're insignificant; you're too unclean; you're just a little nothing, there is no good thing of value in you." There's the lie again — the ORPHAN spirit.

> *The* ORPHAN *spirit remains aloof because he believes that his Heavenly Father is aloof. There is no compassion expressed, no sense of a deep hug and kiss. That is not possible for* ORPHANS. *They are alone.*

> *A* SON *realizes the embrace of the Father's Spirit and that Father God kisses His* SON's *forehead, holds him close. Why? Because that is what Father's do.*

This father went further "and kissed him."

A father's loving embrace and kiss — it says, "I approve of this young man, not of what he has done, but deeply of who he is."

Let's put this in perspective. Younger stank. His clothes smelled like pig manure. He had spent days walking on a road in the sun and wind. On the farm we would say he smelled "pretty ripe." But even worse, he was stained with the uncleanness that a Jewish man could not touch. He was rebellious and disobedient, smelled un-Kosher, and others were forbidden to hardly even greet him.

Many homes treat a sinning child this way. "I'll not hug you or embrace you or approve of you until you clean yourself up and pay back what you owe me."

Younger learned that he was accepted and approved of. The judgmental anger he expected was not there. In time, his father would deal with the consequences, but not now, and certainly not with critical words or a list of rules and restrictions. Not before he was reconciled and covered in his father's GRACE.

ORPHANS believe that they cannot be accepted or approved of, so ultimately they cannot accept or approve of themselves.

SONS understand that even when they smell bad, their Father holds His arms open and can't wait to hug them. His Love remains firm, and any corrective actions will always be attached to that Love.

If you can't see this, then you don't yet understand Father. That is what He told His SON Jesus to tell you in this parable about His Love for you. You may say, "My sins are too great; I'm a loser; I'm not valuable like that." Stop telling God how He should react to you! It's another lie!

You have no right to tell God He can't love you like that. You simply look up and let Him scoop you into His loving hug — one of those hugs that take away your ability to breathe for a moment. That is God's Love for you. Confront the lie. Father is not your enemy; He is not your judge. He is your Father and He loves you.

When Younger returned home, his father ordered the servants to bring three items. He did not meet him with a list of offenses demanding payment for each loss. He did not say, "Until you pay up, there will be no joy for you. You'll be lucky to sleep in the stables, because I won't even let you sleep in the servants' quarters until every last cent is paid back. And, I will remind you of that list daily."

No! Instead his father embraced him and called out to the servants to:

Quick, "bring sandals for his feet."

This is extremely significant because sandals represented being part of or belonging to the family. Servants did not wear sandals; sons did. Sandals signified membership in the family as one who is accepted and belongs.

> ORPHANS *do not understand that forgiveness means acceptance and belonging. They try to pay back and beat themselves until they have repented enough.*
>
> SONS *understand that they belong to someone. Father's Love is greater than their failures. Coming* HOME *is not an exercise in being rejected and made to feel bad. Love overcomes because Father has waited for their return home. Mercy triumphs over judgment (James 2:13).*

"Bring the robe."

The robe was not only a sense of protection against the elements, but it also represented a covering of love. This robe visually demonstrates whose son Younger is and says that he falls under his father's protection and shield.

I'm sure the older brother wanted to take him out back. Many of the other fathers in town would have wanted to beat him as well. The robe signified the covering of the father's authority and protection.

The Scriptures tell us that God's "banner over us is love."[101] This becomes an assurance that nothing we face or go through will be outside Father's protective grace. Corrie Ten Boom, author of *The Hiding Place*, fondly quoted her sister Betsie's saying, "There is no pit so deep that God's love is not deeper still."[102]

This is the robe God gives us even though we remember our failings, sin, greed and self-centeredness. Father's Love is the oil poured over our heads. Then He puts a mantel of praise on our shoulders. His cloak guards us against exposure. How Father God loves to protect us from exposure to the Law and ongoing condemnation! How He rejoices to cover our sins in the provision of Christ's blood sacrifice!

Another aspect of covering us is the protection of our dignity. People who make mistakes or commit offenses are often made spectacles of in front of family or business associates. Everyone knows "there is the black sheep," the one who can never "get it right." The cloak placed on Younger's shoulders signified "Back off — this one is under my protection."

> ORPHAN *thinking lives in the lies of the past, digging in graveyards of past sins and broken dreams and does not understand the covering and protection that* GRACE *spreads over our shoulders.*

> SONS *arrive at the Father's feet daily, content to remain there, and instead of encountering exposure and fear, they find covering and protection, tasting the sweetness of* GRACE.

"Put a ring on his hand."

In ancient times, the ring was symbolic of the father's authority. The ring indicated that its wearer was appointed to carry out the father's mission in his authority. It designated the wearer's significance as under appointment to accomplish the task or will of its owner. The ring's design provided the bearer with identification and a type of "power of attorney." When Younger went back into the marketplace, he went as a fully trusted legal representative of his father's estate. He could negotiate sales and business with the authority to represent his father.

Jesus commissioned His disciples saying, "All authority has been given to me in heaven and on earth, therefore go. ..." All authority has been given to Christ, and the Scriptures tell us that we are "in Christ." In Him we have been restored, and in Him all authority has been given. And from that authority, He says, "And all things you ask in prayer, believing, you will receive" (Matthew 21:22).

This is an unquestionable statement of significance and importance.

> For ORPHANS *this gracious demonstration of significance is unthinkable. They must work to repay, must live in shame, can never be forgiven let alone restored to a place of authority.*

For SONS this is what living in GRACE does. Whether in daily struggles with the sinister without or the subtle within, there is a place in Father's heart called "restoration."

APPLICATION: LEARNING TO HEAR FATHER'S HEART

Dialogue with Father for several moments about the "pond" and "garden" of your thinking. Are you starting that displacing process of pouring in Father's incredible Love? I know you *know* God but *are you experiencing His Love on a daily basis?*

1. GET SERIOUS: "I will stand and station myself ..." to wait on God.

I repeat, the first step in hearing the Father's heart is to make time with Him a "non-negotiable." Jesus said God promises blessing to "those who hunger and thirst for righteousness, for they shall be satisfied." The promise will be granted if you are hungry and thirsty for Him. Engage in the contemplative time set aside, whether in a busy coffee shop or on a picnic table in a forest campground. Shut down the noise. Rest, sense joy, and let His peace calm the emotional "waves" of your life.

2. BE FOCUSED: "and I will keep watch to see what He will speak to me."

Keeping watch is being ever alert, focused on Father's heart. It is our privilege to simply approach Father God with great confidence. Inhale God's Love for you then exhale self-dependence. Ask Father to send His Spirit to open your eyes to your world-based thinking. Make this a practice. Think back over the past week, the last few days and even the last few hours. Note when you were angry, upset, irritated, sad, depressed — What was the "life" vine being threatened? Have you seen yourself as an ORPHAN or a SON? Stand and watch to see as God's Spirit shows you these toxins in your life.

3. PRACTICE AUTHENTIC HUMILITY: "how I may reply when I am reproved."

As soon as your Heavenly Father shows you a false vine, reply to Him. Tell Him your fears and tell Him your desire to be rid of them. Let this STARTING QUESTION probe your heart: *"I know you know God, but do you believe He loves you, and are you experiencing Him as Father on a daily basis?"*

Meditate on Psalm 73:25-26. "Whom have I in heaven but thee and besides thee I desire nothing on the earth. My flesh and my heart may fail; but God is the strength of my heart and my portion forever." Does that describe you or is it just another verse? Dissolve your *self-dependence* into *God-dependence*. Get into the Christ Vine; abide in His Love; let His joy flow through you and bring you back to peace and rest. Hear what He says to the Church of Ephesus, "I have this against you, you have left your first love … therefore remember … repent … redo."

4. WRITE IT, CHECK IT, RUN IT: "Record the vision and inscribe it."

Don't forget to journal your time with Father God. Write down your dialogue with Him. Picture yourself in a hug so big it takes your breath away, walking with Him as He drapes His arm across your shoulders, accepting you are HOME. See yourself stopping to sit at the side of the road with this Father. Hear Him sniff back tears of relief because you are back HOME. Visualize your joyous homecoming. Every. Single. Day. Re-centered.

IF YOU HAVE NOT APPLIED THE PRECEDING CHAPTER TO YOUR

LIFE, PLEASE DO NOT MOVE FORWARD WITH THIS BOOK.

You will simply turn it into another formula.

CHAPTER 14: LANDFILLS, WEEDS AND ROCKS

Watch over your heart with all diligence, for from it flow the springs of life.
— Proverbs 4:23

LET'S REVIEW: *Displacement thinking* (renewing your mind) requires four steps. Step one is *finding and shutting down toxic world values.* Step two is *displacing the stagnant pond with the pure, clean water of God's Love through re-centering daily in His Presence.*

But obstacles exist that restrict your ability to hear the Father's voice through His Word and His Spirit. It's like discovering a landfill underneath your pond, or realizing that the stream that feeds the pond is choked with weeds and rocks. So you must learn to identify the obstacles in your life, and find additional ways to clean the pond of your thinking, displacing the blockage and renewing your mind in Christ.

Dealing with Landfills

The ORPHAN spirit is a mindset. It finds its life in a lack of BASIC TRUST to let God go to work on one's self. Paul identified this mindset in Romans 8:5-8. The mind set on the flesh (ORPHAN spirit) is death; the mind set on the Spirit is Life and peace. But there is something much more sinister that infects the mind. The ORPHAN spirit loves to serve this nature. Deep below our mind (our "pond") lies an old — very old — landfill. It is called the "sin nature." Paul deals with this in Romans 6:5-11.[103]

There are three primary cracks from the landfill beneath our lives. We all have them. The Apostle John identified them when he wrote, "For all that is in the world, the *lust of the flesh,* and the *lust of the eyes,* and the *pride of life,* is not of the Father, but is of the world." (Italics mine.)[104]

You can see all three in Younger's words when he goes to leave:

No please

*The younger of them said to his father, 'Father, give me the share of the estate (*lust of the eyes*) that falls to me.' So he divided his wealth between them. And not many days later, the younger son gathered everything together (*boastful pride*) and went on a journey into a distant country, and there he squandered his estate with loose living (*lust of the flesh*).*

Below the level of the three basic desires lurks a core of sin. Problematically (and frankly, sinister), the ORPHAN spirit feeds on this core sin nature and will do anything to deny its existence, cover up its influence and excuse its effects. But as I took brutally honest inventory of my life, I began to see what sin's core really is — *selfishness.* Plain and simple, it is *me putting my will above my Father's will. It is self-dependence.*

Christian counselor Troy Reiner writes:

If we accept the fact that, as a minimum, sin is the basis of at least all psychological problems that result from our free choices, then what is the basis of sin? It is based on our free choice to try to direct our own lives in order to meet our needs without God. Each of us is driven to meet our most fundamental psychological needs of the self: love, security, worth and significance. Attempting to meet these needs of the self, in our own strength, is called self-centeredness or selfishness, and it lies at the core of our sin nature. These needs provide the motivation for everything that we do or attempt to do in the flesh. (Emphasis mine.)[105]

This makes sense to me. The core of my being is *selfishness!* Self-exalting, self-promoting, self-defending, self-sufficient, self-justifying, self-protecting, self-oriented. Once I began seeing my motives in this way, I could see them in others as well.

We can see this sin nature in the prodigal son. Younger began with the words, "give to me." Below the world value-system attractions, came the essence of the problem, the very nature to sin against God. It sounds like this: "Gimme, gimme, gimme, I want, I want, I need, I need, I need, I have to have, I can't live without, I have my rights, it's mine, I want it now …" Ultimately it's about me, my dreams, my goals, my agenda.

The core of sin is self-dependence. At the core of a severed heart is the self-dependence that — like Adam and Eve's — seeks to gain "life" and meet the emotional needs of "life" from the eight world value-systems identified in Chapter 3. The core drive behind Adam's original sin was in Satan's temptation, "In the day you eat you will be like God, knowing good and evil." You will be self-sufficient, no longer dependent; you will be just like God.

Really? Adam and Eve were already like God, created in His likeness. "Let us make man *in our likeness,*" God said at Creation. They already were like God. The key to Satan's deception is that he told them they could be like God based on their own self-effort, their own choice.

Dealing with the sin nature is like driving a car toward an intersection. The "Walk" sign is flashing in its countdown toward "Don't Walk." Then comes a yellow light followed by a red. The time to catch "gimme, gimme, gimme" is at the yellow, or better, when the Holy Spirit is flashing "Don't Walk." When you run the light, it can be devastating to you and others. Sometimes you get by with it, but sooner or later it gets you. Then BAM!

Waiting to deal with a sin behavior by veering away at the last minute before impact involves a much greater struggle. Sometimes, you will be too late to avoid sin's effect, and you'll crash. Injury and damage result. The emotional desires of sin grow exponentially as you get closer to acting on them. Once you express the sin, the emotions are nearly unstoppable. This is especially true when the sin has become a habitual behavior, as in an extramarital affair. Trying to sidestep emotional attachment at the action level is like trying to steer a car away from impact after you have run the light.

Unfortunately, much of this teaching in our churches remains centered on behavior modification and does not actually touch the root of the problem. Interestingly, most counselors and coaches and parents focus on behavior control but few get to the root. Researching hundreds of articles, I found hardly any references to the actual core of sin: selfishness, self-centeredness, and self-dependence. The closest I found was a statement by John Stott that "sin is a form of selfish revolt against God's authority [and] our neighbor's welfare."[106]

The good news of the Word of God is that the connection of the landfill to your pond is broken in the death of Christ. However, the landfill itself has not been removed. It still lurks, full of those lusts on the ready to seep through the cracks and pollute your pond. But your pond is protected by a powerful sealant in the Holy Spirit, who keeps the seepage out so long as you maintain your connection to Him.

As a non-believer, I was chained to my own agenda, connected to the landfill of my own self-dependency and self-sufficiency. In the death of Christ, sin's power was broken; the chain was cut. My old sin nature still lurks nearby, ready to seep its influence back into my mind and the seat of my desires, but its connection to me has been severed by Christ's powerful redemptive work. It's up to me to choose through *displacement thinking* to keep the sealing influence of the Holy Spirit in place to protect me moment by moment.

Pulling weeds

Another problem with your pond is that weeds and rocks may be blocking the stream feeding it. As Proverbs 4:23 says, "Watch over your heart with all diligence, for from it flow the springs of life." So you need to watch over your heart and keep the movement of God's Word and Spirit flowing through.

Today's world offers so many temptations and opportunities to fulfill them — things contrary to God's will and His Word, that is, sins. Isaiah 59:2 describes the seriousness of succumbing to these temptations: "Your iniquities have separated you from your God; your sins have hidden His face from you, so that He will not hear."

But Psalm 119:9-11 provides a solution:

How can a young man keep his way pure? By keeping it according to Your word. With all my heart I have sought You; Do not let me wander from Your commandments. Your word I have treasured in my heart, That I may not sin against You.

Founder of Cru (formerly Campus Crusade for Christ) Dr. Bill Bright taught a simple but effective process called "Spiritual Breathing." It is contained in what was affectionately known as "the blue booklet" describing "How to Be Filled with the Spirit." Recognizing that young Christians could easily be misled by up-and-down emotions, Dr. Bright provided a simple three-step process consisting of 1) desiring to live a life pleasing to the Lord, 2) surrendering one's life "totally and irrevocably" to Jesus, and 3) confessing "every known sin" brought to mind by the

Holy Spirit. Steps 1 and 2 are part of inhaling, confessing sins is exhaling.[107]

Dr. Bright also urged believers to make a list of their sins by letting the Holy Spirit reveal them, writing them down, accepting God's promise of forgiveness, destroying the list and then making restitution where necessary. Personally I believe that the process of Spiritual Breathing should also include reading and listening to God's Word. No spiritual growth can occur apart from being able to answer the question "What does God say?"

Breaking Rocks

Have you ever rafted or canoed down a stream only to come upon a narrow spot blocked with boulders and rocks slowing the flow of water? You have to stop, get out and carry your vessel around the blockage to where the stream can run freely again. Several strongholds act like blockages in the streams that feed your "pond." These strongholds in the displacing/renewing process in your mind are like huge rocks covering the springs of your heart. They distract you, diverting your attention, slowing your spiritual attention to a stop. They must be addressed in your journey into Father's Love.

In 2 Corinthians 10:3-5, the Bible identifies strongholds or fortresses in our minds:

> *For though we walk in the flesh, we do not war according to the flesh, for the weapons of our warfare are not of the flesh, but divinely powerful for the destruction of fortresses. We are destroying speculations and every lofty thing raised up against the knowledge of God, and we are taking every thought captive to the obedience of Christ.*

These mental fortresses are built over many years and encased in thick layers of emotional cement. By my own personal definition a stronghold is "a reflex, belief or structure of thinking which influences our actions, encased in emotional experiences (cement), and requiring no rational thought on our part." It's like a reflex. I'm so used to mentally responding a certain way that I simply don't rationally think about the action or the consequence before I do it.

Dr. Paul Hegstrom provides an excellent description of this process in his book *Angry Men and the Women Who Love Them*. According to

Hegstrom, people perceive information through their senses, which begins the process of deciding what action to take. They rationally think about it, and decide what they feel emotionally. Their intuition is involved, along with logical consideration of pros and cons, possible consequences and decisions to get more information if they need more data.

An almond-sized gland called an amygdala resides in the core of the brain, helping to sort this incoming information and associating it to prior experiences, feelings, and/or past conditioning. The amygdale is like a fortress, controlling one's reflexive behaviors and will reflexively make a decision to act without consulting rational thought, allowing past desire and wounds to become driving forces in one's life.

Here in the amygdale, strongholds exist. They are entrenched, tough and hard, like rocks in our streams. And Satan loves to enthrone himself in the center of these fortresses. Destroying them requires intentional and focused actions that retrain one's brain to do as Paul describes in the passage above.

The strongholds I encounter in my practice with clients are typically:

+ Perfectionism — always having to have things done correctly, because when they are not it is a statement about who I am. I am who I am because I do things precisely, correctly and with little or no margin for failure.

+ Anger — the uncontrolled expression of frustration that injures others and causes us personal damage, expressed without thinking. Anger is the emotion used to conceal or control, manipulate, protect. It is related to apathy, despair and hopelessness.

+ Unforgiveness — the inability to forgive another person, to carry the memory of injury and loss thus affecting one's walk with God and relationships to others. Part of this stronghold is the inability to practice the skill of reconciliation in relationships with others. It is a sister to bitterness and resentment.

+ Immorality — the willing giving over of my physical body or mind to sexually impure thoughts and actions.

+ Rebellion against Authority — inability to respond positively to authority, specifically to a father or mother, teachers, pastors and other leaders God has placed in one's life.

- Rights — inability to live a surrendered life because standing up for what one sees as one's just due is so over-riding.

- Dissipation — misuse of time and the inability to prioritize. Procrastination, laziness and escapism.

- Idolatry — the inability to give up the world values and worshipping or valuing created things more than the Creator.

- Comparison — comparing oneself to others in any way. It's the "rocket fuel" of shame, a powerful stronghold. God establishes one's value and nothing else should have that right.

- Strongholds of Disrespect — lying, bearing false witness, stealing another's property or time, and other actions that demonstrate a breaking of the commandment "Do to others as you would have them do to you."

- Denial — probably the greatest stronghold of all — the inability to look at one's self first, taking ownership of specifically what one has done wrong *before* looking at and blaming others.

If you recognize any of these in your life, then let this be an exhortation to seek out a life coach, trusted pastor, someone who can walk through the process of self-examination and *displacement thinking* with you. Like an old cow in Nebraska, people return to habits of thinking until the trails are deeply entrenched. The thought patterns encased in emotional cement are hard to break, but it can be done. You must break out.

These strongholds can be broken, but in my practice I have found it takes two years, and typically success comes when one consults a godly, well-trained counselor or life coach. I love working with people in this process because the joy, peace and rest on the other side are amazingly freeing.

APPLICATION: LEARNING TO HEAR FATHER'S HEART

Dialogue again with Father's Spirit for several moments about the "pond" and "garden" of your thinking. Are you experiencing His Love and Presence? Are you shutting off the world's values? Clearing the sins in your life daily through confession? Smashing stronghold thinking? Have you figured out the core of your nature, self-dependency? I know you *know* God but *are you experiencing His Love on a daily basis?*

1. GET SERIOUS: "I will stand and station myself..." to wait on God.

Get serious. Get absolutely determined that you are going to seek God with all your heart. Again, the first step in hearing the Father's heart is to make time with Him a "non-negotiable." Shut off the white noise, all the distractions. Find a time when you can stand with firm resolve. Rest, sense joy, and let His peace calm the emotional "waves" of your life. Make this a priority as though you are a guard standing watch over his city. I recommend a book by fellow life coaches Lindon and Sherry Gareis, *Declutter Your Life Now* (Ambassador International, Greenville, SC) who have written extensively about this subject.

2. BE FOCUSED: "and I will keep watch to see what He will speak to me."

Start the listening process. Tell the Lord, "I will to hear You, Father, and You alone." Acknowledge your enemies: the world, your personal sins, self-dependency, and doing things because they "feel" right. Start expecting Him to respond. Watch for it. Look for His touch in your life. Be patient with Him. What you think is a problem may only be superficial. He may want to probe into another place or far deeper.

3. PRACTICE AUTHENTIC HUMILITY: "how I may reply when I am reproved."

Hear yourself talk. "Gimme, Gimme, Gimme ... I want, I will, I need, I can't deal with, I don't like, I can't stand, I can't take, I can't go on, I won't, I have my rights, I don't have to put up with, I'm better than this." Bottom line — the quest is "It's about me." What will this do for me? What do I get out of it? How will this make me feel better? This is the essence of the sin nature and the ORPHAN spirit. They are subtle, sinister, self-defending, self-vindicating, self-promoting and self-righteous. Want to see what it looks like? Take out a pad of paper and ask the Holy Spirit to go over the past week or month and point out all the times you said, "I will, I will, I will, I will ..." Exactly what Satan said to God in Isaiah 14.

Regarding strongholds ... healing your heart in these areas is literally a rewiring process. It takes time and help from those who know what they are doing. Under the conviction of the Holy Spirit, you begin to see the things you are doing. Reading and learning from qualified teachers is a powerful shortcut.

4. WRITE IT, CHECK IT, RUN IT: "Record the vision and inscribe it."

Don't forget to journal your time with Father God. Picture yourself talking to Him at a kitchen table. Say this: "Father, can we get real? As my Father, please show me those areas that my ORPHAN spirit wants to control. Show me sin areas I need to deal with. Help me see my strongholds." Let Him be what He so longs to be ... your trusted ABBA Father. He's the One who loves you and rejoices over you. Write what He reveals to you.

The "rewiring" process takes time and help from others. It wasn't easy for me. But I urge you to stick with it. The results are amazing.

CHAPTER 15: TEARING OUT BEAVER DAMS

Beloved, let us love one another, for love is from God; and everyone who loves is born of God and knows God. The one who does not love does not know God, for God is love ... If God so loved us, we also ought to love one another. No one has seen God at any time; if we love one another, God abides in us, and His love is perfected in us.

— 1 John 4:7–12

HAVE YOU ever seen a beaver dam? Ever had to tear one down? God has so gifted these creatures that when they build a dam, it is like Fort Knox. Many ranchers resort to dynamite to destroy them.

In preceding chapters, you learned to "abide in the vine" to live in God's Presence. Foundational to abiding is *knowing, experiencing* God's Love for you as Father, as Savior and as indwelling Spirit. From that foundation flow the disciplines of being in the Word, hearing God's voice, and the power of prayer.

The Prodigal story featured another son, "Elder." He is an interesting study because ... now please hear this ... he lived in the father's house but never in the father's heart.[108] While Younger was out living the extravagant life, Elder thought he had it all together, but deep in his heart was another form of the ORPHAN mindset. Elder wasn't able to receive his father's love and give it away to others in random acts of humility.

Elder had built up a mighty "beaver dam" of resentment, unforgiveness, self-pity, and self-absorption, to name a few. Beaver dams consist of those things that stop us from pouring out our lives, giving ourselves for others. We plug up the outflow, and the result pollutes our mindset, our "pond." Without an outflow, the pond remains stagnant and increasingly murky.

For example, both the Galilean Sea and the Dead Sea are fed by the same river, the Jordan. But while the Galilean Sea remains a tourist resort area, full of fish, plants, fun and life, the Dead Sea is, well, dead. The difference? The Galilean Sea expels its water at its southern end.

The Dead Sea only takes in water, and never releases any; its waters accumulate so much salt and minerals it is nearly impossible to submerge oneself beneath its surface.

So how can you break up the beaver dams in your life?

Open Your Outflow Valve into Relationships with Others

Jesus said it repeatedly — Your relationships matter. You must stay up-to-date with forgiveness and reconciliation *with others to remain centered in Father's Love for you.* Although we can't control others and how they act toward us — hurts and disappointments they cause us, betrayals they may inflict — *we can control how we act and react to others*, especially those who injure us. Injuries come in all forms, from the daily "bumps" of spouses, children, parents or co-workers to the "nuclear fallout" from betrayals, malicious injuries and even physical abuse. We may not be able to stop the injuries from occurring, but how we react to those injuries is crucial.

To stay re-centered in Father's Love, you must learn to love others no matter what. The Apostle John wrote in 1 John 4:20, "If someone says, 'I love God,' and hates his brother, he is a liar; for the one who does not love his brother whom he has seen, cannot love God whom he has not seen." The love you have and extend to others is a direct reflection of your love for God. Mistreating or overreacting to others devastates the daily re-centered heart, knocking the marble off the base of the bowl, so to speak. That marble won't find its way back to the top on its own.

Confess Your Masks

The next step in transformational change is to learn to challenge the self-defending masks we wear so readily. We must learn how denial causes us to drift from being centered in Father's Love and then learn how to dissolve those denial systems. By denying, self-defending, self-justifying, self-promoting, or self-guarding we keep the painful truth about who we really are or what we have done from changing our thinking. We don't want to think we are the problem. We want our issues to stem from someone or something else.

This process shields us from the truth that would make us feel bad. We must understand the serious nature of the mind mechanism, and that denial is the greatest of all spiritual, mental, and emotional strongholds against change. Denial protects us from the painful revelation of who we really are and thereby keeps us from discovering the lies we believe and live.

I often ask people these questions: "Look behind your life, the road you have taken. How many enemies do you see? How many have you left wounded? How many did you step on to get where you are? How many people were hurt because of you?"

One senior V.P. replied, "Man, my kids don't even want to be around me." But rather than stop everything to change the situation, he simply went back to wearing his mask, his moment of vulnerability over. His work was his "life."

The masks we wear in denial keep us from becoming honest with ourselves. Even with coaches and counselors skilled at penetrating people's shields, we refuse to drop the mask. We use these deceptive defense mechanisms to avoid facing issues of fear, guilt, failure, emotional pain, embarrassment, or the realization we have hurt others.

When we drop the mask, we become vulnerable. We stop trying to make ourselves look good to others, including God. We open up our defenses and let a few trusted people in to see who we really are. And we drop the pretense that we are somehow better than others. We let people speak into our lives.

We drop the mask because we are crucified in Christ, and a crucified man or woman has nothing to gain, no reason to try to make people think he's something special. We open our hearts to listen to others' thoughts of us. We stop hiding and covering and protecting and shielding and defending and justifying and vindicating. "He that covers his sins shall not prosper; but whoever confesses and forsakes them shall have mercy."[109]

Points About Mask Wearing

Wearing masks requires a lot of emotional energy. It takes much effort to keep ourselves from being vulnerable to others. Someone has said, "Anger is the emotion we use to conceal and to control." That is very true. Anger is the emotion of aggressive self-sufficiency; it is the emotion of strength to protect, as opposed to dependence upon God.

This aggressive emotion is used to conceal things that we are afraid others will discover. We keep people at arm's length and are guarded in our conversations. We have learned from experience that many people are untrustworthy with our hearts and feelings. So we wear false faces.

Though we may not be entirely aware of it, deep inside we know only the mask is loved or respected by others, and we are not loved, accepted, approved of, etc. *for who we really are.* We fear that if others knew who we really are inside, with our frustrations and hurts and secrets, they would reject us in a New York minute. When we're asked, "How are you," we respond, "Oh I'm fine, just fine." Someone has said, "FINE" really means, "I'm Freaked out, Insecure, Neurotic, and Emotionally unstable."

Here's the problem: Mask wearers never understand or experience intimacy and connectedness with others. It is impossible for you to know someone in an intimate, connected way when both of you are wearing masks. You can never be welcomed into others' lives as you truly are. I see this in many marriages where two people have learned how to not say something that will make the other person mad. They want people to think they have a great marriage, but in reality one or the other has acquiesced to the other's will.

As our closest relationships, marriage and family are where we demonstrate our relational abilities to connect, to go deeper. This is particularly true with men — husbands and fathers. Men wear masks because for them intimacy means vulnerability and loss of respect. Because they hold up the mask of being "fine" with other people, when they try to develop a relationship with God they find it cold and mechanical. Because I see the mask of denial so often, I have great respect for guys who have developed teachable honesty in their lives.

The word "hypocrite" comes from the Greek word for actor. In ancient Greece, all actors were males, even for female parts. They would simply hold masks in front of their faces to play whatever role was needed. So actors were "hypocrites," people behind masks pretending to be what they were not.

ORPHANS live behind lots of masks, because if they ever let their defense down, they will be exposed to criticism or anger or law, and ultimately they won't belong, won't be important, won't have value, won't be acceptable and won't be protected.

For a SON life is simple. GRACE melts the mask, and kindness leads to ABBA's Presence. SONS know they don't have to care what others think because they are okay with their Father.

Recognize the Masks You Wear and What They Look Like

Masks are denial mechanisms in our thinking — lies to keep us from facing the truth. Here is a list of "mask words" and what they represent:

Mask Words We Use:

"Leave me alone!" (*Isolation, Withdrawal*)

"I don't want to talk about it!" "Don't talk to me!" (*Closed conversation*)

"I'm always to blame; you think you're perfect and never do anything wrong." (*Shifting focus onto another*)

"You are just too sensitive." (*You are the problem*)

"Well, it happened a long time ago." (*Implying it doesn't matter anymore*)

"It wasn't all that important." (*Belittling the act*)

"They made me do it." (*Blaming others for a personal wrong act*)

"There was no other way out." (*Justification of wrong*)

"It was just a little white lie." (*Putting evil on a scale*)

"He/she does not deserve forgiveness." (*Trying to balance the scale*)

"It was only a one-time experience." (*Rationalization*)

"You just don't understand my situation." (*Situational ethics approach*)

"I couldn't help it. I was having a bad day." (*Blaming situation as an excuse*)

"I just lost control temporarily." (*Trying to balance evil with good*)

"Everyone does it." (*Using comparison*)

"I am just human." (*Indirectly blaming God*)

"My opinion is just as good as the next person's." (No absolute right)

"They deserved what I did to them." (*Trying to balance the scales*)

"It's all your fault." (*Blaming others without accepting personal responsibility*)

"Somebody needed to put them in their place." (*Pride covering revenge*)

"I don't have a problem. You are the one with the problem." (*Shift of blame*)

"It was just a practical joke, okay?" (*Denial of intent to do harm*)

"Can't you take a joke?" (*Shift of blame*)

"Well, no one is perfect." (*General comparison to shift the point away from guilt*)

"Everyone needs to let off a little steam sometimes." (*Excuse for anger and violence*)

"Who is he/she to say that I am wrong?" (*No one has authority, or no absolutes*)

"I have the right to do anything that I want." (*Authority unto one's self*)

"I just needed a pick-me-up." (*Excuse for using drugs*)

"I can't help it. My parents were that way." (*Denial of personal responsibility/failure to recognize generational strongholds of sin*)

"You just need to get with it." (*Implies that moral absolutes change with time*)

"I say, if it feels right, do it." (*Morality based upon emotions*)

"Why should I suffer when they can do what they want?" (*Comparison of privileges*)

> ORPHANS *are too busy protecting themselves, trying to look good and feel good based on performance, power or possessions to seek godly counsel or coaching. Therein lies part of the reason they never change.*
>
> SONS *deeply value the input of others — those who are likeminded in their pursuit of Christ and are mentors to assist in dealing with past pain, mistakes, or future steps in their walk with God.*

Beware of Elder Brother Syndrome

If you find yourself drifting away from re-centering in Father's Heart, examine your heart for signs of slipping into Elder's attitude. He lived in their father's house, never leaving, never having a party, practicing all the laws and rules he thought would impress his father, yet never understood his father's heart. With all his hard work, he couldn't see his own critical, bitter and angry spirit. Instead of enjoying the intimacy of home he practiced "should" thinking, concentrating on all the things he and his brother should be doing.

Yes, Younger valued their father only for the cash, and as soon as he received it he was out of there. Yet Elder actually *had the same heart hidden behind performance and outward appearances*! He dwelt in his father's house *but never understood his father's heart* or the motives that drove his father's dealings with others.

Elder was just as clueless about their father as Younger. Elder may have chosen not to act out, but his heart was the same as his brother's. He was probably judgmental, perhaps critical, and may have exhibited an angry edge in his dealings with others. That's what happens when we work to make ourselves look good, but don't experience the Father Heart of God.

I imagine Elder frequently using Younger as the brunt of his judgmental and, dare I say, religious spirit, putting him down, condescendingly finding ways to make himself look better at Younger's expense. When Younger comes home, Elder can't begin to understand why their father doesn't judge him harshly.

We, too, may begin to think that others are more sinful than we are. I find that the longer people are believers, the more they tend to exhibit elder-brother judgmentalism. They show up at church, put money in the offering, attend Sunday school, teach classes, even pastor churches, all the while looking down on others. Like Pharisees, they may think, "I thank You, God, that You didn't make me like that guy over there." I myself write this material with great caution; for in condemning Elder's behavior, I easily slide into my own ORPHAN spirit.

The essence of dwelling in Father's house is not proximity and location, being physically there. It's about back-and-forth relationship. Often during ministry times, I have to stop and allow the Spirit to examine my heart. Am I singing for You, Father, or just going through the motions? Am I teaching with Your heart, staring at Your face, searching for Your smile, or am I looking for the world's approval? Do I give to Your ministry with cheerfulness or am I doing it because You will bless me if I do, or get me if I don't?

See how it works? Elder brothers do the job without the joy of intimacy with Father God. They bow their heads in duty but have long forgotten (or never known) the delight of just being Father's SON. They go through the motions of godliness, but deny its power. They observe rituals and duties, but don't have that sense of joy and peace because they are caught up in Elder Brother Syndrome.

> ORPHANS *love to look good and perform well, so they adapt easily to the elder brother role. They become irritated and frustrated when another is welcomed home, because those who don't perform well or haven't paid the price don't deserve to be loved.*

> SONS, *on the other hand, recognize that maturing in Christ brings another set of responsibilities.* SONS *are learning to humbly accept the failures of others, while joyfully living in the Father's house learning His heart.*

Three Principles of Abiding

You can't give away what you don't own. Learn to be loved by Father and then you can learn to love others like He loves them. My life has become about receiving His Love then giving it out to others in acts of humility and kindness. That's what Jesus did. When I abide in His Love and love as He did, I get Life in return. Do you want to abide in Christ? Then follow these principles:

1. Abide in His Love and love others.

"Just as the Father has loved Me, I have also loved you; abide in My love" (John 15:9). "We love, because He first loved us. If someone says, 'I love God,' and hates his brother, he is a liar; for the one who does not love his brother whom he has seen, cannot love God whom he has not seen. And this commandment we have from Him, that the one who loves God should love his brother also" (1 John 4:19-21).

2. "Watch what God does, then you do it, too, like children who learn proper behavior from their parents.

"Mostly what God does is love you. Keep company with Him and learn a life of love. Observe how Christ loved us. His love was not cautious but extravagant. He didn't love in order to get something from us but to give everything of Himself to us. Love like that" (Ephesians 5:1-3, MSG).

3. Father is opposed to the proud but gives grace to the humble (James 4:6).

> ORPHANS *worship their work, and work at their play, and play at their worship. They use people and love things.*
>
> SONS *learn to reflect Father's Love for others. They use their things to love others, and live by the mission statement of "Receiving His Love, I give it away to others in random acts of humility."*

APPLICATION: LEARNING TO HEAR FATHER'S HEART

1. GET SERIOUS: "I will stand and station myself ..." to wait on God.

Make the determined decision to take a specific amount of time to be alone with God. Write in your calendar an appointment to be alone with God and to stand; station yourself in that place.

2. BE FOCUSED: "and I will keep watch to see what He will speak to me."

Focusing is the skill of listening intently to what He wants to say to you. Focusing on Him means learning to see Him in your spirit. You shut off all the voices and concerns and distractions that vie for your attention. You cannot hear God's voice, or sense His influence and Presence in your life when your eyes and ears are filled with the demands of others and the world. Picture yourself sitting beside Jesus at Jacob's well, meeting Him just as the Samaritan woman did. Put yourself into the scene, walking along the shores of the Galilean sea, and hearing Him speak to your heart the kinds of things He said to His disciples.

3. PRACTICE AUTHENTIC HUMILITY: "how I may reply when I am reproved."

Learning to hear reproof from the Lord is not easy and sometimes it comes through others. And the Holy Spirit is not particular about whom He uses. You will learn the most from those who love you if you listen. You'll even learn from those who stand against you, people who are irregular and even obstinate. Proverbs 6:23 and 12:1 clearly state: "For the commandment is a lamp and the teaching is light; and reproofs for discipline are the way of life," and "Whoever loves discipline loves knowledge, but he who hates reproof is stupid."

Three of the actions points used by various 12-step programs may prove useful to you here:

1. Make a list of people you've harmed, and be willing to make amends to all of them. Jesus would agree: "Do to others as you would have them do to you" (Luke 6:31).

2. Make direct amends to such people whenever possible, unless doing so would injure them or others. Again Jesus urges you to act: "Therefore, if you are offering your gift at the altar and there remember that your brother has something against you, leave your gift there in front of the altar. First go and be reconciled to your brother" (Matthew 5:23-24).

3. This is an ongoing process, not a once-and-done thing. Continue to take personal inventory, and promptly admit when you are wrong. Paul encourages such humility in 1 Corinthians 10:12: "So if you think you are standing firm, be careful that you don't fall."

4. WRITE IT, CHECK IT, RUN IT: "Record the vision and inscribe it."

Don't forget to journal your time with Father God. Picture yourself talking to Him at your kitchen table. Say this: "Father can we get real? As my Father, please show me those areas that my ORPHAN spirit wants control. Show me sin areas I need to deal with. Help me, Father, to see my strongholds." Let Him be what He so longs to be ... your trusted ABBA Father, the One who loves you and rejoices over you. Write what He shows you and speaks to you.

Healing your heart in these areas is literally a rewiring process. It takes time and it takes help from those who know what they are doing. Self-help can accomplish some change, but it is slow and frustrating. *Please consider using a qualified counselor or coach to help in this process.* It isn't easy. It wasn't for me. But the results are worth the pain of stripping off the masks and allowing Father, Son and Holy Spirit to apply GRACE to reveal His Life shining through.

A FINAL WORD: WINNERS USE COACHES

IT'S SUCH a simple formula. Winning competitors know if you want to win big, you get a coach. And there is NOTHING more important than winning at life. I wish I had understood this before I inflicted so much pain on myself and others.

Over my years as a pastor and counselor, I have seen the amazing GRACE of Father's Love — when comprehended, applied and practiced — bring about transformational changes in people's lives. I have been surprised at how quickly people change as they start "getting it" (that is, understanding the value of displacing the ORPHAN spirit, correcting the lies of original-family training, and allowing Father room in their lives). I have also discovered that it takes some time for these disciplines to soak into the fabric of one's belief system. This transformational process is not instantaneous. Developing new patterns of thinking that actually and dramatically change one's life takes years.

I have found I move back into fear and hopelessness, moving off center as soon as I start listening to the father of lies. Life is then reduced to digging in the dumpsters of the world to find counterfeit affection through aggressive striving, competition, and comparison. *When I am off-center, I worry about what I do, how I look, what I feel, what I have, whom I know, who likes me, whom I please, and what I control rather than Whom I trust.* I become a person whose ORPHAN spirit is either striving for control or being controlled by horizontals. The evidence is the "splash from my cup" because there is no peace, no rest, no joy, no freedom, no truth and no Love.

So how can you learn to live as if you have a HOME, as a SON letting that Father-SON relationship work itself out through the pores of your life? Henri Nouwen often said, "You will either live your life as if you have a home or you will live your life as if you don't have a home."

The foundation of the Keys4-Life ministry is learning to daily re-center in Father's Love, where you return every morning to hear, "You are the child I love and in whom I am well pleased." In that place, all you need and want is to be centered in Father's Love and Presence. Simply stated, on a daily basis, you go HOME. You live in Father's embrace at the center of His heart. He is the center of your universe, and there you get LIFE every day. This is your true vine. This is where you abide. HOME is where you realize security, comfort, provision, protection, rest, affirmation, acceptance, belonging, inheritance and identity. It is a place of light and warmth and intimate Love with Father.

Counselors help us deal with our pain; *coaches* help us identify and pursue our potential. Counseling is about *past pain*; coaching is about *future potential*. I urge you to seek a godly counselor or coach for your life. Name a successful NFL team that has no coach. Name a successful athlete with no coach. Most successful marriages get help along the way.

The word "idiot" comes from the Greek word IDIOTES. When a town assembly was called, everyone would close up shop and go to the village center for the latest news, civil decisions, and cultural involvement. These citizens were called the EKLESSIA, meaning the called-out ones. EKLESSIA is the same word the Bible uses to identify Christians, the ones "called out" by God. People who didn't get involved, couldn't be bothered, were called the IDIOTES.

Stop being an idiot. Stop hanging back; engage your growth in Christ! Find a counselor or a coach or other godly person with whom you can sit in Bible study. Be part of their small group and learn from their mistakes. If I could point to the one thing that walked me out of my dysfunctional past, it was that I pursued the truth from any source I could find. I refused to be an idiot.

So Refuse to Live Like an ORPHAN. You Are God's CHILD.

I also, finally, refused to live like an ORPHAN, trying to live the Christian life in my own, ridiculously insufficient strength. I realized that, in the words of Gordon Dalbey,

> *Only the Father God of all time can deliver a man from generations of destruction into manhood — that is, from being abandoned to being a son (see*

Rom. 8:14-16). He's done this in Jesus on the cross, and will do it for any man who invites Jesus into his father-wound. Indeed, Jesus has stepped decisively into the path of the snowballing Goliath, letting it smash against himself and thereby breaking its power over fathers and sons alike. Jesus came to restore relationship with the Father — that is, to remind men abandoned and unfathered for generations that we are beloved sons.[110]

Dalbey reminds us of the key to living and walking in Father's GRACE, the key that unlocks the chains that bind us to our old sin nature and to the father of lies who wants to keep us that way. We were not forgiven our sins at a point in time and left to figure out how to live life on our own. But we are SONS of the living God, adopted into His family and invited by His Number One SON along with "the sinners and the publicans in the kingdom" to call Him, "ABBA, dear Father."

Let's close this book remembering where we started: "You will live your life as if you have a HOME or you will live your life as if you don't." This isn't a once-and-done fix; this walk with Father is a journey. What is your occupation — teacher, manager, engineer, worker, policeman, medical practitioner, missionary, firefighter, pastor, leader, marketing/sales rep, professional speaker? Does your career define you? Or is your goal in life to just be a great SON or DAUGHTER and leave the results to God? Check your self-image. Is it centered on SONSHIP? If not, then question your heart. Fall in love with Father again. Make your life a journey HOME and determine to live now and forever like you have a HOME, you belong, you're important, you have value, you're appreciated and protected there.

And walk the walk HOME, to experience ABBA's Presence in your inner spirit, to live in ABBA's house, an ORPHAN no more.

APPENDIX

A. YOU CAN HEAR GOD'S VOICE!

(*Adapted from* 4 Keys to Hearing God's Voice *by Mark and Patti Virkler.*)

CHRISTIANITY is unique among religions, alone offering a personal relationship with the Creator beginning here and now, and lasting throughout eternity. Jesus declared, "This is eternal life — that they may know God" (John 17:2). Unfortunately, many in the Church miss the great blessing of fellowship with our Lord, having lost the ability to recognize His voice within them. Despite the promise that "My sheep hear My voice," too many believers are starved for that intimate relationship that alone can satisfy the desire of their hearts.

I was one of those sheep who was deaf to his Shepherd until the Lord revealed four very simple keys (found in Habakkuk 2:1-2) that unlocked the treasure of His voice.

Key #1 – God's voice in your heart often sounds like a flow of spontaneous thoughts.

Habakkuk knew the sound of God speaking to him (Habakkuk 2:2). Elijah described it as a still, small voice (I Kings 19:12). I had always listened for an inner audible voice, and God does speak that way at times. However, I have found that usually, God's voice comes as spontaneous thoughts, visions, feelings, or impressions.

For example, haven't you been driving down the road and had a thought come to you to pray for a certain person? Didn't you believe it was God telling you to pray? What did God's voice sound like? Was it an audible voice, or was it a spontaneous thought that lit upon your mind?

Experience indicates that we perceive spirit-level communication as spontaneous thoughts, impressions and visions, and Scripture confirms this in many ways. For example, one definition of PAGA, a Hebrew word for intercession, is "a chance encounter or an accidental intersecting." When God lays people on our hearts, He does it through PAGA, a chance-encounter thought "accidentally" intersecting our minds.

Therefore, when you want to hear from God, tune to chance-encounter or spontaneous thoughts.

Key #2 – Become still so you can sense God's flow of thoughts and emotions within.

Habakkuk said, "I will stand on my guard post..." (Habakkuk 2:1). Habakkuk knew that to hear God's quiet, inner, spontaneous thoughts, he had to first go to a quiet place and still his own thoughts and emotions. Psalm 46:10 encourages us to be still, and know that He is God. There is a deep inner knowing (spontaneous flow) in our spirits that each of us can experience when we quiet our flesh and our minds. If we are not still, we will sense only our own thoughts.

Loving God through a quiet worship song is one very effective way to become still. (Note 2 Kings 3:15.) After I worship and become silent within, I open myself for that spontaneous flow. If thoughts come of things I have forgotten to do, I write them down and dismiss them. If thoughts of guilt or unworthiness come, I repent thoroughly, receive the washing of the blood of the Lamb, putting on His robe of righteousness, seeing myself spotless before God (Isaiah 61:10; Colossians 1:22).

To receive the pure Word of God, it is very important that my heart be properly focused as I become still because my focus is the source of the intuitive flow. If I fix my eyes upon Jesus, the intuitive flow comes from Jesus. But if I fix my gaze upon some desire of my heart, the intuitive flow comes out of that desire. To have a pure flow I must become still and carefully fix my eyes upon Jesus. Again, quietly worshiping the King, and receiving out of the stillness that follows quite easily accomplishes this.

Fix your gaze upon Jesus (Hebrews 12:2), becoming quiet in His Presence and sharing with Him what is on your heart. Spontaneous thoughts will begin to flow from the throne of God to you, and you will actually be conversing with the King of Kings!

Key #3 – As you pray, fix the eyes of your heart upon Jesus, seeing in the Spirit the dreams and visions of Almighty God.

Habakkuk said, "I will keep watch to see," and God said, "Record the vision" (Habakkuk 2:1-2). Habakkuk was actually looking for vision as he prayed. He opened the eyes of his heart, and looked into the spirit world to see what God wanted to show him. This is an intriguing idea.

God has always spoken through dreams and visions, and He specifically said that they would come to those upon whom the Holy Spirit is poured out (Acts 2:1-4, 17).

I had never thought of opening the eyes of my heart and looking for vision. However, I have come to believe that this is exactly what God wants me to do. He gave me eyes in my heart to see in the spirit the vision and movement of Almighty God. There is an active spirit world all around us, full of angels, demons, the Holy Spirit, the omnipresent Father, and His omnipresent Son, Jesus. The only reasons for me not to see this reality are unbelief or lack of knowledge.

In order to see, we must look. Daniel saw a vision in his mind and said, "I was looking ... I kept looking ... I kept looking" (Daniel 7:2, 9, 13). As I pray, I look for Jesus, and I watch as He speaks to me, doing and saying the things that are on His heart. Many Christians will find that if they will only look, they will see, in the same way they receive spontaneous thoughts. Jesus is Emmanuel, God with us (Matthew 1:23). It is as simple as that. You can see Christ present with you because Christ is present with you. In fact, the vision may come so easily that you will be tempted to reject it, thinking that it is just you. But if you persist in recording these visions, your doubt will soon be overcome by faith as you recognize that the content of them could only be birthed in Almighty God.

Jesus demonstrated the ability of living out of constant contact with God, declaring that He did nothing on His own initiative, but only what He saw the Father doing, and heard the Father saying (John 5:19, 20, 30). What an incredible way to live!

Is it possible for you to live out of divine initiative as Jesus did? Yes! Fix your eyes upon Jesus. The veil has been torn, giving access into the immediate Presence of God, and He calls you to draw near (Luke 23:45; Hebrews 10:19-22). "I pray that the eyes of your heart will be enlightened...."

Key #4 – Journaling, the writing out of your prayers and God's answers, brings great freedom in hearing God's voice.

God told Habakkuk to record the vision (Habakkuk 2:2). This was not an isolated command. The Scriptures record many examples of individuals' prayers and God's replies (e.g. the Psalms, many of the prophets, Revelation).

I call the process "two-way journaling," and I have found it to be a fabulous catalyst for clearly discerning God's inner, spontaneous flow, because as I journal I am able to write in faith for long periods of time, simply believing it is God. I know that what I believe I have received from God must be tested. However, testing involves doubt, and doubt blocks divine communication, so I do not want to test while I am trying to receive. With journaling, I can receive in faith, knowing that when the flow has ended I can test and examine it carefully, making sure that it lines up with Scripture.

You will be amazed when you journal. Doubt may hinder you at first, but throw it off, reminding yourself that it is a Biblical concept, and that God is present, speaking to His children. Relax. When we cease our labors and enter His rest, God is free to flow (Hebrews 4:10). Sit back comfortably, take out your pen and paper, smile, and turn your attention toward the Lord in praise and worship, seeking His face. After you write your question to Him, become still, fixing your gaze on Jesus. You will suddenly have a very good thought. Don't doubt it; simply write it down. Later, as you read your journaling, you, too, will be blessed to discover that you are indeed dialoguing with God.

Some final notes: Knowing God through the Bible is a vital foundation to hearing His voice in your heart, so you must have a solid commitment to knowing and obeying the Scriptures. It is also very important for your growth and safety that you be related to solid, spiritual counselors. All major directional moves that come through journaling should be confirmed by your counselors before you act upon them.

*****

For a complete teaching on this topic, order the book *4 Keys to Hearing God's Voice* at www.CWGministries.org or call 716-681-4896. An online catalog of 60 books by Mark & Patti Virkler as well as 100 college courses through external degree is available at www.cluonline.com.

B. EPHESIANS 3:14-21, PARAPHRASED

I bow my knees before You, Father, from Whom
every authority in heaven and on earth derives its name,
that You would grant me,
according to the riches of Your Extravagant Glory,
to be strengthened with power through the intimacy of
Your Holy Spirit in my inner man,

so that I, by faith, may experience
Christ dwelling daily in my heart;

(having been and continuing to live)
rooted and grounded in love

so that I, (by faith) may comprehend, seize, possess as my own
the breadth and length and height and depth,
and to experience
the intimacy of Christ's Love for me
which surpasses all knowledge,

so that I (by faith) may experience being
filled up to all the fullness of God.

Now to YOU, Father, the One Who is able to do
far more abundantly beyond all
that I can ask or think,
according to the power that works within us,

to You, Father, be the glory both in us,
and in Christ Jesus to all generations forever and ever.
I receive this today, and I believe it,
Amen.

C. FATHER'S LOVE LETTER

(Adapted from a compilation of Scriptures as a sermon illustration by Barry and Anneliese Adams in January 1999.)

The words you are about to read are true.

They will change your life

if you let them.

For they come from

the heart of God.

He loves you.

He is the Father you have been looking for all your life.

He longs for you to come to Him.

This is His love letter to you.

My Child…

You may not know me, but I know everything about you. **Psalm 139:1** I know when you sit down and when you rise up. **Psalm 139:2** I am familiar with all your ways. **Psalm 139:3** Even the very hairs on your head are numbered. **Matthew 10:29-31** For you were made in my image. **Genesis 1:27** In me you live and move and have your being. **Acts 17:28** For you are my offspring. **Acts 17:28** I knew you even before you were conceived. **Jeremiah 1:4-5** I chose you when I planned creation. **Ephesians 1:11-12** You were not a mistake, for all your days are written in my book. **Psalm 139:15-16** I determined the exact time of your birth and where you would live. **Acts 17:26** You are fearfully and wonderfully made. **Psalm 139:14** I knit you together in your mother's womb. **Psalm 139:13** And brought you forth on the day you were born. **Psalm 71:6** I have been misrepresented by those who don't know me. **John 8:41-44** I am not distant and angry, but am the complete expression of love. **1 John 4:16** And it is my desire to lavish my love on you. **1 John 3:1** Simply because you are my child and I am your Father. **1 John 3:1** I offer you more than your earthly father ever could. **Matthew 7:11** For I am the perfect Father. **Matthew 5:48** Every good gift that you receive comes from my hand. **James 1:17** For I am your provider and I meet all your needs. **Matthew 6:31-33** My plan for your future has always been filled with hope. **Jeremiah 29:11** Because I love you with an everlasting love. **Jeremiah 31:3** My thoughts toward you are countless as the sand on the seashore. **Psalms 139:17-18** And I rejoice over you with singing. **Zephaniah 3:17** I will never stop doing good to you. **Jeremiah 32:40** For you are my treasured possession. **Exodus 19:5** I desire to establish you with all my heart and all my soul. **Jeremiah 32:41** And I want to show you great and marvelous things. **Jeremiah 33:3** If you seek me with all your heart, you will find me. **Deuteronomy 4:29** Delight in me and I will give you the desires of your heart. **Psalm 37:4** For it is I who gave you those desires. **Philippians 2:13** I am able to do more for you than you could possibly imagine. **Ephesians 3:20** For I am your greatest encourager. **2 Thessalonians 2:16-17** I am also the Father who comforts you in all your troubles. **2 Corinthians 1:3-4** When you are brokenhearted, I am close to you. **Psalm 34:18** As a shepherd carries a lamb, I have carried you close to my heart. **Isaiah 40:11** One day I will wipe away every tear from your eyes. **Revelation 21:3-4** And I'll take away all the pain you have suffered on this earth. **Revelation 21:3-4** I am your Father, and I love you even as I love my son, Jesus. **John 17:23** For in Jesus, my love for you is revealed. **John 17:26** He is the exact representation of my being. **Hebrews 1:3** He came to demonstrate that I am for you, not against you. **Romans 8:31** And to tell you that I am not counting your sins. **2 Corinthians 5:18-19** Jesus died so that you and I could be reconciled. **2 Corinthians 5:18-19** His death was the ultimate expression of my love for you. **1 John 4:10** I gave up everything I loved that I might gain your love. **Romans 8:31-32** If you receive the gift of my son, Jesus, you receive me. **1 John 2:23** And nothing will ever separate you from my love again. **Romans 8:38-39** Come home and I'll throw the biggest party heaven has ever seen. **Luke 15:7** I have always been Father and will always be Father. **Ephesians 3:14-15** My question is…will you be my child? **John 1:12-13** I am waiting for you. **Luke 15:11-32**

Love, Your Dad
Almighty God

D. How Jesus Honored the Father

(Adapted from Humility, *by Andrew Murray.*
http://www.worldinvisible.com/library/murray/5f00.0565/5f00.0565.c.htm)

- ✦ Luke 2:49 From His early life it was the emphasis of His focus. "Why is it that you were looking for Me? Did you not know that I had to be in My Father's house?"

- ✦ Jn. 3:35 Father loves the Son and has given all things into His hands.

- ✦ Jn. 5:17 When healing the paralytic He answered the leaders, "My Father is working until now, and I Myself am working." In verse 18, the Jews try to stone Him for making Himself equal to God.

- ✦ Jn. 5:19 "Truly, truly, I say to you, the Son can do nothing of Himself, unless it is something He sees the Father doing; for whatever the Father does, these things the Son also does in like manner."

- ✦ Jn. 5:20 "For the Father loves the Son, and shows Him all things that He Himself is doing ; and the Father will show Him greater works than these, so that you will marvel."

- ✦ Jn. 5:21 "For just as the Father raises the dead and gives them life, even so the Son also gives life to whom He wishes. For not even the Father judges anyone, but He has given all judgment to the Son, so that all will honor the Son even as they honor the Father. He who does not honor the Son does not honor the Father who sent Him."

- ✦ Jn. 5:30 "I can of My own self do nothing; My judgment is just, because I seek not Mine own."

- ✦ Jn. 5:41 "I receive not glory from men."

- ✦ Jn. 6:38 "I am come not to do Mine own will … but the Father's will and the Father honors me."

- ✦ Jn. 7:16 "My teaching is not Mine but His Who sent Me."

- ✦ Jn. 7:28 "I am not come of Myself … The Father sent me … I am from Him, come from Him and am sent by Him."

- ✦ Jn. 8:28 "I do nothing on My own initiative, but I speak the things My Father has taught Me."

- ✦ Jn. 8:38 "I speak the things which I have seen with My Father."

- ✦ Jn. 8:42 "If God were your Father, you would love Me for I proceeded forth and have come from God, for I have not even come on My own initiative, but He sent Me."

- ✦ Jn. 8:50 "I seek not Mine own glory."

- ✦ Jn. 12:49 "For I did not speak on My own initiative, but the Father Himself who sent Me has given Me a commandment as to what to say and what to speak."

- ✦ Jn. 14:8 Jesus to Philip, "If you have seen me you have seen the Father."

- ✦ Jn. 14:8-10 "The words that I say, I speak not from Myself."

- ✦ Jn. 14:24 "The word which ye hear is not Mine."

- ✦ Jn. 14:28 "The Father is greater than I."

- ✦ Jn. 14:30-31 "I will not speak with you much longer, for the prince of this world is coming. He has no hold on Me, but the world must learn that I love the Father and that I do exactly what My Father has commanded Me."

- ✦ Jn. 15:8 The goal of Christ's ministry was that we would honor Father. (Mt. 5:16, also John 14:13 prayer.)

- ✦ Jn. 15:15 "All the things I have heard from my Father I have made known to you."

- ✦ Jn. 15:23 Hating Jesus is the same as hating the Father.

- ✦ Jn. 17:3 Eternal life knows Him.

- ✦ Jn. 20:21 "As the Father has sent Me, so also I send you."

E. GOD'S GAMBLE

(From Truefaced: Trust God and Others with Who You Really Are *(Colorado Springs, CO: NavPress, 2003) by Bill Thrall, Bruce McNicol and John Lynch*

God says, "What if I tell them who they are? What if I take away any element of fear in condemnation, judgment, or rejection? What if I tell them I love them, will always love them? That I love them right now, no matter what they've done, as much as I love my only son? That there's nothing they can do to make my love go away?

"What if I tell them there are no lists? What if I tell them I don't keep a log of past offenses, of how little they pray, how often they've let me down, made promises that they don't keep? What if I tell them they are righteous, with my righteousness, right now? What if I tell them they can stop beating themselves up? That they can stop being formal, stiff, and jumpy around me? What if I tell them I'm crazy about them? What if I tell them, even if they run to the ends of the earth and do the most horrible, unthinkable things, that when they come back I'd receive them with tears and a party?

"What if I tell them that if I am their Savior, they're going to heaven no matter what — it's a done deal? What if I tell them they have a new nature — saints, not saved sinners who should now 'buck-up and be better if they were any kind of Christians, after all he has done for you!' What if I tell them that I actually live in them now? That I've put my love, power, and nature inside of them, at their disposal? What if I tell them they don't have to put a mask on? That it's ok to be who you are in the moment, with all their junk. That they don't need to pretend about how close we are, how much they pray or don't, how much Bible they read or don't. What if they knew they don't have to look over their shoulder for fear if things get too good, the other shoe's gonna drop?

"What if they knew I will never, ever use the word punish in relationship to them? What if they knew that when they mess up, I will never 'get back at them?' What if they were convinced that bad circumstances aren't my way of evening the score for taking advantage of me? What if they knew the basis of our friendship isn't how little they sin, but how much they let me love them? What if I tell them they can hurt my heart but that I never hurt theirs? What if I tell them I like Eric Clapton music too? What if I tell them they can open their eyes when they pray and still go to heaven? What if I tell them there is no secret agenda, no trapdoor? What if I tell them it isn't about their self-effort, but about allowing me to live my life through them?"

F. ATTACHMENT THEORY

Attachment theory gained influence in the late 1950s when Harry Harlow started asking childhood development questions. He believed that early infancy and childhood bonding had exponential consequences in the development and life of children, deeply affecting how they related as adults. Two of his contemporaries, John Bowlby and Mary Ainsworth, were also studying and expanding this concept. Ultimately they named it attachment theory. According to Bowlby, "Attachment can be defined as the strong bond that develops first between parent and child, and later in peer and romantic relationships."

They demonstrated conclusively early deprivation of needs produces injury and/or a vacuum in the heart that lasts through adulthood. When the inner heart has been deprived of appropriate parenting there is an inability to deal with life in a healthy way, and this inability acts out at varying levels of severity.

In the late 1950s Harlow began his experiments using Rhesus monkeys at the University of Wisconsin. His research basically took monkeys from their mothers and placed them in a cage where they had all their physical needs met, but their form of attachment or bonding was controlled using different mothers: a terrycloth mother, a human substitute, or a monkey made out of wire mesh. I actually saw movies of these experiments in my Psychology 101 class at the University of Nebraska. I remember being told these experiments were finally shut down because the impact of the lack of bonding in a baby monkey through early childhood began manifesting itself in some very aberrant and aggressive ways. The behaviors crossed a wide spectrum from being constantly anxious, fearful, depressed, angry, unable to adapt to a group when introduced to others, antisocial behaviors, all the way to extreme schizophrenia and aggressive sexual aberrancies including rape and homosexuality. Robert Hatfield provided a description of this in his paper:

> *"In his original classic 'wire mother' study, Harlow placed the touch deprived monkeys in a large cage that contained two crude dummy monkeys constructed of wood and chicken-wire. One dummy was bare wire with a full baby bottle attached. The monkeys had been regularly nursed from similar bottles. The other dummy was the same as the first except that it contained no bottle and the chicken wire was wrapped with terry cloth. Placed in this strange environment, the anxious young monkey very quickly attached itself to the cloth wrapped dummy and continued to cling to it as the hours passed by. The infant monkey could easily see the familiar baby bottle no more than a few feet away on the other dummy.   Many hours passed. Although growing increasingly distraught and hungry, the infants in these studies would not release their hold on the soft cloth of the food-less dummy. It was soon apparent that the young monkeys would likely dehydrate and starve before abandoning the terry cloth surrogate mother. As the isolated monkeys grew older, they were observed to display a highly predictable constellation of behavioral symptoms, even when they were later reunited with their mother and social group. ... They included: highly unusual patterns of self-clasping and self-morality; idiosyncratic patterns of repetitive stereotyped activity; an almost total lack of gregariousness or interest in exploring the environment; timidity and withdrawal from virtually all social situations with concomitant self-directed stereotyped behaviors; obvious aversion to physical contact with others; hyper-aggressivity; gross abnormalities in sexual behaviors; and later in adulthood, the inability to nurture offspring, with failure to nurse, neglect, and abusive behaviors being highly predictable. In addition, negative physical health consequences and hormonal imbalances ... have been noted in these primate studies."*

In documenting the consequences of early lack of bonding and its affects, Bartholomew in 1990 expanded the consequences of attachment theory and came up with four behaviors that remain throughout life if the attachment is not there. He identified quadrant one as Secure, with Preoccupation, Dismissing and Fearful as the three other quadrants of human behavior. What if the behaviors we are trying to change are due to primary beliefs and training?

In their article, Hazan & Shaver, working in early adult development with Bartholomew's attachment theory categories, state the following: "Secure adults find it relatively easy to get close to others and are comfortable depending on others and having others depend on them. Secure adults don't often worry about being abandoned or about someone getting too close to them. Avoidant adults are somewhat uncomfortable being close to others; they find it difficult to trust others completely, difficult to allow themselves to depend on others. Avoidant adults are nervous when anyone gets too close, and often, love partners want them to be more intimate than they feel comfortable being. Anxious/ambivalent adults find that others are reluctant to get as close as they would like. Anxious/ambivalent adults often worry that their partner doesn't really love them or won't want to stay with them. Anxious/ambivalent adults want to merge completely with another person, and this desire sometimes scares people away."

Again, is it possible that there is a drive in adults at that BASIC TRUST level that produces this sense of anxiety and a sense of hopelessness?

Another such study concluded, "Intimate relationships formed during infancy, childhood, adolescence, and young adulthood give rise to continuing relationships, and ultimately to individual development. These life stages are associated with richer bodies of knowledge about intimacy than any other."

Rene Spitz explored the development (or lack of development) of institutionalized children. In the 1945 study involving human babies, Spitz followed the social development of babies who, for various reasons, were removed from their mothers early in life. Some children were placed with foster families while others were raised in institutions (e.g., a nursing home). The nursing home babies had no family-like environment. The setting was very institutional. Care was provided by nurses who worked eight-hour shifts. The babies raised in the nursing home environment suffered seriously. More than a third died. Twenty-one were still living in institutions after 40 years. Most were physically, mentally, and socially retarded. (Spitz, R.A. *The First Year of Life*)

The internet site "eHow" stated the following information:

"Touch deprivation is the lack of physical interpersonal contact. Infants who experience touch deprivation may face social and psychological developmental challenges. According to BabyZone.com, infants who are not handled enough may develop depressive symptoms, anger and aggression problems that last into adulthood. According to research published in 1998 in the journal Cutis, *people with the skin condition psoriasis who experienced touch*

deprivation as a result exhibited increased rates of depression. According to research published in 2002 in the journal Adolescence, children who experience touch deprivation, physical abuse and neglect may display impulsive, aggressive behavior; such behavior is associated with increased rates of depression. According to Dr. Robert W. Hatfield, Ph.D. of the Department of Psychology of the University of Cincinnati, children who experience touch deprivation may grow to be adults who are not physically nurturing."

G. VARIETIES OF MASKS PEOPLE WEAR

- *Anger outburst*: the use or expression of anger (voice tone, cursing, facial expressions, body gestures, aggression, and violence) to control a person or situation.

- *Analyzing*: an attempt to explain the cause for one's failure, believing that that may resolve the issue. "I have thought long and hard on the problem and believe that it must have been precipitated from my exposure to too much violence on the TV."

- *Arguing*: bringing up a controversy to sidetrack the other individual. "My position is that ... don't you agree that I am right?" (while knowing well he/she will disagree).

- *Blaming*: laying the judgment for one's problems upon someone else. "I would be a better husband if I had a better wife. It is all her fault."

- *Compensation*: to excel in one area as a cover for inferiority in another. "I know I'm not too great at math, but I do really well in art class."

- *Compliance*: giving in to the wishes of another to avoid confrontation. "OK, I will do whatever you want."

- *Defiance*: daring others to prove that you are wrong. "I challenge you to show me in the Bible where it says that smoking marijuana is wrong." It's being highly controlling or intimidating so that others never get past the mask.

- *Displacement*: transferring a strong emotion from a precipitated object to a safer or more acceptable substitute. (The husband becomes angry at his boss at work then goes home and gripes at his wife.)

- *Distortion*: changing the shape of a reality to make it more acceptable; over-exaggerating a positive spin on things. "Officer, I was just trying to keep up with the other traffic."

+ *Explaining*: describing the problem in minute detail, thinking that may resolve the problem. "I first began to look at porn when I was eight years old. Then when I was 10, I found some of my dad's girlie magazines. When I was 15, I met this girl who was really into pornography and we looked at it and acted out some. Then when I got a computer ..."

+ *Excuses*: the use of logic that may appear to be acceptable to avoid an issue. "I think you can find someone more skilled than I to choose for the project."

+ *Fantasy*: daydreaming or imagining an escape from reality into a fictitious world, a world of success or pleasure. "When I find myself in a bad situation like this, I just like to imagine that I am on a warm beach, sun bathing with the sound of the waves washing away my problems." (This may develop into schizoid fantasy.)

+ *Humor*: making a joke out of a grave or hurtful situation; laughing to cover fear or pain. "It was just a joke. :-) I was just kidding."

+ *Idealization and Identification*: the over-estimation of desirable traits in another. "I would love to be like that person. She does everything so well."

+ *Intellectualization*: the avoidance of unconscious conflicts by the excessive use of an intellectual guise of words, thoughts or debate. "The current research by Dr. So-and-So from Such-and-Such University shows that the reason why people like me get so depressed is because there is a chemical imbalance."

+ *Introjection*: is to assume responsibility for events outside their realistic control. "It's all my fault that our marriage was a failure." A surviving passenger of a plane crash says, "If I hadn't worn this green shirt, the plane wouldn't have crashed."

+ *Isolation*: splitting off a strong negative emotion or mental image from one's consciousness. Being out of touch with one's emotions. In extreme cases there may be Multiple Personality Disorder. "I really feel sad, but I can't figure out why."

+ *Judgmentalism*: placing others on a lower spiritual level to cover one's own spiritual inadequacies. "If you would get some counseling yourself, then I think that I could handle the situation."

- *Justifying*: trying to balance your wrong with the wrong of others. "I wouldn't have to take so many tranquilizers if my husband wasn't angry all the time."

- *Lying*: a blatant lie to cover one's back. "No, sir. I wasn't speeding. I have never broken a traffic law in my life."

- *Manipulation*: trying to indirectly blame someone else for your difficulty then trying to get the other person to straighten up so that you can. "If you will quit bringing home all that fatty food, I will go on a diet."

- *Mind over Matter*: the unconscious changing of a strong negative emotion into a bodily disease or abnormality. "I feel too bad to go in to work today. I probably have a fever."

- *Minimizing*: attempting to make the problem smaller than it is. "It was only a one-night stand. It only happened that one time."

- *Projection*: attributing your own feelings or thoughts to someone else and passing judgment on the other person. "I would never do something like that. You must be the one with the guilty conscience."

- *Questioning*: firing questions at the potential intruder to keep him from bringing up threatening issue in your own life.

- *Rationalization*: avoiding facing responsibility by bending the truth. "My parents did not mean to be bad parents. They did the best that they knew how."

- *Reaction Formation*: doing exactly the opposite of what one desires to do. (A drug addict joins an anti-drug campaign.) "We really need to put all drug dealers out of business."

- *Regression*: reverting back to an earlier stage of immaturity. "I'd rather just sit here and pout." "Have you ever tried putting soda straws up your nose? It is fun." (In more serious cases, the adult may take on the personality of a child.)

- *Repression*: the involuntary exclusion of unwanted thoughts or feelings from consciousness. "I can't remember how I felt that day when that happened. I just don't feel anything."

+ *Self-deception*: deceptive thinking that is usually vocally expressed. "I don't need anyone's help. I can quit drinking anytime that I want to."

+ *Shouting*: using a loud voice to try to control the situation. "Don't tell me to shut up! I will say what I want to say!"

+ *Silence*: using silence to protect one's self from talking about the problem. This is often the case with men in marriage. When confronted with the issue, the individual may just walk away or stand there and say nothing.

+ *Suppression*: the voluntary exclusion of unwanted thoughts from the individual's consciousness. "I just want to forget that whole experience."

+ *Sublimation*: redirecting the emotion into a more socially productive activity. "Here is a really neat short story that I have written about a woman having a sexual affair."

+ *Threatening*: using aggression to avoid facing an issue. "Don't ever bring up that topic again or I will make you wish that you hadn't!"

+ *Undoing*: attempting to make up, atone for or reverse the guilt by doing well in the place of the evil. "Please take this gift. It would really make me feel better after all that I did to you."

+ *Withdrawing*: deliberate removal of one's self from the situation. "This is the last straw. I can't stay in this situation any longer. I am leaving."

BIBLIOGRAPHY

Bibles and Reference

Baker's Evangelical Dictionary of Biblical Theology, http://www.biblestudytools.com/dictionaries/bakers-evangelical-dictionary/

Hodges, Zane Clark, and Arthur L. Farstad, *The Greek New Testament According to the Majority Text*, Nashville: T. Nelson, (1982)

The Holy Bible: New International Version. Grand Rapids, MI: Zondervan, (2005)

King James Bible, Nashville, TN: Holman Bible, (1973)

New American Standard Bible, La Habra, CA: Foundation Publications, for the Lockman Foundation, (1971)

New International Bible, Intervarsity Press, (1973)

Peterson, Eugene H., *The Message*, Colorado Springs, CO: NavPress, (2004)

Strong, James, *New Strong's Exhaustive Concordance*, Nashville, TN: Thomas Nelson, (2001)

Thomas, Robert L., *New American Standard Exhaustive Concordance of the Bible: [including] Hebrew-Aramaic and Greek Dictionaries*. Nashville, TN: A.J. Holman, (1981)

Vine, W. E., Merrill F. Unger, William White, and W. E. Vine, *Vine's Expository Dictionary of Biblical Words*, Nashville: T. Nelson, (1985)

Other Resources

Anderson, Neil T., *Victory over the Darkness*, Gospel Light (2000)

Barna Group, "Most American Christians Do Not Believe that Satan or the Holy Spirit Exist," April 2009, and "Americans Draw Theological Beliefs From Diverse Points of View," October 2002

Bartholomew, K., "Avoidance of intimacy: An attachment perspective," *Journal of Social and Personal Relationships, 7*, 147-178 (1990)

Blackaby, Henry T. and Claude V. King, *Experiencing God: Knowing and Doing the Will of God*, Nashville, TN: Broadman & Holman, (2008)

Boice, James, *The Gospel of John*, Vol. 4, Grand Rapids: Zondervan Publishing House, (1978)

Bruce, F.F., *The Epistle of Paul to The Romans*, Grand Rapids, Michigan:

William B. Eerdmans, Carder, Dave et al., *Secrets of Your Family Tree: Healing for Adult Children of Dysfunctional Families*, Moody Publishers, (1995)

Chen, Diane G., *God as Father in Luke-Acts*, Frankfurt Am Main: Peter Lang, (2006)

Chambers, Oswald, and James Reimann, *My Utmost for His Highest*, Grand Rapids, MI: Discovery House, (1992)

Clinton, Timothy E., and Gary Sibcy, *Why You Do the Things You Do: The Secret to Healthy Relationships*, Nashville, TN: Integrity, (2006)

Cloud, David, *Biblical Repentance*, Fundamental Baptist Information Service, P.O. Box 610368, Port Huron, MI 48061, 866-295-4143, fbns@wayoflife.org Updated and enlarged August 21, 2008 (first published June 13, 1999)

Dillahunty, George, Rev., Sermon " Prayer: Our Access To Almighty God!" Fundamental Baptist Information Service, P.O. Box 610368, Port Huron, MI 48061

Esses, Michael, *Jesus in Exodus*, Plainfield, NJ: Logos International, (1977)

"Father's Love Letter" used by permission Father Heart Communications, Copyright 1999-2011, www.FathersLoveLetter.com

Fausset, Andrew Robert, M.A., D.D., "Definition for 'Adoption,'" Fausset's Bible Dictionary," (1878)

Frost, Jack, *Experiencing the Father's Embrace*, Lake Mary, FL: Charisma House, (2002)

Frost, Jack, *Spiritual Slavery to Spiritual Sonship*, Shippensburg, PA: Destiny Image, (2006)

Gaultiere, William, *Returning to the Father*, Chicago: Moody, (1993)

Genung, Michael, "Healing Father Wounds", http://www.blazingGrace.org/index.php?page=healing-father-wounds

Hanby, Mark, and Ervin, Craig Lindsay, *You Have Not Many Fathers: Study Guide*, Shippensburg, PA: Destiny Image, (1999)

Hanegraaff, Hank, *The Christian Research Institute Newsletter online*, April 2, 2010, http://www.equip.org/hank_speaks_outs/john-griffith-the-bridge-operator

Hatfield, Robert W., Ph.D., V. Bullough, B. Bullough, & A. Stein (Eds.). *Human Sexuality: An Encyclopedia*, Garland Publishing, NY, (1994)

Harlow, H. F., & Zimmerman, R., "Affectional responses in the infant monkey," Science, 130, 421-432 (1959)

Hazan, C., & Shaver, P., "Romantic love conceptualized as an attachment process," *Journal of Personality and Social Psychology, 52*, 511-524, (1987)

Hegstrom, Paul, *Angry Men and the Women Who Love Them*, Beacon Hill Press, Kindle Edition, (2011-01-03)

Hession, Roy, and Hession, Revel, *We Would See Jesus*, Fort Washington, PA: Christian Literature Crusade, (1958)

Hillman, Os, *TGIF (Today God Is First), Volume 2*, Tuesday, May 22, 2012

Hillman, Os, *Experiencing the Father's Love*, Aslan Group Publishing, Cumming, GA (2010)

Jacobsen, Wayne, *He Loves Me!: Learning to Live in the Father's Affection*, Newbury Park, CA: Windblown Media, (2007)

Johnson, Oatman, Jr., "Count Your Blessings," in *Songs for Young People*, Music by Edwin Excell, Chicago, Illinois, (1987)

Kansas State University, "Help Yourself" created by Counseling Services ©1993,1997, http://www.k-state.edu/counseling/topics/relationships/dysfunc.htm

Keathley III, J. Hampton, "Faith Under Fire," Bible.org, 5 April 2011, <http://bible.org/article/faith-under-fire>

Kruger, C. Baxter, *The Shack Revisited: There Is More Going On Here than You Ever Dared to Dream* (2012-10-02)

Lynch, John; Thrall, Bill; McNicol, Bruce, *Truefaced: Trust God and Others with Who You Really Are*, Colorado Springs, CO: NavPress, (2003)

Mahaney, C. J., Humility: *True Greatness*, Sisters, OR: Multnomah, (2005)

McClung, Floyd, *The Father Heart of God*, Bastbourne: Kingsway Publications, (2005)

McGee, Robert S., *The Search for Significance*, Nashville: Word Pub., (1998)

Mcleod, S. A. *Simply Psychology*, "Bowlby Attachment Theory" (2007)

Mcleod, S. A., *Simply Psychology*, "Adult Attachment" (2011)

Miller, Sherod, *Collaborative Marriage Skills: Couple Communication I*, Evergreen, CO: Interpersonal Communication Programs, (2007)

Moffatt, James, *Grace in the New Testament*, New York: Ray Long & Richard R. Smith, Inc. (1932)

Mumford, Bob, *Agape Road: Journey to Intimacy with the Father*, Shippensburg, PA: Destiny Image, (2006)

Nagle, Sherman A., *Signs of the Times*, February 12, 1924, Dale Galusha, http://www.pacificpress.com/signs

Nestler, Eric and Malenka, Robert, "The Addicted Brain," *Scientific American*, March 2004

Packer, J. I., *Knowing God*, Downers Grove, IL: InterVarsity, (1973)

Peck, M. Scott, *The Road Less Travelled: a Psychology of Love, Traditional Values and Spiritual Growth*, London: Rider, (1985)

Piorek, Ed, *The Father Loves You*, Cape Town: Vineyard International Pub., (1999)

Piper, Don, and Murphey, Cecil, *90 Minutes in Heaven: A True Story of Death and Life*, Grand Rapids, MI: Revell, (2004)

Piper, John, *Desiring God: Meditations of a Christian Hedonist*, Colorado Springs, CO: Multnomah, (2011)

Prince, Derek, "No. 17: To Please My Father," *A Derek Prince Teaching Letter: 1-2*

Ramsay, W. M., *A Historical Commentary on St. Paul's Epistle to the Galatians*, Baker Book House, Grand Rapids, MI, (reprinted 1979)

Rainey, Dr. Dennis, "Becoming a Real Father", Jan 15, 2011, http://www.familylife.com/articles/topics/parenting/essentials/fathers/becoming-a-real-father

Reiner, Troy, "Biblical Answers for Life's Difficult Problems Based on Faith Therapy Christian Counseling Methods and Resources," <http://www.faiththerapy.org>

Robinson, Haddon W., *What Jesus Said About Successful Living*, Grand Rapids, Michigan: Discovery House Publishers, (1991)

Salvin-Williams, R. C. and Berndt, T. J., "Friendship and peer relations," in S. S. Feldman and G. R. Elliot (Eds.), *At the Threshold: The Developing Adolescent*, Cambridge, MA: Harvard University Press (1990)

Sarpong, Peter K., *Ghana in Retrospect*, Accra: Ghana Publishing Corporation, (1974)

Seamands, David A., *Healing for Damaged Emotions*, Wheaton, IL: Victor, (1981)

Sichel, Mark, as quoted from "Healing From Family Rifts," http://www.sideroad.com/Family_Life/people-pleasers.html

Slagle, Charles, *An Invitation to Friendship: From the Father's Heart*, Shippensburg, PA: Destiny Image, (1999)

Smedes, Lewis B., *The International Standard Bible Encyclopedia (revised)*, Geoffrey W. Bromiley (ed.), Grand Rapids: Wm B. Eerdmans, (1982)

Spitz, R.A., *The First Year of Life: A Psychoanalytic Study of Normal and Deviant Development of Object Relations*, New York: International Universities Press (1965)

Stanley, Charles, "Emotional Baggage in Ministry," *Christian Counseling Today newsletter/magazine*, Jan 1993

Stibbe, Mark W. G., *From Orphans to Heirs: Celebrating Our Spiritual Adoption*, Oxford: Bible Reading Fellowship, (2005)

Stott, John R. W., *The Contemporary Christian: Applying God's Word to Today's World*, Downers Grove, IL: InterVarsity (1992)

Strong, James, *Strong's Exhaustive Concordance of the Bible, Greek Dictionary of the New Testament*, New York: Abingdon Press, (1890)

Tozer, A. W., *The Root of Righteousness*, Harrisburg, PA: Christian Publications, (1955)

Van Vonderen, Jeffrey, *Good News for the Chemically Dependent*, Nashville: Thomas Nelson, (1985)

Virkler, Mark and Patti, *Communion with God*, Shippensburg, PA: Destiny Image, (2010)

Winter, Jack, and Ferris, Pamela, *The Homecoming: Unconditional Love: Finding Your Place in the Father's Heart*, Seattle, WA: YWAM Pub., (1997)

Young, William P., *The Shack: a Novel*, Newbury Park, CA: Windblown Media, (2007)

Wagner, Dr. Maurice, *The Sensation of Being Somebody: Building an Adequate Self-Concept*, Grand Rapids, MI: Zondervan (1985)

"Alcoholism in Family Systems," http://en.wikipedia.org/wiki/Alcoholism_in_family_systems

Wilson, Douglas, *Father Hunger: Why God Calls Men to Love and Lead Their Families*, Nashville: Thomas Nelson, (2012)

Wolter, Dwight Lee, *Forgiving Our Parents: For Adult Children from Dysfunctional Families*, Compcare, (1995)

270 Grace: ORPHANS No More

Woodward, C., "Poll: Most Americans Believe in Angels," The Hour, December 24, 2006

ABOUT THE AUTHOR

Dr. James Johnson, Ph.D.
Executive Director, Keys4-Life:
Faith-based Counseling and Coaching
Contact: James@Keys4.org
www.drjamesgjohnson.org/graceorphansnomore
www.keys4-life.org
Facebook: Keys4-Life

ENDNOTES

[1] Proverbs 4:23.

[2] Luke 6:43-45.

[3] Matthew 15:10-20.

[4] Henri Nouwen, http://www.youtube.com/watch?v=-AAHT4l3jVY.

[5] George M. Stratton (1896), "Some Preliminary Experiments on Vision without Inversion of the Retinal Image," Psychological Review 3 (6): 611-7. DOI: 10.1037/h0072918.

[6] John 8:32.

[7] John 16:13.

[8] David Seamands, *Healing for Damaged Emotions*, David C. Cook, (Colorado Springs, 1981). The entire paragraph reads as follows:

> *"Early in my pastoral experience I discovered that I was failing to help two groups of people through the regular ministries of the church. Their problems were not being solved by the preaching of the word, commitment to Christ, the filling of the Spirit, prayer or the sacraments. I saw one group being driven into futility and loss of confidence in God's power. While they desperately prayed, their prayers about personal problems didn't seem to be answered. They tried every Christian discipline, but with not results. As they played the same old cracked record of their defects, they would get stuck in repetitive emotional patterns. While they kept up the outward observances of praying and paying and professing, they were going deeper and deeper into disillusionment and despair. I saw the other group moving towards phoniness. These people were repressing their inner feelings and denying anything that was seriously wrong, because, Christians can't have such problems. Instead of facing their problems, they covered them with a veneer of Scripture verses, theological terms, and unrealistic platitudes. The denied problems went underground, only to later reappear in all manner of illnesses, eccentricities, terribly unhappy marriages, and sometimes even in the emotional destruction of their children."*

[9] The American Medical Association (AMA) said it was 60 percent but surveyed only addictive behaviors. Other researchers come in with a much higher percentage. The 82 percent comes from Shiloh Place Ministries (http://www.shilohplace.org) and is a direct quote of Jack Frost, whom I believe gave it the most conservative point of view. After my ministry experiences, I lean toward more than 90 percent.

Codependency guru John Bradshaw (an unbeliever who defines codependency as the internalization of shame) blames codependency in part on Christians who teach doctrines of original sin, total depravity, and eternal punishment, adding that Adam's problem was the result of "toxic shame" rather than sin. This theory holds that virtually everyone in this country is a product of a "dysfunctional family," a whopping 96 percent of us, and that we have all experienced some form of traumatic abuse as children. In turn, this childhood "abuse" inevitably results in some form of adult dysfunctional behavior — often some form of addiction — the solution for which is a concerted effort to "heal the inner child" through 12-Step programs. This is the same John Bradshaw who "heartily recommends" *Love is a Choice: Recovery for Codependent Relationships*, a best-selling "Christian" recovery book which Minirth and Meier co-author with Robert Hemfelt (of Serenity Bible fame). [*Toxic Faith*, a book authored in part by professing believer Stephen Arterburn, the CEO of New Life Treatment Centers (now Minirth-Meier New Life Clinics), teaches many of the same concepts as Bradshaw, only dressed up in Christian terminology.]

Analyst Doreen Fellows states that 2000 U.S. Census figures indicate that more than 60 percent of all American children are from divorced families. According to the AMA, 72 percent of American homes harbor someone with an addiction. http://www.chacha.com/question/what-is-the-percentage-of-dysfunctional-families-in-america.

According to "Exploring The Low Percentage Of Victims That Actually Escape Dysfunctional Families" from Atlanta Live Christian Radio, only 2 out of 10 escape their dysfunctional family roots. See more at: http://www.atlantalivenews.org/a-low-percentage-of-victims-escape-dysfunctional-families/#sthash.cB2QUiSz.dpuf.

In reality it is impossible to accurately arrive at a percentage. The AMA only considered addictive behaviors. The qualifications vary with each sample. So I really don't know how to quantify this correctly.

[10] Charles Stanley, "Emotional Baggage in Ministry, *Christian Counseling Today* magazine, January 1993, p. 35.

[11] A.W. Tozer, *The Root of Righteousness*, Christian Publications, (Harrisburg, 1955).

[12] John 10:27.

[13] Colossians 3:16.

[14] James 4:6.

[15] Mark and Patti Virkler, *Communion with God*, Destiny Image Publishers, (Shippensburg 2010).

[16] http://www.cwgministries.org.

[17] Proverbs 8:27.

[18] Roy and Revel Hession, *We Would See Jesus*, CLC Ministries, (Fort Washington, 2005).

[19] Genesis 2:15-17.

[20] Ephesians 2:1, 4-5.

[21] *Vine's Expository Dictionary of Old and New Testament Words* states about "ZOE":

> *Zoe, is used in the NT of life as a principle, life in the absolute sense, life as God has it, that which the Father has in Himself, and which He gave to the Incarnate Son to have in Himself, John 5:26, and which the Son manifested in the world, 1 John 1:2. From this life man has become alienated in consequence of the Fall, Ephesians 4:18, and of this life men become partakers through faith in the Lord Jesus Christ, John 3:15.*

[22] Wikipedia contributors, "Maslow's Hierarchy of Needs," *Wikipedia, The Free Encyclopedia,* http://en.wikipedia.org/wiki/Maslows_hierarchy_of_needs (accessed July 10, 2012).

[23] ibid.

[24] ibid.

[25] Robert S. McGee, *The Search for Significance,* Thomas Nelson (Nashville, 1998, 2003).

[26] Matthew 6:25-34; Luke 12:22-32.

[27] Mark 10:21.

[28] Mark 10:21.

[29] Luke 16:13.

[30] John 19:11.

[31] Jeremiah 17:5-8.

[32] Mark Sichel, "People Pleasers," http://www.psybersquare.com/family/family_pleaser.html, (July 12, 2012), *Psybersquare.*

[33] Craig Groeschel, "Characteristics of People Pleasing Pastors," September 23, 2008, http://swerve.lifechurch.tv/2008/09/23/characteristics-of-people-pleasing-pastors, (July 12, 2012) Swerve.

[34] 1 Corinthians 4:3-4.

[35] After His resurrection, as told in Matthew 28:18-20, in preparation for His final ascent to heaven, Jesus charges His disciples with the following fourfold task, which is known as the Great Commission:

> *And Jesus came up and spoke to them, saying, "All authority has been given to Me in heaven and on earth. Go therefore and make disciples of all the nations, baptizing them in the name of the Father and the Son and the Holy Spirit, teaching them to observe all that I commanded you; and lo, I am with you always, even to the end of the age."*

[36] http://adamsmemorial.org/the-adamses/brooks/.

[37] "Idolatry," *Wikipedia, The Free Encyclopedia*, http://en.wikipedia.org/wiki/Idolatry (July 14, 2012).

[38] Merriam-Webster, s.v. "Worship."

[39] Romans 1:25.

[40] Psalm 115:8.

[41] Psalm 135:18.

[42] Matthew 24:35; Mark 13:31; Luke 21:33.

[43] Eric J. Nestler and Robert C. Malenka, "The Addicted Brain," *Scientific American* (March 2004).

[44] Matthew 6:33.

[45] Vine's Online Dictionary.

[46] John 15:7.

[47] In *The Gospel of John, Vol. 4* (Grand Rapids: Zondervan Publishing House, 1978) commentator Dr. James Montgomery Boice has written:

> *"It would be a strange vinedresser who immediately cuts off such a branch without even giving it a chance to develop properly. But it would be wise and customary for him to stretch the vine on an arbor or use some other means of raising it to the air and sun ... to translate the word* AIRO *by 'lifteth up' gives a proper sequence to the Father's care of the vineyard, indicated by the verb which follows. Thus, He first of all, lifts the vines up. Then He prunes away the unproductive elements, carefully cleansing the vine of insects, moss, or parasites which otherwise would hinder the growth of the plant."*

[48] Isaiah 66:2.

[49] Romans 5:1-2.

[50] W.R. Moody, *The Life of D. L. Moody*, New York: 1900.

[51] Hession, *We would See Jesus*. More fully, this section reads:

> So often people speak of this as some blessing which we receive from God at special times. We have, however, sought to use it in the strictly New Testament sense of the word. There, it is the great word of our salvation and of all God's dealings with us; for it is written, "By Grace are ye saved through faith." Nothing is more important than that we should apprehend its meaning in both our minds and experience. Missing this, we miss everything. In the New Testament, Grace is not a blessing or an influence from God which we receive, but rather an attribute of God which governs His attitude to man, and can be defined as the undeserved love and favor of God. Romans 11:6 says, "And if by Grace, then is it no more of works; otherwise Grace is no more Grace." The whole essence of Grace is that it is undeserved. The moment we have to do something to make ourselves more acceptable to God, or the moment we have to have a certain feeling or attribute of character in order to be blessed of God, then Grace is no more Grace. Grace permits us to come (nay, demands that we come) as empty sinners to be blessed, empty of right feelings, good character, and satisfactory record, with nothing to commend ourselves but our deep need, fully and frankly acknowledged. Then Grace, being what it is, is drawn by that need to satisfy it, just as water is drawn to depth (by gravity) that it might fill it. This means that when at last we are content to find no merit or procuring cause in ourselves, and are willing to admit the full extent of our sinfulness, then there is no limit to what God will do for the poor who look to Him in their nothingness. If what we receive from God is dependent, even to a small extent, on what we are or do, then the most we can expect is but an intermittent trickle of blessing. But if what we are to receive is to be measured by the Grace of God quite apart from works, then there is only one word that adequately describes what He pours upon us, the word which so often is linked with Grace in the New Testament, "abundance!" The struggle, of course, is to believe it and to be willing to be but empty sinners to the end of our days, that Grace may continue to match our needs.

[52] EN AGAPE ERRIDZOMENOI KAI TETHEMELIOMENOI.

[53] 1 John 4:16-18.

[54] Gary Smalley and John Trent, *The Blessing*, Pocket Books (New York, 1986).

[55] James Moffatt, *Grace in the New Testament* (New York: Ray Long & Richard R. Smith, Inc., 1932).

[56] Sermon by John Piper, PhD., http://desiringgod.org/resource-library/sermons/quest-joy-found-christ.

[57] Matthew 5:3; 11:28.

[58] Max Lucado, *God Thinks You're Wonderful*, Thomas Nelson (Nashville, 2003).

[59] Luke 15:11-32.

[60] The Roman historian William M. Ramsay wrote that in Roman law "a man can never put away an adopted son, and that he cannot put away a real son without good ground. It is remarkable that the adopted son should have a stronger position than the son by birth, yet it was so." (Sir William Mitchell Ramsay, *Historical Commentary on St. Paul's Epistle to the Galatians* [1900; reprint, Grand Rapids: Baker Book House, 1965)]).

[61] J.I. Packer, *Knowing God*, (Downers Grove, IL: InterVarsity, 1973). This quote is taken from pages 200-206, which reads in part:

> *What is a Christian? The question can be answered in many ways, but the richest answer I know is that a Christian is one who has God as Father ... You can sum up the whole New Testament of teaching in a single phrase, if, you speak of it as a revelation of the Fatherhood of the Holy Creator. In the same way, you sum up the whole of New Testament religion if you describe it as the knowledge of God as one's Holy Father. ...*
>
> *If you want to judge how well a person understands Christianity, find out how much he makes of the thought of being God's child, and having God as his Father. If this is not the thought that prompts and controls his worship and his prayers and his whole outlook on life, it means that he does not understand Christianity very well at all. For everything that Christ taught, everything that makes the New Testament new ... is summed up in the knowledge of the Fatherhood of God. "Father" is the Christian name for God. ... Adoption ... is the highest privilege that the gospel offers: higher even than justification. ... To be right with God the Judge is a great thing, but to be loved and cared for by God the Father is a greater. ...*
>
> *Everything that Christ taught, everything that makes the New Testament new, is summed up in the knowledge of the Fatherhood of God.*

[62] Matthew 5-7.

[63] Diane G. Chen, *God as Father in Luke-Acts* (New York: Peter Lang, 2006).

[64] John 4:23.

[65] Douglas Wilson, *Father Hunger: Why God Calls Men to Love and Lead Their Families*, (Nashville: Thomas Nelson, 2012) 204-205.

> *The most obvious feature of the Father of Jesus Christ is His generosity. He is generous with His glory (John 1:14), with His tasks (John 5:18), with His protection (John 10:28–32), with His home (John 14:1–2), and with His joy (John 16:23–24). The Father gives (John 3:34–36). The Father gives His Son (John 3:16; 18:11); the Father gives His Spirit (John 14:16–17); the Father gives Himself (John 14:22–24). Learning this about the Father who is a Spirit, who is intangible, should stir us deeply. He is seeking worshipers who will worship Him in Spirit and in truth — in short, who will become like He is. And what is He like? He is generous with everything. Is there anything He has that he has held back? And what should we — tangible fathers — be like? The question is terribly hard to answer, but not because it is difficult to understand.*

[66] Ephesians 5:1-2, *The Message.*

[67] Bob Mumford, *The Agape Road: Journey to Intimacy with the Father*, (Shippensburg, PA: Destiny, 2006) 29. The entire quote reads:

> *God as a Father is an important concept in Scripture. He was Father before He was Creator or a Redeemer. He was the Father of the Lord Jesus Christ in eternity before the world began, so that through fatherhood we can come to know him (see John 17:3). Nothing in American societies has been more twisted and damaged than the concept of the Father. No one in the history of the world has been more misrepresented than God the Father. He is easy to malign, condemn, and speak against, because He does not defend himself. However, in damaging the concept of Father our whole society is bereft of security, identity, and belonging. It is urgent that we see the Fatherhood of God restored. This is what Jesus came to do (see John 14:6).*

Mumford goes on to say:

> *As we come to know this God, the one who revealed Himself, we start feeling comfortable in His presence. We have a wonderful Father! How I wish that when I was young and afraid, someone would have helped me to more clearly understand that Christ came to take me to His Father. My idea of being a Father was making displays of male testosterone in a futile attempt to acquire, possess, and control. I knew little to nothing of His character or the hidden attributes of God's nature.*

[68] Haddon W. Robinson, *What Jesus Said About Successful Living: Principles from the Sermon on the Mount for Today* (Grand Rapids, Michigan: Discovery House Publishers, 1991).

[69] Ephesians 1:3-5, 2:7; Romans 8:15-23; John 1:12; Luke 18:12; Galatians 4:5.

[70] John 5:18, 6:28, 17:1-6.

[71] Matthew 6:9; Luke 11:2-4.

[72] John 16:25.

73 Luke 1:14-17.

74 Romans 2:4.

75 Michael Esses, *Jesus in Exodus* (Plainfield, NJ: Logos International, 1977).

> *The fifth commandment tells us: that your days may be long upon the land that the Lord your God gives to you. (Exo.20:12) Why did God put this commandment on His side of the tables of statutes? Logically, it seems to belong among the ordinances showing us how to conduct our relationships with other people. But God put the honoring of parents with the commandments dealing with our relationship with Him because He knew that if we did not honor our earthly parents, we could not possibly honor our heavenly Father. If we cannot show respect, reverence, awe, and fear of our mother and father, the persons who stand before us as representatives of God Himself, we cannot possibly love and honor God. Proper respect toward parents may sometimes involve immeasurable hardship. Yet the duty remains. Jesus said that one of the signs of the end times would be the disobedience and dishonor of children to parents.*

76 Douglas Wilson, *Father Hunger: Why God Calls Men to Love and Lead Their Families*, Thomas Nelson, Inc. (Nashville, 2012).

77 Micah 7:18-19.

78 Hank Hanegraaff, "John Griffith, the Bridge Operator," *The Christian Research Institute Newsletter*, April 2, 2010, http://www.equip.org/hank_speaks_outs/john-griffith-the-bridge-operator.

79 2 Corinthians 5:21 (NIV).

80 1 Corinthians 2:9

81 Elisabeth Kübler-Ross, *The Wheel of Life: A Memoir of Living and Dying*, Scribner (New York, 1998).

82 Timothy E. Clinton and Gary Sibcy, *Why You Do the Things You Do: The Secret to Healthy Relationships*, Integrity (Nashville, 2006).

83 An excellent compilation of statistics can be found on my website: drjamesgjohnson.org/fatherlessness.

84 Paul Hegstrom, *Angry Men and the Women Who Love Them: Breaking the Cycle of Physical and Emotional Abuse*, Beacon Hill Press (Kindle Edition, 2004).

85 Hegstrom's words are a summary but the amount of research on this is overwhelming.

86 ibid.

87 Jack Frost, Tape Series, *From Slavery to Sonship*.

[88] David M. Carder, Earl R. Henslin, John S. Townsend III, William Henry Cloud, Alice Brawand, *Unlocking Your Family Patterns: Finding Freedom from a Hurtful Past*, The Moody Bible Institute of Chicago (1991).

[89] I would recommend purchasing Jack Frost's messages on *Experiencing the Father's Embrace*, and *From Slavery to Sonship* and his two corresponding books.

[90] The table below describes various attachment styles and their parental origins with resulting adult characteristics:

Attachment Style	Parental Origin	Resulting Adult Characteristics
SECURE	Aligned with the child; in tune with child's emotions	Able to create meaningful relationships; empathetic; able to set appropriate boundaries
AVOIDANT	Unavailable or rejecting	Avoids closeness or emotional connection; distant; critical; rigid; intolerant
AMBIVALENT	Inconsistent and sometimes intrusive parent communication	Anxious and insecure; controlling; blaming; erratic; unpredictable; sometimes charming
DISORGANIZED	Ignored or didn't see child's needs; parental behavior was frightening / traumatizing	Chaotic; insensitive; explosive; abusive; untrusting even while craving security

[91] "Researchers at Johns Hopkins Medical School set out on a thirty-year study to find out if a single related cause existed for mental illness, hypertension, malignant tumors, coronary heart disease, and suicide. After studying 1,377 people over a thirty year period, the single common denominator was not diet or exercise. Not at all. They found instead that the most significant predictor of these five calamities was a lack of closeness to the parents, especially the father."

McDowell further states on his website and in his materials that when there is no relationship with the father especially, suicide rates in 12- to 14-year-old teens is 300 percent higher. And in 15- to 16-year-olds it jumps to 400 percent higher. Think how many people are suffering because of this?

[92] The people we tend to look up to, especially Christian leaders, can look good outwardly, and we think they have no history or past issues. One of the best series on marriage in the Christian market today is a series by Emerson Eggerichs, titled "Love and Respect." This man is a Christlike example from whom we can learn much. And yet he had much to overcome. In a September 27, 2010, blog, Eggerichs wrote that he came from a violent and alcoholic home where his father was an abusive man whom his mother eventually divorced. Later in life, his dad accepted Christ as his Savior, and after much time, the marriage was ultimately restored. And yet this was the family of origin that Eggerichs had to deal with in his own life.

93

WHAT IS A DYSFUNCTIONAL FAMILY? Family dysfunction can be any condition that interferes with healthy family functioning. Most families have some periods of time where functioning is impaired by stressful circumstances (death in the family, a parent's serious illness, etc.). Healthy families tend to return to normal functioning after the crisis passes. In dysfunctional families, however, problems tend to be chronic and children do not consistently get their needs met. Negative patterns of parental behavior tend to be dominant in their children's lives.

HOW DO HEALTHY FAMILIES WORK? Healthy families are not perfect; they may have yelling, bickering, misunderstanding, tension, hurt, and anger — but not all the time. In healthy families emotional expression is allowed and accepted. Family members can freely ask for and give attention. Rules tend to be made explicit and remain consistent, but with some flexibility to adapt to individual needs and particular situations. Healthy families allow for individuality; each member is encouraged to pursue his or her own interests, and boundaries between individuals are honored. Children are consistently treated with respect, and do not fear emotional, verbal, physical, or sexual abuse. Parents can be counted on to provide care for their children. Children are given responsibilities appropriate to their age and are not expected to take on parental responsibilities. Finally, in healthy families everyone makes mistakes; mistakes are allowed. Perfection is unattainable, unrealistic, and potentially dull and sterile.

[94] In December 1999, Dr. Paul Hegstrom was quoted from his book *Angry Men and the Women Who Love Them* in the article "Wounds of Childhood" by Brenda Branson, http://www.focusministries1.org/articles/WoundsofChildhood.pdf, who cites the following:

There are four broad categories of trauma that most commonly arrest the development of the child: rejection, sexual abuse (incest or molestation), emotional abuse, and physical abuse. Any one of these or a cluster of them can freeze the development of the child and cause him or her to shut down emotionally. The pain is simply too great for one so young to handle. The child does not have the ability to see the reality of the situation that causes the trauma. Instead, he or she assumes responsibility for the deviant behavior of the adult and thinks, What did I do to cause him [or her] to do that to me?

[95] Dalbey, Gordon, *Sons of the Father: Healing the Father-Wound in Men Today*, Civitas Press, Kindle Edition.

[96] http://www.blazinggrace.org.

[97] Romans 12:1-2.

[98] Sermon by John Lynch, "TrueFaced," April 2011.

[99] An in-depth study on this topic in terms of Attention Deficit Disorder (ADD) is "Healing ADD" by Daniel G. Amen, M.D.

[100] In his online devotional, Os Hillman presents an excellent example of confronting worldly lies then turning toward home as the godly response in his online devotional:

> *"Jerry had grown up with a father who was a successful workaholic. Although he lacked for nothing materially, he never sensed much warmth or compassion from his parents. Then, when Jerry was still in his early teens, his father died very suddenly. His large family was left with little support, and insecurity and fear became the dominating factors in the young man's life. Vowing to himself that he would never lack financial need again, Jerry worked hard at his business. A stronghold of idolatry brought reliance on the wealth he had accumulated rather than a prayerful dependency on God. Arguments over money dominated his marriage. Distrust and greed permeated his home and business relationships. No one could "stand in his face" and tell him what to do. Finally, as his marriage disintegrated and his business gave signs of going under, Jerry renounced the strongholds of insecurity and fear that had made money his idol and had shaped his disbelieving view of God's ability to meet his need. As the Holy Spirit brought conviction of the sins he had committed against so many people, he purposed to approach each one to seek forgiveness and make restitution wherever appropriate. His priorities shifted to God and family, then to close friends and business. God began to restore balance and intimacy with God and others as a result." Os identifies "Jerry" as himself.*

TGIF Today God Is First, Volume 2, Tuesday, May 22 2012, Online Devotional. tgif@marketplaceleaders.org.

[101] Song of Solomon 2:4.

[102] http://en.wikipedia.org/wiki/Corrie_ten_Boom.

[103] Romans 6:5-11:

> *For if we have become united with Him in the likeness of His death, certainly we shall also be in the likeness of His resurrection, knowing this, that our old self was crucified with Him, in order that our body of sin might be done away with, so that we would no longer be slaves to sin; for he who has died is freed from sin. Now if we have died with Christ, we believe that we shall also live with Him, knowing that Christ, having been raised from the dead, is never to die again; death no longer is master over Him. For the death that He died, He died to sin once for all; but the life that He lives, He lives to God. Even so consider yourselves to be dead to sin, but alive to God in Christ Jesus.*

[104] 1 John 2:15-16. For an interesting side study, look at what happened to Eve in the garden. All three lower desires were there, "When the woman saw that the tree was good for food (flesh), and that it was a delight to the eyes (eyes), and that the tree was desirable to make one wise (pride), she took from its fruit and ate (Genesis 3:6). If you want to take this further look at the temptation of Christ in Luke 4, where Satan tempts Him in all three basic desires.

[105] Troy Reiner, "Biblical Answers for Life's Difficult Problems Based on Faith Therapy Christian Counseling Methods and Resources," http://www.faiththerapy.org.

[106] John Stott, *Contemporary Christian, Applying God's Word to Today's World,* InterVarsity Press (Downers Grove, 1992).

[107] Bill Bright Transferable Concepts

> *Though you are filled with the Holy Spirit by faith and faith alone, it is important to recognize that several factors contribute to preparing your heart for the filling of the Spirit. First, you must desire to live a life that will please the Lord. You have the promise of our Savior, "Blessed are those who hunger and thirst for righteousness, for they will be filled." Second, be willing to surrender your life totally and irrevocably to our Lord Jesus Christ. Paul admonishes in Romans 12:1, 2: "I urge you, brothers, in view of God's mercy, to offer your bodies as living sacrifices, holy and pleasing to God — which is your spiritual worship. Do not conform any longer to the pattern of this world, but be transformed by the renewing of your mind. Then you will be able to test and approve what God's will is — his good, pleasing and perfect will." Third, confess every known sin which the Holy Spirit calls to your remembrance and experience the cleansing and forgiveness which God promises in 1 John 1:9: "If we confess our sins, he is faithful and just and will forgive us our sins and purify us from all unrighteousness." I call this process "Spiritual Breathing." Just as you exhale and inhale physically, so you also breathe spiritually. You exhale spiritually when you confess your sins.*

http://www.cru.org/training-and-growth/classics/transferable-concepts/be-filled-with-the-holy-spirit/07-steps-to-being-filled.htm.

[108] Luke 15:25-32:

Now his older son was in the field, and when he came and approached the house, he heard music and dancing. And he summoned one of the servants and began inquiring what these things could be. And he said to him, "Your brother has come, and your father has killed the fattened calf because he has received him back safe and sound."

But he became angry and was not willing to go in; and his father came out and began pleading with him. But he answered and said to his father, "Look! For so many years I have been serving you and I have never neglected a command of yours; and yet you have never given me a young goat, so that I might celebrate with my friends; but when this son of yours came, who has devoured your wealth with prostitutes, you killed the fattened calf for him."

And he said to him, "Son, you have always been with me, and all that is mine is yours. But we had to celebrate and rejoice, for this brother of yours was dead and has begun to live, and was lost and has been found."

[109] Proverbs 28:13.

[110] Here's the full quote in context:

Only the Father God of all time can deliver a man from generations of destruction into manhood— that is, from being abandoned to being a son (see Rom. 8:14-16). He's done this in Jesus on the cross, and will do it for any man who invites Jesus into his father-wound. Indeed, Jesus has stepped decisively into the path of the snowballing Goliath, letting it smash against himself and thereby breaking its power over fathers and sons alike. Jesus came to restore relationship with the Father— that is, to remind men abandoned and unfathered for generations that we are beloved sons. Quoting Hebrew scholar Joachim Jeremias, theologian Marvin Wilson notes that men in the Old Testament occasionally referred to God as "Father," but never as "my Father." Traditional Judaic prayers used the term, "our Father." Jesus, however, not only referred often to God as "my Father," but used the intimate Hebrew term abba, or "Daddy." ADOPTION BY FAITH "The same childlike closeness," Wilson declares, "is central to the sonship that is at the heart of the Christian gospel; for those who, by faith, have been adopted into the Father's family as children may also address him as Abba" (see Rom. 8: 15; Gal. 4: 6). Thus, the striking significance of this revolutionary term used by Jesus: With Abba we are . . . confronted with something new and unheard of which breaks through the limits of Judaism. Here we see who the historical Jesus was: the man who had the power to address God as Abba and who included the sinners and the publicans in the kingdom by authorizing them to repeat this one word: "Abba, dear Father."

Gordon Dalbey, *Sons of the Father: Healing the Father-Wound in Men Today,* Civitas Press, Kindle Edition.

CPSIA information can be obtained
at www.ICGtesting.com
Printed in the USA
FSOW01n2007280915
11548FS